THE AMERICANIZATION OF
CARL SCHURZ

THE UNIVERSITY OF CHICAGO PRESS
CHICAGO, ILLINOIS

THE BAKER & TAYLOR COMPANY
NEW YORK

THE MACMILLAN COMPANY OF CANADA, LIMITED
TORONTO

THE CAMBRIDGE UNIVERSITY PRESS
LONDON

THE MARUZEN-KABUSHIKI-KAISHA
TOKYO, OSAKA, KYOTO, FUKUOKA, SENDAI

THE COMMERCIAL PRESS, LIMITED
SHANGHAI

THE
AMERICANIZATION
OF
CARL SCHURZ

By

CHESTER VERNE EASUM

THE UNIVERSITY OF CHICAGO PRESS
CHICAGO · ILLINOIS

COMPOSED AND PRINTED BY THE UNIVERSITY OF CHICAGO
PRESS, CHICAGO, ILLINOIS, U.S.A.

PREFACE

THE author frankly hopes that some of the readers of this book will be disappointed in it —sorry that it does not continue the story on to the end of the long and active life of its subject. It is, in fact, with the greatest regret that the study of the record is temporarily abandoned.

Many phases of the life of Schurz invite the attention of the student. As a "political general" of the highest type—one who realized, as did Lincoln and von Clausewitz, that war itself is but one phase of the political activity of a government and not an end in itself—Schurz had a highly interesting career. Elected to the Senate in the first year in which his years of residence in the United States made him eligible, he became one of the greatest orators in that assembly, quite fulfilling the promise shown in his active campaign for the election of Lincoln in 1860. As Secretary of the Interior in the cabinet of Hayes, he was a sponsor of the merit system before the passage of the Civil Service Act, and a pioneer in the fostering of a national conservation policy. As the great Independent and civil service reformer in politics, he always brought upon himself much bitter criticism as a political turncoat and trouble-maker; but he usually defended himself well enough. No one was keener or quicker in

v

debate, or better equipped to master facts and marshal them in support of his political position. In a sense he outlived his generation. Always an anti-imperialist, the Lincoln Republican was not quite at home among the McKinley and Roosevelt Republicans; but he found even less in common with the Populist-Democratic followers of Bryan, and made a strong fight for "sound money." These later periods of his life also deserve intensive study.

Schurz was always an ardent patriot but never an unquestioning follower of any leadership. He was always proud of his German origin and of the many real virtues of the German people, and he always loved his native tongue; but nothing so aroused his ire as any imputation that he was not a good American. It is the development of that militant American patriotism, during his first ten years in the United States, that suggested the title of this study of that portion of his life. The growth of his attachment to America during the interval of nine years which elapsed between his arrival as an outlawed immigrant and his return to Europe, clothed in the dignity of the diplomatic representative of his adopted nation at the court of Spain, is a study in Americanization as interesting as his phenomenal rise to prominence was romantic. Bismarck later remarked to an American that, as a German, he was "proud of Carl Schurz"; the way to Germany was open to him, but *something* had made an American out of him. How "the brilliant German" was made into a devoted American citizen, and his influence upon public affairs even while the process of his Americanization was going on, it has been the chief purpose of this study to discover.

The author is glad to take advantage of this opportunity to give expression to his feeling of gratitude to those who have assisted him in the preparation of this volume. He is particularly indebted to Dr. Frederic L. Paxson, of the University of Wisconsin, under whose stimulating supervision most of the research work upon which it is based was done, and to Dr. Frederic Bancroft, of Washington, and Dr. Joseph Schafer, of the State Historical Society of Wisconsin, who so generously shared with him their extensive knowledge of the sources of information about Schurz, and their enthusiasm for the quest of it.

TABLE OF CONTENTS

LIST OF ABBREVIATIONS

MOST COMMONLY USED IN FOOTNOTES

C.S.—Carl Schurz.

C.S., *Rem.*—Carl Schurz, *Reminiscences.*

C.S., *S.C.&P.P.*—Carl Schurz, *Speeches, Correspondence, and Political Papers,* edited by Frederic Bancroft.

C.S., *Lebn.*—Carl Schurz, *Lebenserinnerungen.*

C.S. MSS., W.H.S.—Carl Schurz Manuscripts, Wisconsin Historical Society.

C.S. MSS., L.C.—Carl Schurz Manuscripts, Library of Congress.

A.H.R.—*American Historical Review.*

Die deutschamerikanische u.s.w.—Betz, *Die deutschamerikanische patriotische Lyrik der Achtundvierziger und ihre historische Grundlage.*

Mil. Sen.—*Milwaukee Daily Sentinel.*

N.A.R.—*North American Review.*

"Pol. Act. of Wis. Ger."—"Political Activities of Wisconsin Germans, 1854–1860," *Proceedings of the State Historical Society of Wisconsin,* 1901.

St. Jour.—Madison, *Wisconsin Daily State Journal.*

Watertown Dem.—*Watertown Democrat.*

CHAPTER I

BEGINNINGS

SUCH is the power of suggestive phrase, particularly when pronounced in striking or dramatic fashion or at moments of psychological tension, and so far has popular thought been commonly conventionalized, that the author of some such phrase has often, with or without such intent on his own part, lent a distinctive character to the whole picture presented by a people to its own eyes or to those of others. We are still painfully conscious, for example, of the repercussions of bitter disappointment following the very incomplete realization of the extravagant anticipations aroused by the two famous promises to make England "a land fit for heroes" and the world "safe for democracy." Even if exaggeration or other inaccuracy has been avoided by the maker of a popular catch phrase, himself, excess of zeal on the part of those who adopt it, or of hostility on the part of those who like it not, quite commonly attach to it a significance, and entail for it consequences, far beyond the intentions of its author. The man who summarized thoughts already old to himself and many others, in the blazing trilogy of words, "an irrepressible conflict," thought that he was only describing a condition; but the words meant far more than that to friend and foe alike.

Another descriptive phrase, which lived long after
its immediate purpose had been served, and influenced
the popular American view of America long after its
origin had been forgotten, was that which characterized this country as "The Melting-Pot." There was
sufficient verisimilitude in the picture suggested, to
gain it popular acceptance; and in the decade before
the World War people were willing generally to take
for granted the genuineness and the excellence of the
metal poured from the pot into the molds. There were
men then, and there are many more now, who did
and do question the assimilative capacity of the "melting-pot," and not only the possibility but even the desirability of turning out, from an indiscriminate con-
glomeration of elements, a stamped and thoroughly
standardized product. They cannot even yet agree as
to whether this product stood the tests of heat and
stress, in the war years, well or badly.

But without entering at all into the discussion as
to the efficiency or the beneficence of the melting-pot,
one may still question the accuracy, or the complete-
ness, of the picture presented by it to the mind. For it
is a part of the connotation of that phrase that the ma-
terials thrown in are, in themselves, shapeless, un-
formed lumps of ore or baser metals, or broken scraps
of little use or value until reduced to a molten mass,
refined and fused into a finer metal, and formed into
the desired and pre-designed product; and that they
do not, themselves, affect either crucible or mold in the

process. Such a picture of America has commonly so filled the frame of popular vision as to leave little room in it for a view of this country as a magnet, which has had the happy power to attract to itself rare specimens of the finest metal, already refined by training and tested in the fire of experience, and already sufficiently fixed in form and hardened in substance to be spared, or to resist, the melting-down process, and themselves to produce a positive effect upon the whole of which they become individual parts. Such immigrants are usually Americans by choice; and whether they have come from preference, as did Albert Gallatin, or because of too stubborn a resistance to some other smelting process, as did Francis Lieber, or because rejected by governments which wanted men of different mold and more malleable metal, it has been one of the glories of the American system of government that it could draw to itself such men, or hold and use them even when thrown off in its direction, without their own volition, by some turn of the wheel in Europe.

Such an immigrant was Carl Schurz. He landed in New York on the seventeenth of September, 1852,[1] as a precociously mature young man who had already developed and revealed many of those peculiar qualities of mind and character which later made him so distinctive and colorful a figure in the history of two

[1] Carl Schurz, *Reminiscences* (3 vols.; New York: McClure Co., 1906–7), I, 406; II, 3.

generations. While the determination to stay permanently in this country had by no means, at that time,
taken any such definite shape in his mind, it did gradually do so in the course of the next few years. By the
end of a decade the republic had bound him irrevocably
to itself and had conceded to him positions and distinc-
tions which would be truly amazing if one did not consider both the peculiar timeliness of his arrival and
the outstanding, incisive qualities which he already
possessed at the time of his immigration, and which
enabled him to exert a positive influence upon the course
of events even while consciously shaping his own course
to them.

His own recollections of his early life and experiences in Germany were written late in life, after
he had acquired such mastery of the English language
as to use it as freely and felicitously as he could his
native tongue. Yet he found that, for writing about
his German experiences, the German language lent
itself more readily to his use. So he used it; and Volume I of his *Reminiscences* was translated into English
for him by Mrs. Eleanora Kennicutt,[2] and then read
and approved by him before publication. These "reminiscences" were written by him about a half-century

[2] C.S., *Rem.*, I, 4. Conversely, Volume II of the *Lebenserinnerungen* was later translated from English into German, partly by his
daughter, Miss Agatha Schurz, and partly by Miss Mary Nolte, of
Bremen, under Miss Schurz's guidance. That part of Volume III of
the *Reminiscences* which was written by Mr. Schurz himself (i.e., up
to his taking of the oath of office in the U.S. Senate in 1869) is in-

after his immigration;[3] but their standard of accuracy
was raised by the diligence with which he collected contemporary letters and in other ways verified his memory of details;[4] and they are well supplemented by the
many contemporary letters that are still extant, some
of them published[5] and some not.[6]

As to the school and university career of Schurz,
the letters supplement the *Reminiscences* without con-
tradicting them in any important particular. In the
latter, for example, he speaks of the stimulating influence of his mother;[7] in the letters, she appears more
plainly as a woman of strong character and sincere
Christian faith, constantly demanding of her boy, away
in school, his best efforts. It is evident that the small
successes of a schoolboy were a source of pride to his

---

cluded in the second volume of the *Lebenserinnerungen,* with the exception of the last half-dozen paragraphs, dealing with relations between himself and President Grant. The remainder, with a number of
letters, makes up the third volume of the German edition, which in
that respect differs most widely from the English.

[3] In the years just before and after 1900.

[4] C.S., *Rem.,* II, 328.

[5] *Speeches, Correspondence, and Political Papers of Carl Schurz,*
selected and edited by Frederic Bancroft on behalf of the Carl Schurz
Memorial Committee (6 vols.; New York: G. P. Putnam's Sons,
1913); Carl Schurz, *Lebenserinnerungen,* Band III, *Briefe und Lebensabriss* (Berlin: Georg Reimer, 1912) (the *Lebensabriss* by Bancroft
and Dunning, translated into German by Max F. Blau, Princeton).

[6] Carl Schurz Manuscripts Collections, Library of Congress and
Wisconsin Historical Society.

[7] C.S., *Rem.,* I, 25.

parents, and particularly to his father, who was inor-
dinately fond of showing off his son's musical accom-
plishments, since his more purely academic ones lent
themselves less readily to purposes of display.[8] But
they were not merely accepted as a source of pride;
they were demanded, as a just return for the very real
sacrifices necessary to maintain him in the "Gymna-
sium" and as befitting the talents which teachers,
friends, and parents assured him he possessed.[9] Going
up, then, from the village schools of Liblar and Brühl,
son of a village schoolmaster, and grandson, on his
mother's side, of a *Burghalfen*, or tenant-in-chief, of
Count Wolf Metternich, from whom he seems to have
inherited much of his exceptionally resilient physical
vitality, as well as some of the tendency to dominate
which later marked him, it is not surprising that he
was but little tempted to frivolous use of time or money, either at Cologne (Köln) or, later, in the University of Bonn. Neither is it surprising that, under such
insistent pressure from home, and friendly recognition from teachers and associates, his ideas and expres-

[8] There is a somewhat pathetic, but very appealing, story to the
effect that, to the end of his days, the old gentleman was unable to resist the temptation to inform chance acquaintances that "Carl Schurz
is my son."

[9] Letter, Marianne Schurz, to her son, Carl, January 3, 1844, in
C.S., *Lebn.*, III, 2: "It depends solely on your industry and deport-
ment; you have talent. . . . . Where will you find a father who needs
his money so much, and who is spending and has already spent so
much on his child?"

sions should have been marked by ambition and brilliance more than by humility. But under the guidance
of such teachers as Bone, Pütz, and Kinkel, he developed much more than the mere superficial attributes
of precocity; and long before the revolutionary movement of 1848 put an end to his peaceful preparations
for a professorship of history in some German university, he had developed, and revealed in correspondence,
many of the traits of mind and character which marked
him, later, in his life in America.

One of these was a serious and philosophical turn
of mind. The Franconia, a student club to which he
belonged and in which he found most of his intimate
associates, must have in it no members merely for con-
geniality or to fill out its numbers, but must choose
only those of outstanding scholarship and character
and must be marked first by a higher standard of scholarship for *all* of its members.[10] *Manfred* and *Faust*
were elaborately analyzed and compared, and Byron
and Shakespeare similarly weighed up in the balances
soon after an evening spent in seeing *Hamlet* and reading *Werner*.[11]

His own literary ambition was unbounded but
lacked direction. At one time he was writing a novel,
the theme of which was "the contrast between the ideal
world in the mind of a young poet, and the crass prose

[10] Letter to Theodore Petrasch, a friend for many years, 1846, in
C.S., *Lebn.*, III, 24.

[11] Letter to Petrasch, November 17, 1845, *ibid.*, p. 3.

of every-day life."[12] At another, he was trying his
hand at poetry and was seriously concerned about himself because "only occasionally a lyric came" to him
and, while aspiring to be a dramatist and to write
something of national interest, seemed to be making no
progress at all with an epic.[13] Again, during vacation,
he had written a Latin treatise.[14] Speaking with an
old man's tolerant condescension of the effusions of
his early youth, many years later, after his *Life of
Henry Clay* had been widely acclaimed as an excellent
contribution to American literature as well as for its
historical value, Mr. Schurz congratulated himself,
probably with good reason, upon the fact that these
early writings were lost or burned, and never published.[15] But the general amazement occasioned by the
literary qualities of his early lectures and addresses,
even in the alien tongue of his adopted country, would
have been considerably lessened by a more general
realization of the thoroughness of his philological
training and of the early inception and constant

[12] Letter to Petrasch, January 27, 1846, *ibid.*, p. 6. "Richard
Wanderer," Carl Schurz Manuscripts, Library of Congress. Not without merit, but valuable chiefly as psychological source for his early
youth, being largely autobiographical.

[13] Letter to Petrasch, February 6, 1846, in C.S., *Lebn.*, III, 9.

[14] Letters to Petrasch, September 23, 1846, *ibid.*, p. 22, and November 7, 1846, Carl Schurz Manuscripts, Wisconsin Historical Society.

[15] C.S., *Rem.*, I, 92. A few poems, as well as "Richard Wanderer," did survive, in MS.

strength of his ambition to make a name for himself in literature.

The question of religious belief was approached in a fashion no less earnest than those of scholarship and literary endeavor. In common with many of his contemporaries, he rejected the orthodox doctrine of the Catholic church. In his case, this rejection came at the time of confirmation and was occasioned by what appeared to him as the narrowness of a doctrine which was presented to him as denying salvation to any but true Catholics and even to unbaptized infants.[16] This apostasy, and occasional rather unfavorable references to the Catholic church, later in life[17] exposed him to numerous charges of atheism and infidelity. Presumably with these in mind, he said in his *Reminiscences* that he had never adopted, nor been able to understand or sympathize with, or even to tolerate, the disrespectful attitude of the scoffer in matters of religion.[18] How far from atheism the remarkably thoughtful boy really was at the time of his revolt from Roman Catholicism will appear from a reading of another letter to Petrasch.[19] In it he argued that "indifferentism" was not possible; "A man has to know what he knows and what he believes." Tracing the universality and

[16] C.S., *Rem.*, I, 70.

[17] As in his address on "True Americanism," Faneuil Hall, Boston, April 18, 1859.

[18] C.S., *Rem.*, I, 71.

[19] From Cologne, February 16, 1846, in C.S., *Lebn.*, III, 14.

noting the strength of the belief in God and immortality, and characterizing it as "the religion of humanity," he pointed out that the belief of all the philosophers actually far exceeded their knowledge, and came to the conclusion, which he announced as his unalterable conviction, that it was impossible not to believe in God. A boy who, at fifteen, had done the thinking indicated by this letter was a fitting father of the man who, at thirty, showed such independence of character and such supreme confidence in the correctness of his own conclusions on any question which he had thoroughly considered.

This trait of intellectual independence was shown also in matters less weighty than religion. The Franconia must have among its members "no men who would be entirely under the influence of others," but men of real individuality capable of original thought and firm convictions. These views were expressed before he was himself a member. He would "much rather be thought awkward than insignificant"; and if he must conform in all things to the views of a leader or a majority, he would refuse an invitation to join.[20] An actual refusal would probably have been a definite one.[21]

He was quite capable of criticizing his associates,

[20] Letter to Petrasch, from Cologne, August 6, 1846.

[21] "Was ich nicht will, das thue ich nicht, eben weil ich es nicht will. . . . . Ein fester Wille lässt sich nicht zwingen," letter to Petrasch, June 4, 1847, in C.S. MSS., W.H.S.

in friendly but very frank fashion, for failure to show
similar independence, and of characterizing as a weak-
ness any concession to circumstances.[22] But he was
quite capable of participation in the most violent differences of opinion, and in the most heated arguments,
without permitting his feelings of friendship to be at
all affected by them, provided that he considered the
opposing opinions to be honestly held. When nearing
the age of nineteen, he could write, after a heated
argument which had apparently had a stormy ending:

> I have respect for every conviction as soon as I know it to
> be an honest one, and would never oppose it with extrinsic per-
> sonalities. . . . . Let us prove that we are not reckless boys, and
> that we know what it means to show proper respect for honest
> opinion.[23]

No such forbearance was shown, either then or later,
where he did not consider his opponent's "conviction"
to be an honest one; but even in such cases he consistently refrained from the use of "extrinsic personalities," although he found, to his pained surprise, that
the game of American politics was not universally
played by such gentlemanly rules. Among his friends
in later years, as with Petrasch in youth, he continued
to debate with vigor any difference of opinion, and to
furnish them, as a friendly duty, unbidden advice and
opinions as to their conduct. Even Lincoln was not

[22] *Ibid.*; also, February 6, 1846, in C.S., *Lebn.*, III, 9.

[23] Letter to Petrasch, December 21, 1848, in C.S., *Lebn.*, III, 37.

spared,[24] and even Lincoln did not spare him some extremely sharp rejoinders;[25] but he retained the friendship of the mature Lincoln[26] as he did that of the
youthful Petrasch.

Student life, however, was not all theology, literary criticism, or philosophy, nor entirely devoted to the
dangerous duties of the self-appointed censor. His
teacher in the art of speech, Professor Gottfried Kinkel, found in him not only an ardent proselyte in the
doctrines of political liberalism but an agreeable com-
panion in social and musical enjoyments; while Frau
Johanna Kinkel, the professor's wife, shared with him
her knowledge and appreciation of music, so that he
learned to find in it much of his keenest artistic pleasure and even a medium of expression for his own emo-
tions. This love of music was a permanent part of his
life.[27]

This association with the Kinkels and their friends,
all older than himself, and also with his fellow-mem-

[24] Letters to Lincoln, November 8, 1862, in C.S., *S.C.&P.P.*, I,
209; November 20, 1862, *ibid.*, I, 213 (original draft in C.S. MSS.,
L.C.).

[25] Letters from Lincoln, November 10, 1862, in C.S., *S.C.&P.P.*,
I, 211; November 24, 1862, *ibid.*, I, 219; in C.S., *Rem.*, II, 394.

[26] C.S., *Rem.*, II, 396.

[27] It was, in part, his playing in the White House during an evening in the early spring of 1861 that earned him from John Hay, then
one of President Lincoln's private secretaries, the humorous but admiring cognomen, "the elegant Teuton." Letter of John Hay, quoted
by W. R. Thayer, *Life and Letters of John Hay* (2 vols.; Boston and
New York: Houghton Mifflin Co., 1915), II, 443.

bers of the Franconia, was very fortunate for him.
For by them the introspective youth was drawn somewhat out of himself and saved from excessive egoism;
and he developed not only the ability to meet people
easily and to impress them favorably[28] but also the more
endearing quality of a real genius for friendship.
Those who knew him best in his later years[29] speak
of him still in terms of genuine affection; the letters
of the associates of his most strenuous period breathe
the same spirit;[30] and his Cologne and Bonn letters
show that happy faculty of giving and of winning affection to have been already developed at that early
period. This trait of lovableness among his intimates
adds much to the attractiveness of the character of a
youth who would appear, superficially, to have been
almost painfully high-minded, strenuous, and self-
conscious.

That he did have this human and lovable side later
is quite abundantly shown by the unpublished letters in
English in the collection of manuscripts in the Library

[28] Note his striking social success at the Jefferson Day dinner and
private dinners in Boston, 1859; and L. P. Harvey's testimonial of
friendship "as strong . . . as I ever remember to have experienced
on so brief an acquaintance as with yourself" (letter to Schurz, December 20, 1857. C.S. MSS., L.C.).

[29] Notably Mr. Oswald Garrison Villard and Dr. Frederic Bancroft.

[30] Letters of D. L. Buttrick, Milwaukee, September 15, 1861, in
C.S. MSS., L.C., and of Halbert E. Paine, former law partner, April
4 and October 12, 1861, *ibid.*

of Congress, particularly those to and from Charles Sumner, and by the family letters in German in the Wisconsin Historical Society collection. How much he himself felt he owed to his friends of school days was indicated in his own words, in a revival of the Petrasch correspondence, after an interruption of fifteen years, occasioned by the revolutionary movement of 1848:

> Far separated in time and experience, we may have been able to lose one another in life and in countenance. But the recollections of the cherished days of youth, when we clung together like brothers, nothing can destroy in me. . . . . We were at the age when a couple of years' difference means much. I was younger than you. . . . . I often wondered how you could become thus attached to me, and . . . . I still do not understand it. I leaned upon you with enthusiastic friendship; you drew me out of the narrow sphere which my circumstances and training built about me, and gave me a glimpse into life. You taught me first to overcome my anxious bashfulness. I have to thank you for every encouraging word because you were the first to awaken in me the consciousness that I did not belong to the commonplace. Then, when I had just gained courage to stand on my own feet and power to be something to you, the vortex of life seized us both and drew us asunder, and only now do I receive a word from you and you from me.[31]

All of the activities and relationships described above were designed to prepare the young man for a life of peace; and he pursued his philological and historical studies and his artistic avocations with such a life in prospect. But such a mind as his was fertile soil

[31] Letter from camp at Catlett Station, Virginia, September 24, 1863, in C.S., *Lebn.*, III, 225. Schurz was then a major-general in the Army of the Potomac.

for the seeds of political liberalism. While he had chosen the history of Germany at the time of the Great Reformation as the field of his special study,[32] the character of that period who interested him most was Ulrich von Hutton; and the source of that period's attraction for him was the semblance of strength and unity with which the historian had clothed the "holy Roman empire of the German nation." The University of Bonn must have been an exceptionally congenial environment for one following such a nationalistic trend of thought; for Dahlmann, Duneker, Sybel, Arndt, and Treitschke were all connected with it, at one time or another, either as teachers or as students. In contrast with the period of disunion and impotence which opened the nineteenth century, the unity of the past took on, in the mind of the student, a reality probably never attained in fact; while a future union of the German people was viewed rather in the light of its eminent desirability than of its immediate, practical attainability.

It was the opinion of the more democratic theorists that this union, of course, must be of a liberal sort and must rest upon a broad popular basis and constitutional forms.[33] As early as 1845, Schurz had developed in his mind, to the point of outlining it in a letter to Petrasch, a political philosophy of a sort entirely incompatible with the forms of government then existing in the German states. Using Shakespeare as

[32] C.S., *Rem.*, I, 110.   [33] *Ibid.*

an example, he maintained that the excellence of his portrayals of characters of the lower walks of life was due to the fact of his own common birth, and that anyone so born could understand the class or classes above himself far better than they could understand him; that, therefore, since the people understood their rulers better than the latter understood the people, and since it was easier for a man to lift himself, in his own thinking, into a plane above his own than it was for one to reverse that process, government ought to come from below rather than from above. It could not properly be imposed upon a people. He had also made a speech, "basing soul life and development wholly on the conception of freedom."[34] And interest in the Reformation had not excluded the French Revolution from his consideration.

Thinking thus, even before coming so much as later under the influence of the revolutionary Kinkel, or beginning to wear under his coat the forbidden black-red-gold ribbon of the Burschenschaft societies,[35] it was not surprising that when the outbreaks of 1848 and 1849 occurred, he should quickly have become involved in them. That happened. It is notable, however, that, although he was still but nineteen years of age when the word came from France which set up great convulsive movements in Central Europe, he had already developed not only those political convictions

[34] Letter to Petrasch, November 17, 1845, in C.S., *Lebn.*, III, 3.
[35] C.S., *Rem.*, I, 35.

which seconded the impulses of youth in plunging him into them but also many of those distinctive traits of mind and character which survived, with little change, all the vicissitudes of revolt, exile, and emigration, and which made of him such an individualist but at the same time so useful a ready-made citizen of the United States.

The following words, written by himself just before the surrender of the fortress of Rastatt in 1849, when faced, as he believed, by the alternatives of a quick death or lifelong imprisonment, were at once a consciously accurate self-characterization and an unconsciously true prophecy. "I knew my life would be full of storms and dangers, because I was too proud to evade them. But I always imagined that I should die like a man whose memory should encompass a rich life, charged with distinguished achievements."[36] He could not then know that his life was to be spared until the laudable ambition, then expressed as a regretful wish, should be abundantly realized.

[36] Letter to parents from Rastatt, July 21, 1849, *q.v.* below, chap. ii.

CHAPTER II

WANDERINGS

WHEN the news of the overthrow of the monarchy of Louis Philippe reached Bonn, it was assumed by the young liberals there that "something of course must happen" there, too,[1] though they seem to have had rather vague ideas as to just what it would be. Still, emotionally and psychologically, they were quite ready to act. In spite of repressive measures typified by the Karlsbad decrees, the hopes aroused during the war of liberation by royal promises or half-promises, such as the manifests of Kalisch, had never died out. In Prussia they had acquired new strength since the accession of Frederick William IV; and when at last, early in 1847, he summoned an assembly consisting of members of the provincial diets already formed,[2] it was assumed by many that arbitrary government was about to give way to a constitutional monarchy, wherein the popular will might find expression through constitutional channels.

[1] *C.S., Rem.,* I, 112.

[2] *Ibid.,* p. 107. The decree by which the Landtag was created was dated February 3, 1847. Carlton J. H. Hayes, *Political and Social History of Modern Europe* (2 vols.; New York: Macmillan Co., 1924), II, 126; E. F. Henderson, *Short History of Germany,* 343; J. A. R. Marriott and C. Grant Robertson, *The Evolution of Prussia* (Oxford: Clarendon Press, 1915), pp. 307, 308.

General disappointment and increasing discontent, rather than complete disillusionment, followed Frederick William's refusal to concede any such powers to the assembly. Coexistent with this demand for popular participation in government, in the minds of the reformers, had been the aspiration toward a national union of the German states. It was even farther from realization in February of 1848. But the French revolution of that month, far from furnishing the Germans with a new idea, seemed only to have set them an example of the speedy and successful accomplishment of purposes already familiar. Republicans were not wanting; but republicanism was no essential part of the reform program, even in Rhenish Prussia, the Bavarian Palatinate, or Baden where the influence of the "Gallicized radicals of the Rhineland" and of Polish and Swiss refugees made it strongest. Schurz wrote, in June: "We head fellows are, all and sundry, republicans, but with measure and moderation."[3]

It is perhaps needless to say that, in naming himself as one of the "head fellows," he referred to the student federation in Bonn University and not to any national revolutionary movement. There were at that time, unfortunately, no such national leaders; and if there had been, a student of nineteen years would hardly have been numbered among them. The whole movement lacked coherence; and the efforts of Schurz

[3] Letter to Petrasch from Bonn, June 26, 1848, in *Lebn.*, III, 33; Marriott and Robertson, *op. cit.*, pp. 309, 315.

and others were then being devoted to an attempt to
form a union of all the student clubs and of fencing
and other corps among the young men of Bonn.[4] Going as organized groups of speakers to address meetings
in the city and neighboring towns, writing articles for
the *Bonner Zeitung*, a newspaper started and edited by
Kinkel, and, presumably, talking endlessly among
themselves, he and his friends devoted almost their entire time to political activity. But they met with but
indifferent success. The number of those accustomed
to independent or political thinking was small; and
the number of those capable of showing initiative or
willing to hazard anything remained small. Although
he had himself been content, only two years before, to
lie in a window and watch with sympathetic but idle
amusement a midnight clash of the populace with the
military in Cologne, Schurz could not now understand
the indifference of others.[5] During these early months,
however, the active ones did at least succeed in gaining
official recognition from the University for their political organizations;[6] and when the Prussian national
government, feeling itself forced to make similar temporary concessions, summoned a diet in Berlin, Kinkel
went up to it as delegate from Bonn, leaving the active
editorship of the *Bonner Zeitung* in the hands of

[4] Letter to Petrasch, June 26, 1848, *supra*, n. 3.

[5] *Ibid.*

[6] *Ibid.*

Schurz, while still maintaining his connection with it and writing articles for it from Berlin.[7]

Kinkel's mantle as general leader of the local agitation, as well as conductor of its journalistic enterprise, seems to have fallen upon the shoulders of his youthful protégé and to have thrown him into a state of the greatest excitement and kaleidoscopic changes of emotional reaction. Free for the first time, because of the removal of the censorship, to write his views for publication rather than the private perusal of his friends only, he reveled, like an errant schoolboy, in the noise he could make and in the unfavorable notice he was quickly able to win from the academic senate. He was delighted to find himself odious to that body, and, encouraged by the approval of his friends, fancied he held in his own hands the control of the local movement. The government having as yet taken no action, he saw no prospect of failure but considered the uprising permanent and assured Kinkel that Bonn was "the most un-quiet city on the Rhine."[8] In the same letter, however, he sobered himself to give a scrupulously careful account of his stewardship and to make repeated requests for advice and active guidance from his absent superior. He did not restrain himself from offering suggestions freely as to changes of procedure and policy, but the changes proposed were those of the

[7] Letter to Kinkel, March 20, 1849, in C.S. MSS., W.H.S.; Lebn., III, 39.

[8] Ibid.; Marriott and Robertson, op. cit., p. 316.

pupil who suggested ways in which the paper might, he thought, be made to bear more clearly the imprint of the teacher's control and to present his political views more effectively.[9]

The very old boy of 1848, thus suddenly converted into the very young man of 1849, and still alternating between self-confidence and humility, and similarly between regretful recognition of his youth and inexperience at one moment,[10] and self-congratulations at another, that for some years yet he could hope to escape being called up for service in the Prussian army,[11] and disturbed still further, in the early spring of 1849, by the recurring fear that he might, after all, be "stuck in the muskets for a couple of years,"[12] had naturally even less opportunity for quiet reflection, or for viewing himself or the liberal movement in any sort of perspective, than in the preceding year.

Once, in September, 1848, he used an expression in a letter which showed that he had at least made an attempt to keep his sense of proportion. He suffered from disillusionment after seeing the Frankfort parliament forced already to call upon the princes of Germany for protection against the people of the region because of its abandonment of the cause of the Ger-

[9] Letter to Kinkel, *supra*, n. 7.

[10] *Ibid.*

[11] *Ibid.*; letter to Petrasch, March 23, 1849, in *Lebn.*, III, 43.

[12] Letter to Petrasch, March 23, 1849, *supra*, n. 11.

mans of Schleswig-Holstein.[13] He was further disillu-
sioned after attending a general students' conference
at Eisenach, where in an atmosphere charged with
excitement youthful orators stimulated themselves still
further with liberal potations, drinking numerous
toasts, giving voice to some startling sentiments and
even indulging in some mild disorder, without attracting the attention of the authorities either favorably or
unfavorably.[14] He began to realize the inertia that had
to be overcome and the lack of solid weight behind the
movement for reform. Perhaps with those experiences
in mind he wrote: "If the German nation makes itself
ridiculous now, it will be ridiculous for a long, long
time."[15] Another illusion was lost when Karl Marx,
in whom he had expected to find all the qualities of
wisdom and greatness, showed at a conference in Cologne such didacticism and intellectual arrogance as
totally to unfit him for the rôle of a popular leader.[16]
With increased activity and a growing sense of importance, as has been indicated, this questioning attitude
of pessimism had given place to a more optimistic and
perhaps less critical one by the time the revolutionary
movement was a year old and still unchecked by government.

That the period should have been one of confusion was perhaps inevitable, and that the counsels of

[13] C.S., *Rem.*, I, 141–43; Hayes, *op. cit.*, II, 136.

[14] C.S., *Rem.*, I, 145–51.

[15] Letter to Petrasch, September 18, 1848, in *Lebn.*, III, 27.

[16] C.S., *Rem.*, I, 139, 140.

the reformers should have been marked more by earnestness than by unity or steadiness of purpose was but
natural. When added maturity and years of life in
America had enabled him to review the activities of
1848 and 1849 as he could not do at the time, Schurz
summarized, as follows, the effects of the old censorship and the consequences of its sudden removal. The
censorship had not stopped agitation but had only driv-
en it under cover and increased its bitterness and the
extravagance of its designs.

> The strangest doctrines of political and social organization
> were thus propagated, and the most adventurous plans of fu-
> ture action seriously formed and entertained. All those who felt
> sensible of the pressure of an absolute government, grasped at
> this forbidden fruit with morbid avidity. Sense and nonsense
> were taken in promiscuously by all those who had not accus-
> tomed themselves to a regular mental discipline; everything op-
> positional, however extreme or strange, was secretly but fervid-
> ly applauded,—because everything that resisted the pressure
> from above seemed to cheer and relieve the minds of the people.
> . . . . [In 1848 the censorship was removed.] Writing and
> speaking [went on] everywhere, and yet no two men seemed to
> understand each other. Most of them certainly did not under-
> stand themselves [Demagogism then became a danger] . . . .
> because the people had been deprived so long of the instruction
> and discipline that free speech brings with it; because the peo-
> ple . . . . were apt to believe that everything that sounded
> well was right, and that everything that pleased their imagina-
> tion was reasonable.[17]

[17] Address on "Free Speech," Boston, December 11, 1860, in
Schurz, *Speeches* (Lippincott, 1865), pp. 222 ff.; Hayes, *op. cit.*, II,
126.

It may be regrettable, but is not surprising, that conditions should have been as just described. A year was spent in agitation and discussion, during the latter part of which the Frankfort parliament was in session and during which it earned the esteem of liberals by the personal respectability of its membership and the high moral and intellectual standard set by its debates, while incurring the disrespect of worshipers of success by its failure to overcome its own inhibitions and the more or less active hostility of the hereditary rulers of the German states. The princes of the smaller states were naturally opposed to both liberalism and nationalism.

As early as September, 1848, Prussia successfully disregarded the wishes of the Frankfort parliament in the matter of the Danish peace. In April, 1849, her king refused the crown of a proposed united German state, proffered to him by the parliament;[18] and the concern shown by Schurz in the matter of military service[19] was not without reason, for affairs then began to move rapidly on to a crisis. In the first week of May the parliament, having finished the work of making a national constitution, appealed to the German people

[18] Marriott and Robertson, *op. cit.*, p. 326; F. H. Henderson, *op. cit.*, pp. 362–65; Hayes, *op. cit.*, II, 141 and 142. Schurz later thought timidity, the fear of Austria, to have been his chief reason for doing so, and quoted him as having said: "If you could have addressed your appeal to Frederick the Great, he would have been your man; but I am not a great ruler" (C.S., *Rem.*, I, 169).

[19] Letter to Petrasch, March 23, 1849, *supra*, nn. 11 and 12, p. 22.

to uphold it and to secure its adoption. This was taken as an appeal to arms in the Bavarian Palatinate, Baden, and Saxony. The king of Saxony was restored to his throne by aid of Prussian troops; and in the second week of May disorder broke out in Rhenish Prussia, evoked largely by the government's proposal to call out the *Landwehr* for similar use in the suppression of the revolt in Baden and the Palatinate.

An abortive attempt was made on the night of May 10 by the Bonn revolutionists to seize arms for their prospective forces and to anticipate the mustering, next day, of the *Landwehr* by the seizure of the nearby Siegburg arsenal. Plans for the attempt were but half-made, and with almost no secrecy at all, and were carried out in bungling fashion; so the government had but to send out a single handful of cavalry, who were permitted to trot unwittingly through the double handful of half-hearted insurrectionaries who had started on the road to Siegburg but who, at the approach of the troops, took to the fields in the darkness and again sought the security of their homes.[20]

The principal speaker in the mass meetings which resolved upon the Siegburg expedition had been Kinkel, who had returned to Bonn after the dissolution of the Prussian diet; and such military leadership as it had was furnished by Fritz Anneke and Josef Gerhardt. An active and trusted lieutenant of the leaders in both

[20] C.S., *Rem.*, I, 170–77.

phases of the otherwise insignificant affair was Carl Schurz. Having thus made themselves conspicuous, these men would have found it doubly dangerous to have returned home and stood trial for their efforts to incite and to conduct a treasonable attack upon a government arsenal. Smarting, moreover, under the humiliating realization of the dismal and complete failure of an action so incommensurate with their ambitions and anticipations, they chose to associate themselves with such insurrections elsewhere as had not broken down or been suppressed. Schurz went on reluctantly, and only because he thought himself too badly compromised to return.

After pushing on, with two others, to Siegburg and Elberfeld, and being convinced that nothing but noise and confusion could be expected of the popular demonstrations there, Schurz traveled alone up the Rhine to Kaiserslautern, where he rejoined Kinkel and Anneke. The latter had been made chief of artillery in the revolutionary forces of the Bavarian Palatinate, and made Schurz a member of his staff. These forces were officered in part by men of Prussian training, who later showed, in the American Civil War, some real ability as commanders. Among them were Blenker, Mahler, Beust, and Schimmelpfennig, the last named of whom in 1862 and 1863 was a brigade commander in Schurz's division of the Eleventh Corps of the Army of the Potomac. Franz Sigel, who in 1862 com-

manded that corps, was in 1849 a major in the revolutionary forces in Baden.[21]

The Badisch forces were attacked first by the
Prussians in the performance of their self-appointed
task of the pacification of their neighbor states. Schurz,
serving with the men of the Palatinate, saw his first
military actions at Brucksaal, where he received a
slight wound in the leg, and at Ubstadt, in June, in an
attempt to protect the flank of the retreating Badisch
army. The first real stand was made at the fortress of
Rastatt (Rastadt), where the insurrectionary forces
were able to endure a siege of some weeks but were
finally induced to surrender, upon being convinced of
the general and complete failure of the uprising, elsewhere.[22]

With the curious logic of oppression, the Prussian
government, which considered it proper for its own
troops to intervene in the neighboring states in the interest of reaction, found it a doubly serious offense
on the part of Prussian subjects to have participated
in the revolts there. Prussians among the garrison
therefore had to face the prospect, on surrender to the
Prussian army, of more rigorous treatment under mar-
tial law than their comrades would probably receive.

[21] *Ibid.*, pp. 188, 190.

[22] *Ibid.*, p. 203; Becker und Esselen, *Geschichte der süddeutschen
Revolution des Jahres 1849* (Genf.: Gottfried Becker, 1849), pp.
323–29 and 439–50; also *Nachträgliche authentische Aufschlüsse
über die badische Revolution von 1849,* in "Sammlung social-politi-
scher Schriften" (Zurich, 1876), XX, 150–55 and 169–71.

Such a fate, in fact, befell Kinkel, who was wounded, and so captured, outside Rastatt.[23] For "having fought among the insurgents in Baden with arms in his hands against Prussian troops,"[24] he was tried before a court-martial of Prussian officers. By his spirited defense and eloquence they were moved to pronounce, "instead of the penalty of death," only the sentence that he should lose the Prussian cockade and be confined for life in a fortress. This sentence was reviewed by the royal auditor-general and the king, and by them changed to a more severe and dishonorable form of imprisonment as a felon in a house of penal servitude. Some others were executed, including the senior officers of the garrison.[25]

The facts as to Kinkel's fate (except that of his capture) were, of course, unknown to Schurz on the day of the surrender of Rastatt, July 23, 1849; but he knew only too well that some such fate awaited him, as a Prussian, at the hands of the Prussian troops. Seeing, therefore, his life "ending where it ought to begin,"[26] and given ample time as well as food for

[23] C.S., *Rem.*, I, 235; *Aufschlüsse über die badische Revolution des Jahres 1849*, p. 450.

[24] Quoted from public announcement of Commanding General von Hirschfeld, Freiburg, September 30, 1849, as given in C.S., *Rem.*, I, 247.

[25] *Ibid.* Henderson says many were sentenced to death (*op. cit.*, p. 367). Becker and Esseling, (*op. cit.*, p. 449), name thirteen; the *Aufschlüsse über die badische Revolution* name the same ones as executed at Rastatt, and ten others, executed elsewhere.

[26] Letter to friends cited in n. 29.

thought in the closing days of the siege, which were
devoted to a fruitless attempt to secure more favorable
terms of surrender than "at discretion,"[27] he gave expression to his reflections in two extremely interesting
valedictory letters—one to his parents[28] and one to his
friends[29]—placed in the hands of his host, Mr. Nus-
ser, to be posted as soon as communications were re-
opened and as soon as the fate of the Prussian prisoners
had been decided.[30] To the reader who knows that the
day of surrender was actually made to be the day of
escape, the dramatic effect of these letters is somewhat
affected by a certain sense of anticlimax; but although
the second of them was dated on that day, no evidence
is apparent to disprove his own statement that it was
written in the morning and that the idea of escape occurred to him suddenly and not until about noon.[31]

Under such circumstances he would not have been
himself and he failed to realize the dramatic possibilities of the situation; yet he wrote with marked re-

[27] C.S., *Rem.*, I, 213.

[28] Dated July 21, 1849, in *Lebn.*, III, 45; mentioned in C.S.,
Rem., I, 215.

[29] Dated July 23, 1849, the day of surrender (*Lebn.*, III, 49).

[30] C. S., *Rem.*, I, 215. Only one of these letters, that to his parents, is here mentioned; and it is spoken of as having been written on
the day of surrender, given as July 23. But in the *Lebenserinnerungen*
the two letters appear, dated as above, nn. 28 and 29.

[31] *Ibid.*, p. 216. The statement was made, however, about the
letter to his parents, actually dated two days earlier. The letter to his
friends is not mentioned in the *Reminiscences*.

straint and absence of heroics. One part of the first
letter was, in fact, almost apologetic:

> I tried to pass judgment on great situations, although I had
> not seen them and *because* I had not seen them. I would partic-
> ipate in great affairs, although and because I had not considered
> the necessity of a far-reaching organization, or because, in a
> measure, I thought such an organization superfluous. If I have
> deceived myself, I have merely suffered the fate of common
> men, and a heavy penance will expiate a trivial fault.

To his parents, he expressed his thanks as a dutiful
son for their sacrifices for his education, now apparently thrown away, and sorrow that they must face
old age without his support.[32] While filled with regret
for the pain occasioned for them by his course, he
found none to express for his acts themselves, and
hoped that he could, like Kinkel, "die like a man, because he had lived like one."[33]

In writing to his friends, he showed more concern
about self-justification. He claimed credit for no brilliant military exploits and asked them only to believe
that he had not been afraid in battle. In defending
himself against supposititious charges of having sacri-
ficed his usefulness by being overeager, excitable, and
intolerant of opposing views, he produced a somewhat
naïve but singularly revealing picture of himself:

[32] His only brother, Herbert, had died in boyhood.

[33] Letter to parents, *supra*, n. 27. In the same letter, he wrote:
"At this moment, which in its devastating reality banishes every romantic illusion, the pleasant consciousness that I have done my duty
with spirit and honor becomes doubly clear. I have never been prouder
than now, for I know I have never had a better right to be."

I did not want to be second where I could be first; I did not want to serve where I understood how to command. But subordination under superiority has never come hard for me; and I have never denied recognition to superior power wherever I found it. . . . . [But] there was in me a certain untamableness . . . . [and] I was on the way to become an intolerant person.

Men could have been found among political managers and placemen in America, years later, who might have suggested that these tendencies had revived in Mr. Schurz, in spite of this early recognition and confession of them; and some, even, of his political friends may have considered that his recognition of superiority was never too easily won.

The letter concluded in a tone of true nobility with a simple but eloquent sentence that deserves to be remembered as a tribute to unsuccessful and impractical idealists of all times, everywhere, and as an antidote to the condescension with which they are often so described. It read: "Remember occasionally a friend who pledged his life for the realization of an idea before knowing the means of achievement; whose greatest sin it was, contrary to his own theory, to be too regardless of egoism."[34]

The story of the escape of Schurz with two companions from the fortress of Rastatt on the day of the surrender of the garrison is told in the *Reminiscences* (I, 214–46) and in an undated fragment in the col-

[34] Letter to his friends, *supra*, n. 29.

lection of German manuscripts,[35] the two accounts apparently written at different times but differing only in relatively unimportant details. As so given, and without the imaginative embellishments with which it was later adorned by others,[36] it is a romantic and thrilling one reminiscent of, and not much inferior in interest to, that of the experiences of Jean Valjean in the sewers of Paris.

With less than an hour to spare before the time set for the surrender, he remembered having once noticed the existence of a tunnel, or drain, for the purpose of carrying off the surface water of heavy falls of rain, and resolved to make an attempt to escape through it. His orderly-servant, "Adam," when told of the scheme, resolved to accompany him, as did also an artillery officer named Neustadter, a Prussian like himself. Entering the tunnel near the center of the town, they were forced to wait till darkness before attempting to leave it at its outer opening, beyond the wall. Threatened with drowning by rising water in the tunnel during a heavy rain, they at last reached the outer mouth of the tunnel only to find it closely guarded, and were forced to retrace their harrowing course back into the town. Ejected there next morning from the stable of a relative of Adam's because of the imminent arrival of Prussian troops to use it, they at last found refuge in a small loft over a shed, also used

[35] C.S., MSS., W.H.S.

[36] Cf. nn. 37 and 38.

by cavalrymen.[37] After lying concealed there for
three days and nights, befriended and fed by a sympathetic laborer whose cottage stood near by, they
slipped again at night into the tunnel[38] and, finding
its outer opening unguarded since the surrender, succeeded after many more adventures in making good
their escape across French territory to Switzerland.

Letters are again available, as a record of the
period of exile there. It is significant that in the first
of them,[39] after the natural announcement of his escape and after requests for news and money, he at
once began to canvass schemes for the future. He
would first raise some money by publication of his
diary, which, because of his daily contact with the com-
mandant, he said, contained very important and authentic information on the surrender of Rastatt as well
as the Badisch revolt (but which has, unfortunately,

[37] In one legendary account published in the *Easton* (Pennsylvania) *Times* in September, 1860, his companions were lost sight of
and this loft had shrunk to the narrow dimensions of a mere beam,
barely wide enough to conceal his body, as he lay prone along it, over
the heads of the troopers. Quoted in *Chicago Press and Tribune,* September 21, 1860.

[38] As late as January, 1928, a certain Mrs. Earl, aged resident of
a Soldiers' Home in Quincy, Illinois, added another item to the legend
of this escape by telling a reporter of the *Quincy Herald-Whig* that
she had, as a little girl in Germany, unwittingly and without their
knowledge, greatly endangered Schurz and his companions by artlessly
telling the soldiers that they had been sheltered in her mother's home
the night before.

[39] From Dornachbruck to his parents, July 31, 1849, in *Lebn.,*
III, 53.

not been found among his papers). He must then find
a place of refuge farther from the border and so safer
from arrest and internment or extradition. Furthermore, being himself a man whose intellectual needs
guaranteed intellectual activity, he began at once to
criticize his fellow-refugees for "sinking in a slime
of idleness."[40] A student friend, Adolph Strodtmann,
hurried to him with money and word of his people;
and his ambition and his spirits revived accordingly.
While still forced to write home for such things as
shirts—colored ones preferred, as more practical—he
determined to support himself, as far as possible, by
writing for the Cologne paper edited by Dr. Carl
Becker,[41] and to settle down again to scholarly life.[42]

While at the beginning of his exile he would have
welcomed any honorable opportunity to return home,
he was less inclined to do so after the rehabilitation of
confidence which followed his establishment at Zurich, perhaps because of the influence of the other refugees already there. Becoming conscious of the possession of a reputation in Germany, he refused to hazard
it by making a personal request for amnesty. Submission would "go against his nature" and "be an impos-
sibility" for him. Amnesty must be complete and must
be offered to him, although his friends might be

[40] Letter to parents from Zurich, August 15, 1849, *ibid.*, p. 59.

[41] C.S., *Rem.*, I, 245. Some articles found by Dr. Schafer, 1928.

[42] Letter to parents from Zurich, August 18, 1849, in *Lebn.*,
III, 59.

secretly induced by the budding young politician to solicit the offer. He would not return as a suppliant for mercy; but "as a man to whom his honor and his principles are dearer than his happiness, so [do] I renounce all clemency of a ruler."[43] There is a tone of grandiloquence in this letter which causes it to appear in unfavorable contrast with the two written at Rastatt;[44] and in it his natural jealousy of his right and his commendable sense of responsibility as a representative of the revolution are overshadowed to a degree by an equally human but less attractive solicitude for his personal reputation.

Within less than a week, however, in a much milder tone, he wrote for news about an individual amnesty and intimated that he would gladly return, even on a temporary permission to do so, if it could be secured and if he could first know its terms. The old repulsion for compulsory military service found expression again; he feared that, even if granted amnesty, he would be "stuck for two years in a regiment," which he might "just as well spend in prison," especially after having done so much to earn the disfavor of the authorities, who might single him out for specially severe treatment.[45]

[43] Letter to father from Zurich, October 3, 1849, in C.S. MSS., W.H.S.

[44] *Supra.*

[45] Letter to parents from Zurich, October 9, 1849, in C.S. MSS., W.H.S.

Living thus from day to day and from hand to mouth, while trying to share the confidence of his fellow-exiles in the speedy revival of the revolution, in which they should all be successful and prominent,[46] he found the making of plans even for the immediate future to be practically impossible; but it is characteristic of him that he made the attempt.[47] A quiet winter in Italy,[48] private tutoring or study toward a doctorate and a professorship of history in Switzerland,[49] were considered as possible courses of action or as "doors to be kept open in case of accident"; while a possible new uprising in Germany was kept constantly before him as his brightest hope of return. Meanwhile his earnings, although he was again writing for the *Bonner Zeitung*, were not sufficient for his support, and money from home, raised largely among his friends, was still a necessity. But, having learned caution, he hesitated to exchange even so unpleasant a situation for a totally uncertain future in Belgium or any other of the countries then open to him as places of refuge.[50]

As the winter passed without the realization of any of his hopes, his situation became more and more precarious. His dependent position, his suspicion of police

[46] C.S., *Rem.*, I, 243–45.

[47] Letters of October 3, n. 43, and of October 9, n. 45.

[48] Letter of October 9, n. 45.

[49] Letter to father from Zurich, October 20, 1849, in *Lebn.*, III, 60.

[50] *Ibid.;* also February 8, 1850, *ibid.*, p. 64.

interference with his letters,[51] fear of expulsion by
Switzerland at the instance of Austria,[52] and the in-
creasingly unfriendly and malicious attitude of the
Zurich police toward the refugees generally, apparently
designed to make Switzerland uncomfortable for
them, combined to keep him in anything but a comfortable frame of mind.[53] To this state of unrest,
knowledge of Kinkel's trial and sentence contributed
not a little. There was widespread sympathy for the
popular teacher and liberal, and Strodtmann was ex-
pelled from Bonn University for writing "The Spinner's Song," alluding to his prison labor.[54] His friends
would raise funds for his rescue if someone would
make the attempt; and Schurz, after the receipt of a
particularly moving letter from Frau Kinkel, decided
to make it.

So he requested his cousin, Herbert Jüssen, whose
age and general description were not too different from
his own, to secure a passport for Germany, Switzerland, and France and send it to him. So equipped,
passing as Herbert Jüssen and furnished by the exiles
at Zurich with names of people in various cities whose
sympathy could be counted upon, he visited several
towns of southern and southwestern Germany, calling
upon those previously named to him as trustworthy

[51] Letter to parents from Zurich, January 31, 1850, *ibid.*, p. 63.

[52] Letter to parents from Zurich, February 8, 1850, *ibid.*, p. 64.

[53] Letter to parents from Zurich, February 18, 1850, *ibid.*, p. 65.

[54] Letter to parents, *supra,* nn. 50 and 52.

friends of the revolution and reporting what he learned of existing conditions to the group of exiles in Switzerland. This and the formation of committees of correspondence they supposed to be the purpose of his journey, no intimation of his intentions regarding Kinkel being given them.

On a brief secret visit to his home in Bonn he saw Frau Kinkel,[55] but no one else was admitted to the secret of the attempt to be made for her husband's liberation. Money was contributed for it by friends and admirers of the poet-teacher; and the management of the affair was left to Schurz, whose identity was not known, even to the donors.

All action in the matter had to be delayed, for late in April Kinkel was brought from the penitentiary at Naugard[56] to stand trial at Cologne for his share in the attempt on the Siegburg arsenal. Ten persons, among whom Schurz was included, were accused "of an attempt to upset the present constitution of the kingdom" by attempting to arm themselves and to incite others to do so and to revolt.[57] Only four of the defendants were present, the others, like Schurz, having fled the country. Again Kinkel was able to speak in his own defense, this time before a jury; and this time, he won full acquittal for himself and his

[55] C.S., *Rem.*, I, 255.

[56] *Ibid.*, p. 249.

[57] *Ibid.*, p. 264.

co-defendants.[58] So Schurz was freed from that accusation; but he would still have been subject to trial
for the more serious offense for which Kinkel was
already under sentence and at once reincarcerated, being transferred to the prison at Spandau, near Berlin.

During these proceedings, Schurz naturally found
it prudent to absent himself from the vicinity. So after
brief visits to Cologne and Brussels, he took up his temporary residence in Paris.

After the excitement over Kinkel's second trial
had somewhat subsided, he returned again to Germany,
still bearing his cousin's passport and still acting in two
secret capacities: as agent and correspondent of the
group of exiled revolutionists at Zurich and as self-appointed rescuer of Kinkel. The former of these activities served the latter admirably by getting him into
touch with those most likely to aid him but least likely
to burden their own minds with incriminating knowledge of his plans and movements.

About six months were thus spent in Germany,
nearly three of them in bachelor lodgings of student
friends in Berlin, to which he says he was often admitted by the pass-key of the police watchman when
returning late from his nocturnal errands in Spandau.[59]
It is again characteristic of the man that he was thus
emboldened to go repeatedly to see the French actress,
Rachel, then making a great sensation in Berlin, until

[58] *Ibid.*, p. 271.   [59] *Ibid.*, p. 276.

he was deterred by the practical certainty of recognition.

For two weeks of Schurz's stay in Berlin he was a cripple, confined to bed by a leg injury incurred in a fall. At some time during that confinement, "September, 1850," he wrote to someone not now known the one letter which seems to have survived from that period.[60] In it he expressed the greatest disillusionment as to the "few and mean occurrences of 1848" and bemoaned the lack of "any great memories" from them, drawing the most unfavorable comparisons between them and the great events of the French Revolution of 1789 and even between Berlin and Paris as centers of historical interest.

After several failures to secure Kinkel's release by bribery of jailers, he found it necessary to give the suspicion so aroused some time in which to die down, while he journeyed to other cities of Germany, returning later to pose as a medical student, living with Dr. Falkenthal in Moabit, a suburb of Berlin. At last, a jail guard named Brune, bolder than the others, was found, who agreed to unlock cell and prison and to deliver the prisoner for a certain sum of money. The first plan failed by an unfortunate coincidence, but next night Brune lowered his man from a window by a rope; and by hard night driving and the connivance

[60] *Lebn.*, III, 66. Brought to light at trial of Dr. Falkenthal, *(q.v. infra)*; published in part in the *Vossischen Zeitung*, No. 236 (1912). Leg injury mentioned in letter to wife October 21, 1855.

of friends, Schurz and Kinkel escaped to Warnemunde
and thence, by sea, to Edinburgh.[61]

So well had secrecy been preserved throughout
that all of Schurz's accomplices were able either to escape suspicion entirely or to convince the authorities
that they had no real knowledge of him or his movements, with the single exception of Brune, who had to
serve a brief prison term, after which he was able to
retire in modest comfort on the gratuity paid him in
advance.[62] Because of this secrecy and of the fact that
it had still to be preserved for the protection of the
others, Schurz received in popular estimation all of the
credit of which only a part, though of course a large
one, was really due him. He found himself suddenly
famous and was a marked man among Germans
thenceforth. He even figured as Wolfgang von Hohenstein, and Kinkel as Dr. Münzer, in Friedrich Spiel-
hagen's *Die von Hohenstein*.[63] Ten years later the
story was still being retold in American newspapers,
with many unauthentic and inaccurate additions,[64] for

[61] C.S., *Rem.*, pp. 290–336; Henderson, *op. cit.*, p. 367; Ernest
Bruncken, *The Germans in Wisconsin Politics*, "Parkman Club Papers" (1896), p. 235.

[62] C.S., *Rem.*, I, 339–40.

[63] Georg von Skal, *History of German Immigration in the United States*; and *Successful German-Americans and Their Descendants*
(New York, F. T. and J. C. Smiley, 1908), p. 45.

[64] The *Milwaukee Daily Sentinel*, September 9, 1857, told of his
attracting Kinkel's attention by playing the flute outside the prison at
Naugard. When Kinkel was in Naugard, Schurz was in Switzerland;

the enhancement of a reputation which by then rested on a more solid foundation and had but little need of it; while scores of scattered persons claimed connection with the affair.[65]

The rapid rise of Carl Schurz in American politics would have been impossible without his brilliant intellectual and personal gifts and his solid contribution to American political life; but it was his fame as a German, among Germans, won in the German exploits of the escape from Rastatt and Kinkel's *Befreiung,* which earned him his first political opportunities in America.

On shipboard, en route across the North Sea, both of the fugitives utilized the opportunity to compose letters. One from Kinkel to Christian Schurz, father of Carl, referred to his meeting the older Schurz, in the summer of 1848, searching among the prisoners in the crowded casemates at Rastatt for his son.[66] With a confidence which could not, under the circumstances, have been based on any complete knowledge of current conditions, he predicted a successful revolution, and in it, a high place for his rescuer, by virtue of "his character and intellect as well as his unheard-of wonderful

---

and the flute story is pure fable. So is another version, according to which he used a barrel-organ for the purpose; but in Germany he was even shown in pictures with it.

[65] Letter of T. O. Howe, Green Bay, Wisconsin, to Schurz, December 2, 1858, in C.S. MSS., L.C.; cf. also n. 38, p. 34.

[66] C.S., *Rem.,* I, 235.

luck."[67] Schurz himself, writing at the same time to
his parents, had less to say about the revolution and
more about his luck.[68] He was becoming a conscious
opportunist, and often, in the next few years, spoke of
"trusting a little always to his luck." Both his boldness
and his optimism were measurably sustained during
years of uncertainty by his happy ability to do so.

Until his second sojourn in Paris, whither he soon
went from England, and where he remained for six
months after the reunited Kinkel family had returned
to London and settled there, his confidence in the prospect of successful revolution seems to have been on the
wane. What he had experienced in Switzerland and
seen in Germany had not been encouraging; and his
Berlin letter, quoted above, had been quite pessimistic.
In Paris, however, even that hope revived; and in letters to his parents he expressed confidence that revolution would again spread from France to Germany.[69]

It is interesting to note, in the correspondence of
that period, sentiments and phrases which were later to
become familiar as recurring frequently in his best-
known speeches. He was already using expressions
such as "the nature of things" and "the logic of events"
to prove the inevitability of democratic reform in Eu-

[67] *Lebn.*, III, 72.

[68] *Ibid.*, p. 70.

[69] Letter from Paris, January 1, 1851, *ibid.*, p. 77; April 7,
1851, in C.S. MSS., W.H.S.; from London, October 25, 1851, in
Lebn., III, 84; in C.S., *Rem.*, I, 374.

rope,[70] exactly as he later used them to demonstrate
that slavery must disappear in America. Another, to
the effect that it was "fine, to see one's fate bound up
with that of a suffering people," he was also to use
later, when momentarily less sure that it was so
"fine."[71]

While maintaining himself by the resumption of
his old occupation of writing for the German papers,
perfecting himself in the use of the French language
and continuing the study of the great French revolution, which later contributed materially to his support
in America, he was yet much troubled by difficulties in
which his parents were involved and by his own ability
to send them only insufficient assistance.[72] To those
troubles there soon was added a new one with the police. The campaign biography printed in the *Easton*
(Pennsylvania) *Times* in September, 1860, told that
in a pamphlet of the Paris police of 1857 he was characterized as "the most adroit and audacious" of the
exiles and as one who was constantly active though
never ensnared into acts warranting extradition.[73] Be

[70] Letters to parents, January 1, 1859, in *Lebn.*, III, 77.

[71] Letter to Friedrich Althaus from Madrid, December 9, 1861,
ibid., p. 211. Cf. chap. x, nn. 109 and 120.

[72] Letter to parents from Paris, March 7, 1851, in C.S. MSS.,
W.H.S.; *Lebn.*, III, 81.

[73] Quoted in *New York Tribune*, September 15, 1860. Cf. A. C.
Wheeler ("Nym Krinkle"), *The Chronicles of Milwaukee* (Milwaukee, 1861), p. 298. Schurz was similarly listed as a "dangerous subject," and his participation in the revolts in the Palatinate and Baden,

that as it may, he was arrested and kept in prison for some days, with no cause shown, and released only at the instance of his friends and when he announced his intention of going at once to England. He was, in fact, encouraged to go.[74] On the day of his release he wrote: "It was thought that I was on the point of overthrowing the government of France. It was found, however, that the French alone could accomplish this feat, and so they let me out again, today."[75] He later supposed his arrest and virtual expulsion to have been a part of the preparation for the *coup d'etat* of Louis Napoleon,[76] and, when lecturing on "Democracy in France," assigned to that monarch no very high or honorable place in its development.

As a matter of fact, he had already written to his people, two months before, that while he wanted to stay in Paris for some time yet, he expected soon to go to London.[77] The Kinkels were already making a suc-

---

his escape from Rastatt, and his rescue of Kinkel were mentioned in a Prussian police handbook published in 1854, entitled *Anzeiger für die politische Polizei Deutschlands auf die Zeit vom Januar, 1848, bis zur Gegenwart. Ein Handbuch für jeden Polizeibeamten.* This book was seen in the Stadtbibliothek of Berlin in 1927 by Mr. Robert Wild, of Milwaukee, one of the best-informed and most enthusiastic of the students of the life of Schurz.

[74] C.S., *Rem.*, I, 360.

[75] Letter to parents from Paris, June 2, 1851, in *Lebn.*, III, 82.

[76] C.S., *Rem.*, I, 361 ff.

[77] Letter to parents from Paris, April 7, 1851, in C.S. MSS., W.H.S.

cessful new start in life there, the Professor teaching
and lecturing and Frau Kinkel teaching music. They
had taken one of his sisters to live with them and had
undertaken her education.[78] There, with Professor
Kinkel as sponsor, he was able to secure enough pupils
in German and music to earn a steady and reasonably
sufficient income.[79]

To an old man, the little German colony in St.
John's Wood would have been a welcome haven of
refuge; for a young one of nervous temperament, it
was altogether too quiet. He wrote that the climate was
bad for him, and teaching injurious to his health.[80]
The fact seems to have been that he fretted with impatience at the vaporings of his fellow-exiles and found
no sort of satisfaction in his own share of their activities, in which he had come to believe but half-heartedly
without actually bringing himself to the point of di-
vorcing himself from them. Influenced not only by
Kinkel and other German refugees but also by repeated contacts with Kossuth and Mazzini, and still
trying, as he had said a year before,[81] to "believe what
he wished to believe" although "just nothing had come

[78] Antonie Schurz. Later, in America, she married her cousin,
Edmund Jüssen, of Madison and Chicago. She died in Milwaukee, at
the home of her daughter, Mrs. Charles E. Monroe.

[79] Letter to Adolph Meyer from London, in *Lebn.*, III, 86; C.S.,
Rem., I, 367.

[80] Letter to parents, May 19, 1852, in *Lebn.*, III, 90.

[81] Letter to parents from Paris, January 1, 1851, *ibid.*

of it," he tried to supply by activity what he lacked in conviction. But he found no happiness in it.

One plan formed by the exiles was the raising of a "German national loan" on the credit of the government which they were going to set up with its proceeds, whenever they should find such a course possible. In the interest of this plan, Schurz made another venturesome trip to the Continent, in October, 1851, revisiting Paris and getting out two hours before the arrests of all foreigners began, going to Strassburg, spending two weeks among the German refugees still in Switzerland, and, after staying secretly twelve days more in Paris, returning again to London, more confident than ever in his personal "luck" but no more so in the strength of the cause he had gone there to serve.[82]

In the interest of the same scheme Kinkel made a tour of America, just before that of Kossuth, meeting a reception only a little less cordial than Kossuth's but achieving results but little more substantial than his.[83] While he was gone, Schurz served once more as his lieutenant, carrying on a voluminous correspondence, sending out printed "interim receipts" and circularizing the Germans in America in the interests of the loan.[84] The national-loan project did attain some strength, and enough funds were raised to become

[82] Letter to parents from London, October 25, 1851, in *Lebn.*, III, 84; C.S., *Rem.*, I, 374.

[83] Ernest Bruncken, *op. cit.*, p. 235.

[84] Letter to parents, *supra*, n. 82.

a subject of discussion for ten years thence, it being proposed at certain times to turn them over to a sort of international league of revolutionists to be used wherever possible, and again, to give them to Garibaldi.[85]

Schurz had interviews with Kossuth in London both before and after the personally triumphant but financially and politically unsuccessful tour of the great Hungarian leader in the United States; and he noted on the second occasion the change in his bearing.[86] But while he had then some idea of the reason for it, he was, of course, in no such position to understand it as he was many years later when he wrote his account of Kossuth's interview in December, 1851, with Henry Clay. In it, he described how high Kossuth's hopes had been raised by the friendly attitude of the United States government toward the movement for Hungarian independence in the days of its initial success, by his own journey on board a United States warship from asylum in Turkey to a rapturously admiring reception in the United States, by Webster's famous Huelsemann letter, and by many speeches he had heard since his arrival. He then told how the aged

[85] Kinkel, as custodian of the fund, was ordered to do this by the German loan-committees of St. Louis and New York but refused. Letters: Schurz to Kinkel, January 23, 1855, in *Lebn.*, III, 119–21; and Kinkel to Schurz, August 19, 1860, in C.S. MSS., W.H.S. The total amount seems to have been about $20,000.

[86] C.S., *Rem.*, I, 384 and 402; II, 50–53.

Clay, in startling contrast, had expressed his disappointment that France had so submitted to the *coup d'etat* of Louis Napoleon, and warned his visitor that hopes of intervention by the United States in the interest of republicanism in Europe were quite without foundation. The biographer then commented:

> This was not what Kossuth had come to hear. But it was what the American people really thought when sobered from the fascination of Kossuth's presence, and what other American statesmen would have said to him had they frankly expressed their sentiments.[87]

The fulness of knowledge and maturity of understanding with which he wrote the foregoing words a full generation later were naturally not his when a young exile in London. On one point, however, he was already in full agreement with Clay. The submission of France, in December, 1851, destroyed his last hope of a speedy revival of the Republican movement elsewhere and of his own early return to Germany.

To that extent, the dramatic account, in his *Reminiscences*, of the formation of his own decision to come to America seems to be literally true. In it, he describes himself as sitting on one end of a Hyde Park bench while Louis Blanc sat on the other, plunged in deepest dejection and admitting hopeless defeat: *"C'est fini."* Viewing this scene in retrospect, almost half a century later, he described himself as thinking:

[87] Schurz, *Henry Clay* (2 vols.; Edinburgh: David Douglas, 1887), II, 394 and 395.

The fatherland was closed to me. England was to me a foreign country, and would always remain so. Where, then? "To America," I said to myself . . . . *Ubi libertas, ibi patria* —I formed my resolution on the spot. I would remain only a short time longer in England to make some necessary preparations, and then—off to America.[88]

As a matter of fact, his emigration to this country did not take place for more than eight months thereafter. The length of that period of preparation may have been partly due to the fact that during it he fell in love with the sister-in-law of another German refugee, Miss Margaretha Meyer, of Hamburg, to whom he was married, July 6, 1852.[89]

During the spring and early summer of that year, several letters were written which have a direct bearing upon the formation of his decision to come to America. To his prospective brother-in-law, Adolph Meyer, a member of a prosperous commercial family of Hamburg, who had, as Margaretha's protector, made some very natural inquiries as to his plans and prospects, he wrote that he was quite able to earn enough in London, by teaching, to support two people comfortably, and that, too, without taking Margaretha's property into the reckoning. But "mere bread" was not enough.

[88] C.S., *Rem.*, I, 401.

[89] *Ibid.*, p. 402. His own story of the meeting and courtship, written for his children at their request, is in the German manuscripts; but there appears no historical reason for introducing it here, while his expressed wish is a superfluous one for not doing so.

The foreigner here is always a foreigner. Under such circumstances, I cannot feel at home. What I seek in America is
not only personal freedom, but the chance to gain full legal citizenship. If I cannot be a citizen of a free Germany, then I
would at least be a citizen of a free America.

The situation of his parents, moreover, impelled him
to the same decision. Because of him, they had for
more than a year suffered almost uninterrupted interference and annoyance from the Prussian police; so
that they were in real distress and it seemed imperative
that he effect their migration to Wisconsin, where several of their relatives were already well established.
So, "immediately after the unfortunate events of
December, in France," he had decided to migrate.
That was before he had met Margaretha; but she was
willing to go with him; and by lecturing in American
cities on the recent history of France, he hoped to earn
a living from the start. He even hoped that Margaretha, who, because she had "never known what it was
to provide her own living" had "not yet learned to
enjoy it," would be happier there.[90]

That the failure of the French, then, again to set
a successful and contagious example for the republicans
of Germany, was the determining factor in his decision
to emigrate seems to be well substantiated. That he
found the life of a professional political exile empty
and irritating, rather than merely enervating, has al-

[90] Letter to Adolph Meyer from London, April 19, 1852, in
Lebn., III, 86–88.

ready been suggested. That the circumstances of his
parents were genuinely uncomfortable is apparent from
the distress he showed in a letter of May 19, sending
them money and regretting his inability to send more,
and expressing concern as to their ability to hold out for
six months more while he preceded them to the land
of asylum and opportunity and prepared a place for
them there.[91]

But that he had actually planned, either then or
earlier, a really permanent transfer of his interests and
allegiance to the new fatherland, or had yet abandoned
hope of an eventual return to the old, is made to appear extremely doubtful by a group of letters written
just before he left England with his bride. In them he
described the same plan as to Adolph Meyer, to lecture
on the history of France from 1789 to 1852, the subject about which he knew most and Americans least.
Unable to content himself with far distant prospects
in Europe, he would thus make his "time of exile fruitful." The other exiles were again showing great interest in a scheme for the formation of an international
revolutionary league with membership on both sides of
the Atlantic, the American members (apparently) to
furnish the funds and the Europeans the agitation and
political activity on their side, while the early grant of

[91] Letter to parents from London, May 19, 1852, *ibid.*, p. 90.
His wife was also subjected to some unpleasant experience with the
Prussian police when on a visit to Germany as late as 1855. Letter to
her, November 5, 1855, in C.S. MSS., W.H.S. Cf. also n. 73.

the suffrage and similar concessions were demanded in
the United States. Schurz showed greater skepticism
toward this plan than he had ever yet expressed, saying
that it sounded good but meant little. The Germans
newly arrived in America, the "greens," would have
but little influence; while "the grays," already well
established there, whose support would be most valuable, would be frightened away from the project by
the noise they made. Such an institution would hold
together only so long as it did not attempt to do anything. But while thus doubtful of the prospect of any
successful uprising to be induced by any scheme then
apparent, he still declared himself as hopeful of sometime seeing one and as willing to serve it when it should
occur. So he "said farewell to Europe, with the certainty of being there again at the proper time."[92]

Viewed in the light of these letters, his move to
America appears to have been that of one who was a republican in opinion, to be sure, but still a German republican in feeling. Maintaining, as was natural, the
strong bond of sympathy between himself and his
revolutionary associates, he wished for them a success
for which he was willing to work in America; and in
the earning of the enjoyment of which, if it should
come, he expected to return and have a share. In the
meantime, he was too restless and too ambitious to en-

[92] Letters to Friedrich Althaus, another Bonn University associate and fellow-exile in England. From Hampstead, July 12; Malvern,
July 26; and Hampstead, August 8, 1852, in *Lebn.*, III, 91–95.

dure the fatuous futility of the life of a political exile
while his parents suffered the petty persecutions of
despotism and America's call of invitation to active
youth went unanswered.

So without the voluntary severance of any of the
ties which bound his affections to the old fatherland,
he came over to the new, which must then knit new
and stronger ties through half a score of years, to
attach him to itself and make him irrevocably its own.

CHAPTER III

SOUNDINGS

THE exact meaning of the hyphenated term "German-American" varies greatly according to the circumstances of its use and the attitude or intention of the user. As applied to Carl Schurz, quite often named as "the greatest German-American,"[1] there came a time when it could be properly used only without the hyphen, as a term indicative of the parentage and birthplace of a man who had come to be as thoroughly American as if he had been born in Boston of Mayflower ancestry or as the son of pioneer log-cabin dwellers of the frontier. In the first few years of his life in America, however, the hyphen had a more real significance. While the contemporary record of the period from 1852 to 1854 in particular is less adequate than that of any other, it is at least sufficient to indicate a real division of interest and of

---

[1] "Germany's best gift to the American Republic" (Georg von Bosse, *Das deutsche Element in den Vereinigten Staaten* [Stuttgart: Chr. Velsersche Verlagsbuchhandlung, 1908], 289). "Der im offentlichen Leben der Vereinigten Staaten hervorragendste und bedeutendste Deutsch-Amerikaner. . . . . Unbestritten der bedeutendste Deutsch-Amerikaner" (Deutsch-Amerikanischer National-Bund, *Das Buch der Deutschen in Amerika* [Philadelphia: Walthers Buchdruckerei, 1909], p. 595). "The greatest German of that migration" (Channing, *A History of the United States*, VI, 127).

activity between Europe and America, between the old
and the new. No question of loyalty, happily, was involved. It was a question, rather, of psychology as affected by conditions and events. The Americanization
of Schurz was a gradual process, during which the
conscious opportunist deliberated upon the choice of
his most promising opportunity while the idealist in
him was drawn less deliberately, but no less strongly,
into the fight against slavery in America. Meanwhile
the desire to return permanently to Germany diminished even more rapidly than the prospect of being able
to do so receded.

It is this process of adaptation, Schurz's reaction
to the new environment, and the growth of his feeling
of attachment to this country which furnish the most
interesting field of study of the years before his active
entry into politics, in 1856.

At the age of twenty-three, Schurz, accompanied
by his young wife of eighteen, landed in New York on
September 17, 1852. An illness of Mrs. Schurz detained them there for a brief time, after which they
went on to Philadelphia, whither they were attracted
by the presence of German friends. Among these was
Adolph Strodtmann, who had carried money to Schurz
in his first exile in Switzerland and had later earned the
distinction of dismissal from the University of Bonn
for arousing sympathy for Kinkel by his "Spinner's
Song." There, also, was Dr. Heinrich Tiedemann,

brother of the unfortunate commander of the garrison at Rastatt.[2]

It was natural that the young couple should seek the company of other Germans; but they avoided the mistake that he had made in England, of neglecting to learn the English language. There are several partial explanations of that failure, none of them quite satisfactory. In London he had been associated chiefly with other Germans; and, the German language being fashionable there at that time, he had not found it difficult to make acquaintances even with English persons who could use it or French.[3] But even so, there must have been some difference other than in the mere need for it, to account for the fact that the same man who in Paris so improved upon his schoolboy knowledge of French as to be considered an almost perfect linguist, should have lived twice as long in London without learning even to carry on a conversation in English.[4] Probably the real explanation is to be found partly in the fact that he needed the French language in Paris and the English in the United States, and, in addition to that, his own feeling that "in England, a foreigner is always a foreigner." Or he may have been over-optimistic as to the adequacy of German in the United States.

But even granting all that, his failure to learn the language of America remains inexplicable, except

[2] C.S., *Rem.*, II, 3, 8, and 9.

[3] *Ibid.*, I, 369.   [4] *Ibid.*, II, 3.

upon the hypothesis that he did not know for any great
length of time before he came that he was going to
come and to stay permanently. As an envoy to the
German-Americans, he would have found German
sufficient; as a bona fide immigrant, or as the American
diplomatic agent of the German radical group, he
would need English. This need, apparently, he did not
realize even when forming his first resolutions to make
the voyage; and it seems to be a fair inference that the
ultimate purposes which only the English language
would serve did not form a conscious part of his plan as
first conceived.

Just what did constitute his original conception of
his mission in America would be more easily demon-
strable if the contemporary record were more complete
and less obscure. It appears nebulous at best, perhaps
because it was nebulous; but it can be traced, after a
fashion.

His first task, as already suggested, was to learn;
and for six months or more in Philadelphia and for
about a year in Bethlehem, Pennsylvania (a place
which would have been congenial to him by virtue of
its musical attractions, if not for other reasons), he
devoted himself assiduously to study. In six months he
had acquired a serviceable knowledge of the language,
though five years elapsed before the delivery of his first
public speech in it,[5] and more before his specialized

[5] In campaign of 1857 (C.S., *Rem.*, II, 69 and 81; also letter
to Kinkel, December 1, 1856, in C.S. MSS., W.H.S.).

studies in "Democracy and Despotism in France," counted upon beforehand,[6] and written in part during his first six months in America,[7] began actually to yield a revenue on the lecture platform.[8]

He began the study of the language by a laborious reading of the newspapers, with the aid of a dictionary. Promotion was rapid in his self-taught private school, and he soon went on to the novels of Scott, Dickens, and Thackeray, then to Macaulay's historical essays, Blackstone's *Commentaries*, and Shakespeare, translating chosen passages into German and then back again into his own words in English, for comparison with the originals.[9] But he still made it his chief business to study the actual working of American governmental institutions for his own information, and the state of public opinion for the benefit of those who still looked to America for support for a prospective German republic.[10]

A part of his reactions to what he learned on the

[6] Letters to Adolph Meyer and Friedrich Althaus, *supra*, chap. ii, nn. 89 and 91.

[7] Letter to Kinkel, from Philadelphia, April 1853, in C.S. MSS., W.H.S.

[8] At Watertown, Madison, Janesville, and other Wisconsin towns, early in 1858. *Watertown Democrat*, January 7 and 20, 1858; *Wisconsin Daily State Journal*, January 11, February 2, 1858; *Janesville Standard* quoted in *Milwaukee Daily Sentinel*, February 1, 1858.

[9] C.S., *Rem.*, II, 10.

[10] Letter to Kinkel, *supra*, n. 7.

first of these points was recorded in two early letters, written in the autumn of 1852. In one, written only about a month after landing, he was still seeing in America what his earlier romantic idealization of the republican form of government had led him to hope and expect to see.

The abuse of the good does not tempt the American to abolish it. The abuse of liberty does not tempt him to curtail liberty.[11] The American knows that liberty is the best means of education, and that it is the highest guarantee for the Republic. We [in Europe] have not yet seen how a free people exercises its freedom. We have not seen in real life the practical application of the principles which we preach. Here all is spread before our gaze in a vast tableau. There is only one shrill discord, and that is slavery in the South.[12]

The slightly mixed metaphor with which the foregoing passage was concluded is interesting both superficially and fundamentally—superficially, as the words of a musician who would brand something inharmonious as a "shrieking false note," even when writing of a tableau; and fundamentally, as evidence that a month in America had sufficed for slavery to make a distinct impression upon the man whose strongest at-

[11] He had not yet, apparently, encountered any of the "temperance" laws which so irritated him and his fellow-Germans a few years later.

[12] Letter to Charlotte Voss from Philadelphia, October 20, 1852, published in the original in C.S., *Lebn.*, III, 100, and a portion of it in translation in C.S., *S.C.&P.P.*, I, 4.

tacks upon it, later, were based upon its incompatibility with free governmental institutions.

Shortly afterward he thought he had rid himself of his illusions and had got down to the facts about the working of republicanism and could write quite condescendingly of those who had not. He had found America to be not at all what was envisioned by the revolutionary idealists of Europe—"hot-headed professional revolutionists" and "strong-minded ladies of the educated class, with their sentimental ideas about democracy," who were all of them too insistent upon "improving things quickly and positively." It was too much to expect that everything should be logical and consistent in a country where enlightenment and ignorance, bigotry and tolerance, lived side by side equally free, and where, for example, those to whom he referred as the "Jesuits" were "not opposed with the weapon of official power but simply with that of public opinion." Really healthy reforms derived their vitality from public opinion which, while it might be cultivated, could not be coerced. Far from being discouraged by the contradictions which he saw, he found much to admire in what he called the "productivity of freedom" as exemplified by the activity and initiative of private enterprise. It is to be noted that the aspects of democracy which he most admired were those of a strictly Jeffersonian type.

Here . . . . you can see how little a people needs to be governed. . . . . We learn here how superfluous is the action of governments concerning a multitude of things in which in Europe it is deemed absolutely indispensable.[13]

By far the most significant letter of that first year is one written to Kinkel from Philadelphia, April 12, 1853, and hitherto unpublished.[14] On some matters it suggests more than it reveals, but it sheds at least an indirect light upon a number of questions not mentioned at all by Mr. Schurz himself in his *Reminiscences*. One of these questions, and a very intriguing one, is as to the exact nature of his connection with the revolutionary group of exiles in London. It would not be entirely unnatural to assume that he had been sent to America by them and was in their pay; but the evidence available for this study offers no proof to sustain such an assumption except the very dubious "argument from silence." What would contribute most to its plausibility is the fact that the money troubles which had filled so much space in his earlier correspondence, if they did not cease, at least cease to appear in his letters. Nor do letters or the *Reminiscences* mention his

[13] Letter to Malwida von Meysenbug, autumn of 1852 or early winter of 1852–53. Published in her *Memoiren einer Idealistin,* II, 77–82; in translation in C.S., *S.C.&P.P.,* I, 5; mentioned and quoted in part, C.S., *Rem.,* II, 16–18. Quoted in part by Channing, as showing the effect upon an educated immigrant of his first contact with American democracy, and characterized as "of great interest to students of political institutions" (*op. cit.,* VI, 127 ff.).

[14] C.S. MSS., W.H.S. This letter was published in translation in 1928, with the others of this collection and many of those in the third volume of the *Lebenserinnerungen,* by Dr. Joseph Schafer, of the Wisconsin Historical Society.

engaging in any gainful occupation for more than three years, except the writing of a few articles on America for the English papers; while during that period money was found for two return trips to Europe, an extended stay in Switzerland, two journeys to Wisconsin, and some purchases of real estate. It has already been pointed out, moreover, that lecturing did not prove to be a source of income then, as it was later.

But all these circumstances really prove nothing at all as to his being in the pay of his old associates. Mrs. Schurz was a member of a well-to-do family and had property interests in Hamburg, so it is not at all inconceivable that he may have decided, after all, to "take Margaretha's property into the reckoning."[15] Both he and his wife had been seriously ill in England shortly after their marriage, and their voyage to America had to be postponed on that account. It may well be that sympathy induced by their plight may have caused her brother to turn over to her at that time some portion of her share of their inheritance. Or Schurz may have earned something, possibly by teaching as in London.

To one who believed that he was actually maintained during those years by funds from abroad, there might occur a certain imputation of duplicity, based upon his maintenance of a connection with a cause in which he had ceased really to believe. To defend him against this imputation would be easier than to disprove

[15] Cf. letter to Adolph Meyer, *supra,* chap. ii, n. 89. See also comment on St. Louis letters, chap. iv.

the original assumption. For, in the first place, it would have been easy for him to convince himself that, by sending them accurate information as to American public opinion and as to the methods of procedure most likely to succeed here, and even by condemning their mistakes, he was rendering to his revolutionary associates a service of the highest order. And in the second place, it would not have been at all inconsistent with the general character of Carl Schurz to have continued to serve a cause because he wished it to succeed after he had ceased actually to expect it to do so.

That this connection was of a very informal nature, and not at all a close one, is indicated by the first two paragraphs of the letter. In the first, he mentioned a period of three or four months during which he had received no direct word from Kinkel, hearing of him only through the newspapers. In the second, the same lack of close touch is indicated. He wrote:

I proposed to you that I should put myself in touch with the loan committees in this country, and as soon as I had received from you any sort of instruction, to pass it on to this or that one. This instruction I awaited in vain, and as you answered absolutely nothing at all, I came to the conclusion that you in London had decided to operate on an entirely different basis, and were following new plans, and so I held my peace. Finally, I learned of the arrival of Willich in New York, and the newspapers carried the plans which he proposed to carry out.[16] About three weeks ago, he came here and called upon me.

[16] August Willich had been one of the principal military commanders in the revolt in Baden. He later settled in the United States, where he was instrumental in effecting the permanent organization of

I soon saw with what illusions he had come here, and realized
that he would not allow himself to be convinced either by arguments or through his own observations. His whole agitation is
a thoroughly bad business. The transformation of the loan committees into little political clubs seems to me purposeless, as in
general all showy undertakings are, all noise-makings, all forcible digging up of old stories, and entirely out of place. You
yourself must have learned what the building up of a so-called
moral force signifies here in America, especially as far as it depends on the Germans. . . . . The Revolutionary League, begun and organized with such great enthusiasm, has failed almost
simultaneously with its creation, because with the first ebulli-
tion, its spirit was spent, and it lacked objectives for its activity.
To that result, to be sure, this beautiful annexations-dream has
contributed. But Willich has expounded to me something of
"the great idea of the actual establishment of the German State
in America, through the loan," which is no less fantastic than
that universal annexation, and is exactly calculated to disappoint
the practical American understanding, which little by little appears also in the Germans. On all that, I have expressed my
opinion to Willich. I have now for seven months quietly observed here, said little, and inquired much, and believe that I
have not been superficial in the forming of my opinions. I believe as follows: Your agitation and Kossuth's and the Revolutionary Alliance have so used up all zeal for transatlantic affairs, and the European events since 1851 have made the Americans so distrustful, that one must give the people rest and quiet,
to recover from their chagrin and disappointment.

The attitude of detachment shown in the foregoing portion of the letter seems to be that of an inter-

---

the *Turnverein*, in 1853. During the Civil War, he was a [Brigadier]-
General, from Indiana (J. H. A. Lacher, *The German Element in
Wisconsin*, Steuben Society pamphlet [1925]).

ested friend, volunteering information, rather than that
of a paid agent making a report. The revolutionary
league referred to was, as indicated, a very nebulous
affair, an outgrowth of the fact that London was, in
1851 and 1852, an asylum for political refugees from
all parts of Europe, including such leaders as Kinkel,
Kossuth, Louis Blanc, and Mazzini. Hoping that the
common people of Europe might be roused to a realization of a community of interest in democratic reform,
the extremists among them talked of an international
group which might, like the first French republic, de-
clare war upon kings and spread republicanism over
central Europe. Lacking the territorial nucleus from
which such a movement might grow, they hoped to find
one in some south German state or possession of Austria and trusted to popular uprisings to spread it from
there.[17] Help from individual Americans was expected, and the most sanguine hoped for official aid
from the government of the great republic as well.[18]
Concerning the prospects of such a scheme, Schurz
wrote, both in this letter and later, as a skeptic confirmed in his pessimism.

As that prospect faded, an older but almost equally
fantastic scheme revived. As early as 1838 there
had been a convention of forty delegates in Pittsburgh
to make plans for the establishment of a German state,

[17] C.S., Rem., I, 380 and 401.

[18] Letter to Althaus, chap. ii, n. 92; Schurz, Henry Clay, II,
394; supra, chap. ii, n. 87.

somewhere in the then western part of the territory
of the United States, which should apply for admission
to the union but should retain its purely German local
laws and customs and be, in fact, a transplanted bit of
Germany.[19] About 1850 that plan was revived; and
in 1851 Watertown, Wisconsin, was the scene of
another German convention for the same purpose.[20]
One group of immigrants even arrived, bringing with
them a bell for the statehouse of their proposed capital and a telescope for the state observatory.[21] The
idea was not completely dropped until 1854.[22]

Schurz, not content with destructive criticism of
projects which he branded as visionary, went on in the
same letter, above quoted,[23] to offer constructive suggestions as to what he thought might be done, and an
account of what he himself was doing to influence
American public opinion and of what he hoped to do
to influence American public men.

> Our task for the present seems to be as follows: We must
> get at the American politicians, to bring before them a true pic-
> ture of political life in Europe, and to center their attention
> upon Germany. They must first learn what conclusions as to

[19] Lacher, *op. cit.*, p. 9.

[20] Dr. W. F. Whyte, "Chronicles of Early Watertown," *Wisconsin Magazine of History*, Vol. IV, No. 3 (1921).

[21] Editorial, *North American Review*, LXXXII (1856), 248–68.

[22] Ernest Bruncken, "Political Activities of the Wisconsin Germans," *Proceedings of the State Historical Society of Wisconsin*,
1901.

[23] Cf. n. 14, and pp. 65, 66.

Germany itself they dare make from the German doings here, which they despise,—etc. If the Americans hitherto have formed no great opinion of the German revolution, no one else is to blame for that but the Germans here. . . . . I have already confided to you the plan of forming a secret association—that is, one that is not public, but not one bound up with any secret hokus-pokus, which shall draw together in itself the intelligent forces of the Germans in this country. It will be a sort of Missionary Society, to convert American politicians. It is in operation, works noiselessly, and has already accomplished something. If it is possible for me, I am going this year for some time to Washington, as a wholly private individual, who is using the library there for the study of American History. On this occasion we must cast our nets, without officially indicating our intention. . . . .

I forgot to give you my opinion in the matter of the loan. That it continues to stand, is a matter of course. But I think one should merely let it stand quietly; the less noise made about it, the safer it will be. It will yield no more money, until some action takes place in Europe. Then, however, it will yield again. Until then, a special agitation for the loan here is a pretty poor affair. . . . .

Be so good as to inform me of your activities from time to time. I am no less attached to Germany in America than I was in Europe. And be not so stingy with your letters.

Your friend,
KARL SCHURZ[24]

From the preceding quotation it appears that, while still German enough to spell his name in the German fashion, and still protesting his devotion to the old fatherland—neither of which, for that matter, he ever quite ceased to do—Schurz was already American

[24] *Ibid.*

enough to sense the American reaction to the Forty-eighters as a group, who were, in fact, too aggressive. Largely freethinkers, and including in their number an admixture of Marxian socialists, they roused dismay by their radical religious, political, and economic ideas;[25] and even those who came as immigrants rather than as temporary residents[26] gave the impression of having come to Germanize rather than to be Americanized.[27] Schurz evidently shared the American reaction to such conduct on the part of the other Forty-eighters. Its effect upon their later position in American public life and on his will be discussed more fully in another place.

The trip to Washington, above proposed, was made early in the following year. Its purpose was not mentioned by Mr. Schurz in his *Reminiscences* except for the general remark that his political education was considerably furthered by it. He undoubtedly went there to learn, but his letters indicate that he was motivated by something more than a purely academic interest in the study. In those to his wife he appears to have

[25] Channing, *op. cit.*, VI, 127; S. E. Morison, *The Oxford History of the United States, 1893–1917* (2 vols.; Oxford University Press, 1927), II, 128.

[26] "At first most of these imagined that their exile would be of short duration; and consequently, during the first few years, took far more interest in the affairs of Europe than in those of the United States" (Bruncken, "Political Activities of Wisconsin Germans," *supra*, n. 22).

[27] Editorial, *N.A.R.*, vol. LXXXII; *supra*, n. 21.

been rather coyly placing himself in the way of an invitation to enter American politics while still trying to decide whether he really wished to accept such an invitation if given the opportunity. At the same time, he avowed to her the hope of influencing the foreign policy of the government; while to Kinkel he wrote as an active ambassador might, to the head of his government, transmitting information as to the motive forces behind governmental policy.

Like many another visitor to a seat of government who has come to pray and remained to scoff, he found his first close view of the actual operation of the governmental machinery, and more particularly of the personalities of the men then serving as its operators, sadly disillusioning. To his wife, he wrote:

> I have learned much from the little I have seen, and much that does not please me. Looking at things as an unprejudiced and disinterested spectator, this confusion of schemes, interests, fears, personal considerations, ambitious plans and claims, manoeuvers, mutual deceptions, etc.—one is involuntarily tempted not to venture further into the turmoil.[28]

His inductor into many of the mysteries of Washington was a German journalist named Francis Grund, who, with presumably no idea of the historical consequences of his cynical exposition, enlightened him especially upon the so-called "spoils system" and upon the supreme importance of "the pickings" in politics.[29]

[28] Letter, March 15, 1854, C.S., *S.C.&P.P.*, I, 8.

[29] C.S., *Rem.*, II, 19–29.

But in spite of all unpleasant revelations, his faith in
the machine increased as his admiration for its operators diminished; and he continued more optimistically
in the same letter:

> However, within this sphere there are great duties, noble
> tasks, momentous decisions, that rise like columns from the dust
> in which vermin crawl. You learn here what good political in-
> stitutions mean. The country is being badly governed at this
> moment, but, however it may be governed, incapable as the men
> at the helm may be, things go well, nevertheless.[30]

If he soon realized that republican institutions were
not so automatic as to render the government capable
of running itself satisfactorily without intelligent direction and vigilant supervision, he at least never
ceased to contrast them favorably with those still subject to the caprices of a Frederick William IV or even
to the arbitrary will of a Bismarck.[31]

Eight days later he was ready to tell his wife something more about his plans and activity in Washington:

> It was my intention to urge upon the people I came in con-
> tact with—especially if I should be able to reach any member of
> the cabinet—*a certain course in their foreign policy* [author's
> italics]. As far as the members of Congress with whom I have
> become acquainted are concerned, I have had some success which
> was quite pleasing. My experience with the President and the
> Cabinet is, in a word, *that they have no foreign policy* [*sic*],

[30] Letter to Mrs. Schurz, March 15, 1854, *supra,* n. 28.

[31] As shown by lectures on France (1858) and on Germany (*ca.*
1868). Manuscripts in C.S. MSS., L.C., and by his striking remark to
Bismarck about the folly of having a policeman posted at every pud-
dle to prevent the people's falling into it.

neither have they a system nor a fixed purpose. They regulate
their foreign policy entirely in accord with the tendency of
public opinion held by the political parties of the country.
Their course of action on foreign affairs is based entirely on the
effect to be made on the nation, and therefore no consistency nor
fixed principles are to be expected of the Administration. . . . .
I have therefore come to the conclusion that there is only one
way of achieving anything, and that is in the first place to work
upon public opinion and so gain a real influence over the Government. *Fortunately at this moment there is no great crisis
looming up in Europe in which America might be called upon
to take part on the side of freedom* [author's italics]. This Administration would be too weak to do anything of that kind.

With the President, he was especially disappointed:

The President presents the sorry spectacle of an individual
who has been placed at the helm of a great Republic without
possessing the necessary strength of character nor the equally
necessary clearness of mind. He has the unfortunate trait of
wishing to please everybody, and consequently he has displeased
all. He agrees with everyone who speaks to him, and so says
something different to each one. There has never been a President in the White House who has to such a degree disappointed
all the good expectations centered on him, and consequently no
one who has so rapidly lost such enormous popularity. This dis-
couraging experience may discourage the people from again
electing such a person, from whom all things are *hoped,* because *nothing* is known.[32]

Within a year he had come to blame an institution
rather than an individual for the failure of his semi-
diplomatic mission. Again in Washington, he wrote to
Kinkel:

[32] Letter to Mrs. Schurz from Washington, March 23, 1854, in
C.S., *S.C.&P.P.,* I, 11.

When you ask me, "when will the United States interfere practically in the interest of the freedom of the peoples of the world?" I answer without hesitation and with unquestioning conviction, "as soon as the slave-holders have ceased to be a political power." The slave-holder fears the propaganda of freedom, because he does not know how far it may go. Even the mere word of freedom has for him a dangerous and ambiguous sound.[33]

Having studied the matter at length, and having sat in the Senate gallery day after day on his previous visit to Washington, listening to the debates on the Kansas-Nebraska bill and forming at least some of those impressions of the pro-slavery and antislavery leaders which are described with such skill in his *Reminiscences*, he was ready to announce his own convictions on the slavery question. As already indicated, he recognized it as a question which would continue to dominate all others until settled, and prevent any other matter from being decided upon its own merits. He favored no further compromise. To Kinkel, he continued:

Whatever may be the considerations that demand compromise, there can be but one question of freedom, and the faithful adherence to that principle is, on the whole, more practical than it sometimes seems. It is not the philanthropic side of the question which has brought me to this conclusion, but the direct and indirect effect of the system upon the whole government of the United States, the aristocratic character of Southern society, the demoralizing influence of the slave power on the politicians of

[33] Letter to Kinkel, January 23, 1855, published in part in *ibid.*, p. 14, and more fully in *Lebn.*, III, 119.

the north; the consequent partisanship of all ideas of justice, and especially the influence upon our foreign policy. . . . . I am decidedly opposed to any extension of the domain of slavery, inclusive of the annexation of Cuba. . . . . Perhaps in the year 1856 we shall completely succeed in breaking up the country-gentry party. I can think of no happier event for the politics of this country.[34]

These early Washington impressions were based upon observation from the galleries and upon numerous personal contacts. He went there, on his first visit, equipped with several letters of introduction, mostly to Democrats. His first call was upon Jefferson Davis, then Secretary of War; another on Senator Shields of Illinois, whom he characterized as a man being carried along by a jovial disposition and a Mexican War record. The third was on Senator Brodhead, who rivaled Francis Grund as a wrecker of illusions, with his

[34] *Ibid.*, Note 33. One needs to be reminded that this analysis of the effect of slavery on American politics was written by an immigrant of twenty-six, after only two years and four months in the country. Note also his later account of the negotiation carried on with Great Britain for the return of fugitive slaves, by John Quincy Adams, President; Henry Clay, Secretary of State; and Albert Gallatin, Minister to the Court of St. James: "The negotiation presents a sorry spectacle; a republic offering to surrender deserters from the army or navy of a monarchical power, if that power would agree to surrender slaves escaped from their masters in that republic! [All the negotiators were half-hearted about it] . . . . It was a mere perfunctory 'going through the motions,' as if in expectation of a not unwelcome failure. But even as such, it is a sorry page of history, which we should gladly miss. Slavery was a hard taskmaster to the Government of this proud American Republic" (C.S., *Henry Clay*, I, 301).

statement: "On the whole, I do not take as much interest in measures and policies as in the management of men."[35]

Initial introductions led to others. Eager to form acquaintanceships, gifted with exceptional aptitude for doing so, and favored by his rather romantic background, he quickly gained some sort of knowledge of all the leaders then in Washington. The accuracy of his own record of the impressions so gained is, of course, open to challenge, as possibly colored by subsequent experience. Sumner, the closest friend of his own later days in Washington, appears in the *Reminiscences* as the man who showed the most intelligent and most courteous interest in him on his first visit. And conversely, a biographer of Douglas, nettled by the far less favorable picture of his hero, writes:

> The *Reminiscences* of Mr. Schurz were not written on the spot, but at a period somewhat late in life, when memories of several uncomfortable campaign engagements with the "formidable parliamentary pugilist" clouded the gentleman's judgment. The likes and dislikes of Mr. Schurz were governed by fortunate or unfortunate experiences, just like those of the common individual, with this difference: he kept a ledger account of his grievances into which a credit rarely found its way.[36]

It is submitted that a worse injustice is certainly here done to Schurz than he can possibly have done to Douglas in either of his brilliant pen pictures of him in

[35] C.S., *Rem.*, II, 23.

[36] Frank E. Stevens, "Stephen A. Douglas," *Illinois State Historical Society Journal*, Joint Number 3–4, 1923–24, p. 490.

his *Reminiscences*.[37] But enough has been quoted from his contemporary letters to substantiate the accuracy of his own summary of the impression made upon him by his first close view of Washington and its leaders—including Douglas:

> I had seen the slave power officially represented by some of its foremost champions—overbearing, defiant, dictatorial, vehemently demanding a chance for unlimited expansion, and, to secure its own existence, threatening the most vital principle of free institutions, the right of free utterance—aye, threatening the Union, the National Republic itself. I had seen in alliance with the slave power, not only far-reaching material interests and a sincere but easily intimidated conservatism, but a selfish party spirit and an artful and unscrupulous demagogy making a tremendous effort to obfuscate the moral sense of the North. I had seen standing against this tremendous array of forces a small band of anti-slavery men faithfully fighting the battle of freedom and civilization. I saw the decisive contest rapidly approaching, and I felt an irresistible impulse to prepare myself for usefulness, however modest, in the impending crisis.[38]

His ambition to enter American public life had, in fact, been growing steadily. As an alternative to a return to Europe it had been in his mind all along, lending a double point to his studies. As early as October, 1852, he had written to Charlotte Voss that he expected sometime to visit the cities of the West with a view to settling in one of them unless something more promising should open up. There, he would become a lawyer, for the sake of the influence he could so attain

[37] C.S., *Rem.*, II, 31, 93–96.

[38] *Ibid.*, p. 37.

as a citizen and as a way into public life, for the lawyers were the politicians.[39] His visits to Washington stimulated this ambition tremendously; and on the first of them he wrote to his wife, as he might more appropriately have done at sixty-five than at twenty-five, that in that atmosphere of political activity he could feel "the old fire of 1848" coursing in his veins "as fresh and young as ever."[40]

Such a rejuvenation, at the age of twenty-five, led inevitably to a comparison of the abilities which he believed himself to possess with those which he saw evidenced by the men around him.[41] He judged the men in Congress to be fairly representative of the average of the people, in intelligence, education, and culture;[42] and having had in his life but little reason, and no encouragement at all from others, to consider himself as anything else than distinctly above the average in those respects, he saw no reason why his qualities

[39] Letter, October 10, 1852, *supra*, n. 12.

[40] Letter from Washington, March 23, 1854, *supra*, n. 32. The events, activities, dangers, and excitements of more than a generation of normal life had, to be sure, been crowded for him into the six years just past, so it is not surprising that he should have looked back as upon a long and eventful life. Many a young veteran looked back in the same prematurely old fashion in 1919.

[41] *Ibid.*; letter to Kinkel, March 25, 1855, in *Lebn.*, III, 123; same, in part, in C.S., *S.C.&P.P.*, I, 19.

[42] He considered "the Frankfort Parliament . . . . the most dignified and orderly, the French Assembly the most turbulent, the House of Commons the most business-like, and the American Congress . . . . the most representative" (C.S., *Rem.*, II, 29).

should not command success. He was strongly encouraged to think so by men in Washington who saw in him a young man sure to be useful to the party which could command his services. From them came the suggestion that he need only establish his residence in one of the new states, where the competition for office would not be too keen, in order as soon as eligible to be returned to Washington as a member of Congress, where they predicted a brilliant career for him.[43] He doubtless seemed to the party managers to be just what they wanted. Here was an able young German, already famous among his countrymen, and likely to be useful in controlling their numerous but none too dependable votes. As a newcomer, and one ambitious for a public career, he would presumably be amenable to suggestions and management. The extent to which these expectations were justified by the event will furnish material for discussion in another place.

The immediate result of the coincidence of the suggestions of his new-found political friends with his own desires and circumstances was an extended trip through the West, in the autumn of 1854, in search of a proper field for his new activity. After his return, he wrote to Kinkel that he had found it in Wisconsin and that he proposed to spend his waiting time in a place and manner which offered promise for the future, in case he should not, after all, be recalled to Europe by a turn of events there.

[43] Letter to Mrs. Schurz, March 23, 1854, *supra,* nn. 32 and 40.

As soon as he could get his parents settled with his mother's relatives, the Jüssens, in Watertown, Wisconsin, he expected to make a trip to Europe on account of his wife's health, which had suffered from the sudden changes of climate in Pennsylvania, they thought, and which they hoped would be benefited by a temporary return to Europe.[44] But lest the purpose of this trip be misunderstood, he wrote, two months later:

You seem to assume that I expect now to return to Europe permanently; and I see that many of my friends are of the same opinion. My intention is that the visit in Europe shall constitute only an interruption in my American existence. . . . . As long as there is no upheaval of affairs in Europe, it is my firm resolve to regard this country not as a transient or accidental abode, but as the field of my usefulness. I love America, and I am vitally interested in the things about me—they no longer seem strange. I find that the question of liberty is in its essence the same everywhere, however different its form. . . . . My devotion to the cause of the old Fatherland has not abated but my expectations have somewhat cooled. I have only faint hopes for the next few years. Even if the revolution should come sooner than I expect, I do not see why I should not utilize the intervening time.

He went on, at considerable length, to discuss the keenness of his interest in the political contests in America, and the strength of his impulse to enter them. He was most optimistic about his financial future in Wisconsin and pointed out that there where the German element

[44] Letter to Kinkel from Philadelphia, January 23, 1855, in *Lebn.*, III, 119–21; in part, in C.S., *S.C.&P.P.*, I, 16 (*supra*, n. 33), p. 74.

was powerful and lacked only leaders he could attain political prominence without "truckling to the nativistic element." And there too, he said, "I hope, in time, to gain influence that may also become useful to our cause."[45]

When one finds a man, usually so marked by decisiveness of character and clarity of expression as Carl Schurz, writing two letters as full of qualifications and contradictions as these two, the phenomenon demands explanation. In January "our foreign policy" was that of the United States, and "we" designated the people who, in 1856, were to break the country-gentry party in America. In March, after his firm refusal to consider America as only a temporary place of residence—unless it should prove to be one—"our cause" had again become that of the German revolutionaries. The explanation seems to be that he was debating less with his correspondent than with himself. The ambitious opportunist in him was attracted by the prospect before him in America, made rosy by the suggestions of Washington friends and by his own faith in his abilities and in his luck; the idealist in him was genuinely drawn simultaneously to the two struggles for liberty, in Europe and in America; and the stubborn, pertinacious German in him still clung with an emotionalized sort of tenacity to a German movement intellectually perceived as hopeless. He was still trying to take a firm,

[45] Letter to Kinkel from Philadelphia, March 25, 1855, in *Lebn.*, III, 123, in full; at length, but not in full, in C.S., *S.C.&P.P.*, I, 19.

unequivocal stand, with a foot planted on each side of the Atlantic, and to turn a hopeful face in both directions at once.

When writing to Germans who were still identified with the German revolution, he naturally gave that interest a disproportionate emphasis. As for him, he would plan a future as if for permanence; but success or failure in America, during the interim, would go far toward determining his course whenever Germany should again be open to him.

CHAPTER IV

EXPLORATION

ON ALL of his first three journeys to the West Schurz traveled alone. It is perhaps well that he did, for the first two of them at least were very arduous ones and would have imposed real hardships upon a young woman of somewhat frail health and timorous nature and upon their infant daughter. He constantly bemoaned his loneliness; but, to the student of the life and character of her husband, there is compensation in the fact that Mrs. Schurz remained behind and let him go off on these journeys, as on numerous others later, alone. For so were written the remarkable series of letters, extending through the years, which form the bulk of the Wisconsin Historical Society collection. On these first two prospecting tours to the West, they consisted largely of descriptions of what he had seen; on the third, Watertown, Wisconsin, was pictured for her as her future home; on later ones, personalities of public men, his own views on current questions, the rigors and emoluments of lecturing, the blare of bands and flare of torchlights in political campaigns, are so realistically reproduced in his letters as to make them fascinating reading.

While there is very little in them to contradict his

own statements in the *Reminiscences* or those concerning him in other accounts of the period, there is much
to supplement them. They have been withheld from
publication until the present time, with a few exceptions,[1] as being "intimate family letters"; and so they
are. But just because they were not written for publication, and are so marked by frankness and freedom
from restraint, they are invaluable as material supple-
mentary to that already available.

The character of Schurz gains far more than it
loses by whatever revelations there are in them. They
do show, on his part, a more intense desire for public
office, especially in 1860 and 1861, than he cared then
or later to admit, although in his *Reminiscences,* while
still saying that the idea did not occur to him during the
campaign, he confesses that he was easily persuaded by
his friends, or convinced himself, after it was over,
that a high-grade appointment at the hands of Lincoln
was his due.[2] They also reveal an honest egoism in
him, a conscious feeling of intellectual superiority
which is not entirely inconsistent with the character of
a theoretical democrat who aspires to be a leader, but
which roused resentment not only among inferior men
who, for their own glorification, insisted that democracy must mean equality in all things but among many
others who were themselves superior men and who
found his didacticism unpleasant. For this trait he was
easily forgiven by his friends, but never by his enemies.

[1] Those found in C.S., *S.C.&P.P.*   [2] C.S., *Rem.,* II, 218.

But if the admiration commanded by his brilliant abilities is in any way diminished by the revelation of such traits as these—the lack of which would have been far more surprising, under the circumstances, than their possession—the loss is more than balanced by the gain on the side of personal attractiveness. In public, he was serious, earnest, and strenuous, almost to excess; in his letters, one sees why his friends all loved him. Only a few of the letters of Mrs. Schurz were apparently preserved; but she appears, reflected, as it were, in his, as a person of less robust temperament and less ebullient vitality than he, but as one capable of holding his constant and devoted affection. It is something in itself that she was the sort of wife to whom a man would write numerous and lengthy letters, marked by both spontaneity and a desire to please, in the midst of the din and confusion of the almost superhuman exertions of the most strenuous political campaigns, on which a very heavy political correspondence was already superimposed.

There was evidently more of kindliness, more of capacity for the enjoyment of shared pleasures, more of humor, more of what he might have called *Lebensgenuss*, in the makeup of Carl Schurz than any but his family and best friends ever knew. These qualities were not shown in his public appearances; but in his correspondence they do become, to a degree, apparent.

The letters written on the first tour of the West have a triple interest. His portrayals of some of the

cities visited are like so many photographs, stamped with
the date "in 1854"; his descriptions of frontier scenes
deserve to live, if for their literary qualities alone,
while showing him to be no frontiersman at heart; and
his observations on the western man in general, and on
the Germans in particular, convey valuable information concerning both their subjects and their writer.

In the first of the series, he wrote an almost po-
etical description of the mountain scenery of western
Pennsylvania on the Pittsburgh route to Cincinnati.
Then:

> We passed through Pittsburgh about three o'clock at night,
> and I saw nothing of it except the yellow burned out fires which
> were lighted in the streets as a defense against cholera.[3]

> Cincinnati lies in crescent formation upon the Ohio, and is
> bounded on the north, west, and east by high steep bluffs. The
> aspect of the city is friendly, not so monotonous as Philadelphia
> nor so bustling as New York, but of course inferior to these
> eastern cities in magnificence. There is so much building going
> on in Cincinnati and the new constructions are on such a mag-
> nificent scale and so splendidly executed that the "Queen of the
> West" may soon proudly compare herself with the great eastern
> cities. . . . . The Germans live together in one division of the
> city, at least most of them, and their streets are easily recognized
> by their distinctive but not very advantageous old-country cus-
> toms.[4]

From Cincinnati he went on to Indianapolis, prof-
iting, wherever he went, in the formation of quick ac-

[3] Letter to Mrs. Schurz from Indianapolis, September 22, 1854, in
C.S. MSS., W.H.S.

[4] *Ibid.*

quaintanceships, from contacts made in Washington, and in his previous heavy correspondence among the Germans. In the Indiana capital, he was well received by Nathaniel Bolton (later United States consul at Geneva), whose wife, Sarah Bolton, he had met in Washington, and by Governor Wright, to whom he was presented by Mr. Bolton. Both of these gentlemen urged him to stay in Indianapolis permanently; and he showed himself then, as later, not immune to "booster" psychology, by thinking seriously of doing so and going into the "gas business," which was then in process of expansion and offered opportunity for investment. His wife must know what Indianapolis was like too; so after a few days there, he wrote:

I now know the city fairly well. Although it has at present only 18,000 inhabitants, it covers a very extensive area. The "great Main Street," with its markets, will not permit us to forget that Indianapolis is a state capital. It presents an extremely lively appearance, not like any one of the chief business streets of Philadelphia and New York; it bears rather a rural character; crowded constantly with a confused mass of farm-wagons and equestrians—(also equestriennes)—it looks more like a permanent annual market-fair. An extraordinary amount of horseback-riding is done here. No farmer comes into the city on foot, and the country women and girls mount their horses in their ordinary clothes, just as they are; and since there is much breeding of horses here, colts follow almost half the riders, and gambol and frolic about as if they were at home.

But in spite of the rustic note introduced by the colts, the animation was so great that the observer could hardly realize that he was nearly 800 miles west of

the Atlantic Coast. Those familiar with the present
suburban tendency of the city will be interested to
note that "the more elegant residences" were already
being built "in the woods, at the ends of the streets."[5]

From there he went on to Chicago. A part of his
description of that city is also given not as a contribu-
tion to census statistics at all but simply as an interesting
and vivid picture of what he saw there and what he
thought of what he saw.

After we had made our way through the broad business
streets, with their magnificent, high, marble buildings, which
cóncede almost nothing to New York's Broadway in the activity
of trade, and had reached the Lake, making our way between co-
lossal warehouses, we reached the great railway station which is
close to the lake and from which four or five railway tracks
built on trestles run out through the water. Suddenly we stood
still before a little wooden building, built of solid logs and
pierced on all sides with loop-holes, which obviously could have
no relation to the present tremendous activity going on around
it. This, I was told, was Ft. Dearborn, which up to about twenty years ago served the few settlers of this place as a protection
against the wild Indian hordes. This fort, the oldest building in
Chicago, the most honored relic, is now thirty years old. The
oldest native inhabitant of Chicago is a girl of twenty-two years.
She was born when only three miserable huts stood there. Now the
city has over 80,000 inhabitants and an incalculable commerce.
As one walks through the streets, one sees the city grow. The
building and the business activity here are indescribable. That
part of the city in which the well-to-do people live, and because
of whose gardens around their houses someone has given the section the name "Garden City," exhibits an elegance of buildings

[5] *Ibid.*

and beauty of streets which is not behind the best I have ever seen. The magnificence of the public improvements and under-takings, in relation to the youthfulness of the city, surpasses anything I have known. The land prices round about are fan-tastically high, since the people well know to what size Chicago will grow.[6]

There is something very ironical in the fact that the man who was soon to be so bitterly disappointed in his own project for selling building-lots cut from a farm on the edge of Watertown, Wisconsin, which is still a farm, should have been told, on this visit to Chi-cago, "If you had been here a year ago, you might have invested money in real estate to great advantage; but it is too late, now."[7]

Another letter, also written in St. Louis, but deal-ing chiefly with his experiences during his first visit to Chicago, tells in most amusing fashion of his difficul-ties in trying to find a place in a hotel there. He had arrived very late from Indianapolis, the shortest rail-way route from Indianapolis to St. Louis being then, he said, via Chicago. From one overfilled hostelry to another he went, until the omnibuses ceased to serve him, then wandered at random until dead tired, sat down on a curbstone, and fell asleep. He was finally awakened by a policeman and conducted to a sort of hotel, where he fought a losing battle with the vermin for the remainder of the night.

[6] Letter to wife from St. Louis, October 2, 1854, in C.S. MSS., W.H.S.

[7] C.S., *Rem.*, II, 44.

But while asleep, according to the letter, he had
had an amazing experience with the rats, which were
then harbored in great numbers under the wooden side-
walks of the city and which ran riot at night.[8] In his
dream he had carried on an extended conversation with
these rats; and as they could speak no German, that
part of the letter was written in English, thus consti-
tuting the only bit of writing in that language in the
entire series of family letters. It is also the earliest
sample of his writing in English now available; which
makes even its errors interesting. And errors there are,
both in grammar and sentence construction, as well as
instances of peculiarly German, rather than English,
word order. The letter was evidently written only for
his own amusement and for that of his young wife;
but its errors show that the use of grammatically and
idiomatically correct English had not yet become so
instinctive or so habitual with him as to be proof against
carelessness.

Where the letter runs most smoothly, it excites
one's curiosity even more. The rats reproached him for
having trespassed upon the streets in the hours when
the city was supposed to be exclusively theirs; and he
confessed to an acute and very human—and not unnatural—case of homesickness, in apologizing for

[8] C.S., *Rem.*, II, 43 and 44. As given in the *Reminiscences,* this
incident is dated as having occurred during his second Chicago visit
rather than the first, and the tale is told quite briefly, but it includes
the wooden sidewalks and the rats.

having trespassed involuntarily, and expressing regret that he had ever left his wife and child and his comfortable home to seek his fortune in a strange world. He so aroused the sympathy of his interlocutors that the rat mayor at once appointed a reception committee, a committee on arrangements, and an entertainment committee. Schurz was made their honored guest; and he and the heads of committees all made mutually laudatory speeches, glibly and aptly burlesquing the rubber-stamp remarks usually made on such occasions. Where had he learned them? He had presumably been entertained now and then by the Germans of various cities; but neither letters nor *Reminiscences* show any record of it; and he made a definite statement in November, 1856, that his part in the campaign of that year constituted his first active participation in politics in seven years.[9] It is a very extravagant bit of foolery; but the remainder of the letter attests, rather than proves, its genuineness by appearing to be an authentic part of an authentic series.

From Chicago he continued his journey to St. Louis.

St. Louis appears very imposing from the waterside. The warehouses and hotels stand in a row on the broad quay like palaces. But in the interior the city is dirty, and the streets of the older part of the city narrow—(that is, according to American standards; in Germany they would be considered very wide).

[9] Letter to his brother-in-law, Heinrich Meyer, from Watertown, November 20, 1856, in C.S. MSS., W.H.S.

It is at once apparent that the city was originally laid out by the French. Some streets are now being developed with great elegance, and accord with the significant business life and incalculable resources of the city. . . . . I found here a large number of old and new friends, and have been able only with difficulty to keep myself free from invitations, etc.

Why in this case he should have tried to avoid invitations he has not here definitely explained. But he did promise to "do what was to be done" there as quickly as possible and to hurry back north as soon as he could.[10] He was there, altogether, less than a week, including the time consumed by a two-day visit to Hecker. His host in St. Louis was a former countryman, a lawyer named Kribben. While he wrote that he was "making a mass of notes and observations" which should be useful later, St. Louis was apparently not then considered at all as a prospective place of abode. Missouri had been advocated by Muench and other protagonists of the scheme as the logical place for the establishment of the German state in America; but as the plan had been almost completely abandoned before 1854,[11] and as Schurz had never been in sympathy with it anyway,[12] his business in St. Louis had presumably nothing to do with that either. The facts that he was soon again in correspondence about the Ger-

[10] Letters to Mrs. Schurz, from St. Louis, October 2 and 5, 1854, *ibid*.

[11] Bruncken, "Pol. Act. of Wis. Ger."; *supra*, chap. iii, n. 22, pp. 68.

[12] Letter to Kinkel, April 12, 1853, in C.S. MSS., W.H.S.; *supra*, chap. iii, nn. 14 and 23, p. 63.

man republican loan with Kinkel, its custodian,[13] and
that so large a portion of his time was spent with Hecker seem to indicate that he went to St. Louis partly to
get into touch with the Germans there and to inform
himself as to their situation and partly to confer with
the famous Hecker as to a line of action. So much for
his personal objectives. Later statements as to his business activities in Watertown indicate that on this whole
trip he may have been commissioned, in a general way,
to act as agent for some Philadelphia company or group
of investors.

This Hecker was one of the firebrands of the
South German insurrection of 1848–49. In the Frankfort parliament he had introduced resolutions calling
for the abolition of the monarchy and the establishment of a confederation modeled upon the government
of the United States; and, upon the failure of his proposal, had withdrawn and raised the standard of revolt
in Baden, acting throughout as such an irreconcilable
extremist as to win unmixed admiration only from en-
thusiasts.[14] Time, however, had made him an increas-
ingly romantic and influential figure among the Germans in America. He was an ardent Republican from
the beginning of the party and was a prominent speaker in Illinois and Wisconsin in 1856 and 1858. Schurz
says in his *Reminiscences* that he and Hecker mutually

[13] Letter of January 23, 1855, in *Lebn.*, III, 119; *supra*, chap.
iii, nn. 33 and 44.

[14] Cf. Henderson, *Short History of Germany*, p. 353.

pledged themselves to meet on the field in a common
endeavor if the antislavery movement should ever need
such service;[15] and it is not impossible that the older
man's influence may have counted toward the younger's decision also to cast his lot with the Republicans.
This interview took place at the beginning of the October previous to the January in which he wrote the
letter above quoted, in which he told what "we" hoped
to do to the country-gentry party in 1856.[16]

St. Louis itself, despite the description of its appearance given above, proved to be the exception among
the cities visited. He found there the least of that
free and unrestrained intercourse and spirit of co-operation between classes which had pleased him most
in other cities. For this he blamed the presence and
the aristocratic pretensions of slaveholding families.
"There the existence of slavery, with its subtle influence, cast its shadow over the industrial and commercial developments of the city, as well as over the
relations between the different groups of citizens."[17]
Perhaps this impression was still with him when, in
1860, he went to St. Louis to make his strongest direct
attack upon slavery as an institution.[18]

[15] C.S., *Rem.*, II, 43.

[16] Letter to Kinkel, January 23, 1855; *supra*, chap. iii, nn. 33
and 44, pp. 74, 80.

[17] C.S., *Rem.*, II, 39.

[18] Speech, "The Doom of Slavery," August 1, 1860. In both editions of *Speeches* and in many contemporary newspapers and campaign
pamphlets.

From St. Louis, he returned to Chicago, where mail awaited him, including an invitation to visit his relatives in Watertown. He went by way of Milwaukee, of which two descriptions were written, one then and one in the following year.

You come from Chicago, by the Lake, to Milwaukee in eight hours; and when I awoke in my stateroom in the morning, I found the chief city of Wisconsin before me. The town is quite pretty, but for some time it has not progressed properly. The immigration into Wisconsin has been forced somewhat too much. The State has anticipated its future a little, and when the formidable competition of Chicago arose, could not quite keep up. Still, things will undoubtedly go better, as soon as the "Territories" to the west of Wisconsin become states, and the trade of Milwaukee is so given a new market. Milwaukee also suffers from the presence of too many Germans. Wherever the German in this country has to live off the Germans things go badly for him. There [in Milwaukee] you can see in the morning as you pass through the streets, the German house-father in dressing-gown and slippers, with his long pipe, standing in the door.[19]

In the following August he was in Milwaukee again, and after a walk through the better residential district he supplemented this description with the following:

No American city, not even Cleveland, has made so favorable an impression on me. Most of the houses combine in the most pleasing fashion the urban with the country-house character; the gardens around them are mostly filled with thick growth, and the almost never-failing and tasteful veranda

[19] Letter to Mrs. Schurz from Watertown, October 9, 1854, in C.S. MSS., W.H.S.

makes the whole thing exceptionally home-like and livable. At dusk, I came upon the height above the lake, where the white light-tower stands visible from afar. From a distance, the lake already made itself heard with a subdued roar, and suddenly I stood on the precipitous edge of the cliff, which revealed to me the light-green, sail-dotted surface in an endless expanse. The appearance of the lake there is not much different from that of the ocean, only the colors are not quite so darkly sombre.

The desire to live here arose strongly within me, especially when I saw through a brightly-lighted window into a family living-room, and involuntarily pictured you and our child in there. . . . .[20]

Of Wisconsin, as a state, he wrote:

Wisconsin is a beautiful land, contrasting very favorably, by reason of its wooded hills and the multitude of its exceedingly lovely little lakes, with the flat Illinois. And I had pictured it as less built-up; for although one is so near the borders of civilization here that in hunting one often encounters Indians, yet the southern half of the State appears as a great blooming, thickly-settled farming district.[21]

That he did not care for the level country was evident all along. After the train trips from Indianapolis to Chicago, and from there to St. Louis, he had written:

The sun was already low in the West, when we crossed the Wabash, and saw on our left the bloody battle-field of Tippecanoe. At twilight we entered the "grand prairie" which occupies the north-west quarter of the State of Indiana. The movement out of the forest into the prairie is comparable to that out of a stream into the high sea. On both sides of the railway track

[20] Letter to Mrs. Schurz from Milwaukee, August 15, 1855, *ibid.*

[21] Letter of October 9, 1854; *supra*, n. 19.

the woods recede farther and farther, just as the stream opens
out into the bosom of the sea; and as you turn your gaze forward over the level endless prairie meadows, your eye finds no
resting-point, save the sharp, straight streak which marks off the
horizon; here and there perhaps a straggling clump of trees or
a small farmhouse, which stand forth like lonely islands from
the great, waveless grass sea. Finally the forest banks right and
left disappear; and wherever you turn your eye you see nothing
but the unbroken, inexorable, dead plains. I believe, there can
be no more profound feeling of abandonment than to be alone
upon a great prairie. The sea is much more alive than the prairie. There at least the waves rise up in grand movement, and
the horizon changes with the heaving of the sea; but even a
storm leaves the prairie still. It must be a remarkable sight to
witness from a distance a railway train rolling over a prairie.
Flowers there are in profusion and in many shades of color; but
when one looks at the prairie as a whole, one forgets the flowers. The "grand prairie" has a rich soil, and in some localities is
already studded with farms; but however much I am compelled
to love the West, at least what I have seen of it, I should not
like to live upon a great prairie.[22]

And again:

The journey through the prairies of Illinois is rather mo-
notonous, and the many places passed en route are neat and
growing rapidly, but otherwise without distinction. From Alton to St. Louis, one travels on the Mississippi. Its dark waters
move majestically between the eternal forests on its banks. Great
herons glide on slow wings over the waves of the stream, swoop-
ing here and there to spear their prey. Swarms of large birds of
prey move across the dark primeval forest of the shore, and
strengthen the melancholy impression which the solitary wild-

[22] Letter to Mrs. Schurz from St. Louis, September 30, 1854, in
C.S. MSS., W.H.S.

ness makes on the soul of the wanderer. For scarcely has the city of Alton vanished from sight, when cultivation ceases on both sides of the river. All is solitude until one reaches the immediate vicinity of St. Louis. Where the broad Missouri mingles its yellow, muddy waters with those of the Mississippi, the color of the stream changes. At first, the water of the latter is clearly distinguishable from that of the former, one side of the stream being dark brown, the other pale yellow. But soon the Missouri with its tremendous mass of water overcomes the Mississippi, and the whole stream becomes clay-colored.[23]

From these quotations, it is evident that it was not for nothing that Teacher Bone had drilled him on description in the village school of Brühl, to impress upon him that every word of a description should denote something definite and something perceptible to the physical senses. But while he could so vividly describe the wilderness, from the point of view of the traveler and observer, it was clear that he was not so constituted as ever to live in it. Neither was Mrs. Schurz, who was not attracted by the prospect of the westward move, in spite of his best efforts to idealize the West for her. The most highly idealized of all the pictures sent back from this journey was the following one of a frontier clearing:

A homestead, taken in the first stage of its development, has about it something quite touching. The log cabin is only large enough to hold a fireplace, a table, a bed, and the assembled members of the family. Stables there are none at first; a shelter covered with boards or often only with boughs takes the place of a barn. The fields are still dotted with trees, but the

[23] Letter of October 2, 1854; *supra*, n. 10.

farmer has girdled these, or has laid a fire under them, and so
they stand leafless and dead, and wait for the first good wind-
storm, which will uproot them. Among them the cattle roam,
and the children among the cattle. The woman is in the house,
busy with the butter, and somewhere around the edge of the
clearing the man is breaking the rich new soil with his plow-
share. The whole picture is framed by thick forest, and only a
road which you often see for miles cutting thread-like through
the forest, maintains contact with the open world outside. Such
woods-roads in Ohio are wonderful, and when I saw one, I have
often wished for no more than to be with you, on horseback,
and to be able to ride such a road to its end.[24]

But even this description followed closely upon a much
more spontaneous reference to the poverty evident in
the clearings and the hardships and privations insepara-
ble from frontier life.

Still, his determination to make the West seem as
attractive as possible to her persisted and, in fact, became stronger after his arrival in Wisconsin, at which
time he seems to have made the tentative decision to
return to that state as a place of residence. So from
Watertown he wrote, continuing the account of his
journey there from Chicago:

I took the night steamer, which brought me across the lake
to Milwaukee. This voyage, on the lake, on an undescribably
lovely moonlight night, was one of the most beautiful of my
travels and for a true revel in enjoyment of nature, nothing was
lacking, but that I should have had you at my side. Certainly,
you must sometime travel with me, and see all that I have seen.
There is so much that is grand and beautiful here, that it well

[24] Letter of September 22, 1854; *supra*, n. 3, p. 86.

repays one for a little expenditure of time and some incon-
venience. I believe that you would quickly lose your antipathy
for the West, if you could once see it.

I will not say that this country surpasses the East, in beauty. On the contrary, the vast plains on both sides of the Mississippi are not even interesting, for long. But there breathes an
infinitely fresh spirit through this land. Whithersoever you turn
your eye, you see something great in progress. Grandeur is the
characteristic of all western life. The whole life appears hopeful, and the fight against the obstacles which oppose civilization
is carried on with the highest confidence of victory.

I have never seen so many cheerful people as here. The
western American, no matter how great his instinct for enterprise or his acquisitiveness may be, does not wear upon his face
the stamp of calculating determination, which one meets so often among the eastern Yankees.

The western man is frank, ready of speech, direct; he
makes acquaintanceships with extraordinary ease, wherever he
may be. The cold reserve of bearing, which in the East often
seemed to us so freezing, is foreign to the "western man." He
is resolute of tongue, as he is of deed, and the complete spontaneity of social intercourse makes one quickly forget that one
must not expect in such a man, finely polished behavior. You
find an extraordinary number of sensible people, [both] men
and women, and in conversation you can usually count upon
finding both an open mind and a sound heart.[25]

There came a time in his life when Schurz was at
least as much at home in the East as in the West and
when his lecture engagements were more numerous in
New England than in any other region. But on a single visit to relatives in Connecticut, soon after their ar-

[25] Letter of October 9, 1854; *supra*, n. 19.

rival in America,[26] his wife and he had apparently not found the general atmosphere of that part of the country hospitable or congenial to them. Schurz had, in fact, excellent grounds for urging that the foreign-born citizen would hardly find a better welcome elsewhere than in Wisconsin.

Before permanently taking up his residence there, however, he returned to Pennsylvania, made a quick trip to Wisconsin early in 1855 to convey his parents thither and establish them with their relatives already there,[27] then another to Washington,[28] then sailed for Europe, April 21, 1855.[29]

Only one return to Europe is mentioned in the *Reminiscences*. The letters show two. Even so, they constituted just what Schurz prophesied, "but an interruption" in his American existence. He returned from the first of them early in July, so had but little more than time enough to take Mrs. Schurz to England, where she remained at a water-cure sanitarium, while he returned to Watertown.[30] During the summer and autumn of that year he was busy with the purchase of a farm near Watertown, planning a home and

[26] C.S., *Rem.*, II, 18.

[27] Letter to Mrs. Schurz from Watertown, March 4, 1855, in C.S. MSS., W.H.S.; *Lebn.*, III, 122.

[28] Letters to Kinkel, January 25 and March 25, quoted in chap. iii.

[29] *Lebn.*, III, 126.

[30] *Ibid.*, p. 127.

a real estate project there, and writing to her a serial account of his activities.[31] In November, 1855, he was in Philadelphia, held there by business of which the *Lebenserinnerungen* gives no details—in contrast with the minuteness with which he had been discussing all matters concerned with life in Watertown.[32] In December he was again in England.[33]

This second journey is apparently the only one which he considered worthy of mention in his *Reminiscences*, unless one is to suppose that there was some other reason than its brevity and small importance for leaving the first unmentioned; and such a supposition does not seem to be justified by the evidence that is available. The only reason for either trip stated by him in letters or *Reminiscences* is the health of Mrs. Schurz. She had suffered a great deal of ill health from some unexplained organic difficulty, and one serious attack of lung trouble. She remained in a sanitarium while he came back to America for nearly six months in 1855; and on the advice of her doctors they both went to Montreux, Switzerland, for some months early in 1856. While there, he carried on a desultory correspondence with Kinkel and Althaus, the letters themselves, as well as the lack of other letters, indicating that there were but few of them. In these letters there is naturally a certain amount of gossip about old Ger-

[31] Series of letters to Mrs. Schurz in C.S. MSS., W.H.S.

[32] Excerpts from four letters from Philadelphia in *Lebn.*, III, 133.

[33] *Lebn.*, III, 134.

man associates—Techow, Schutz, and Damm, who had gone off to Australia,[34] Julius Froebel, who was said to have married a wealthy widow in New York; and so on. There was also a reference to the "thoroughness" with which "August" had done his work,[35] which may refer to some further dark designs upon the peace of Europe or merely to August Willich's organization of the *Turnverein* in America.

As a matter of fact, Schurz and his wife were enjoying a belated, or second, honeymoon in the villa of her brother, Heinrich Meyer; and while he found space in his letters to discuss European politics with those for whom they still constituted a major interest, he confessed that he was so enjoying the idyllic quiet and laziness of life there that he found difficulty in summoning the necessary energy to write some articles on Wisconsin for which arrangements were being made with the English papers. He had no difficulty, however, in rousing himself to write some charmingly beautiful descriptions of their surroundings. One, in particular, of mountains, town, and lake by moonlight, is a model of artistic imagery. It suggests the artist but not the revolutionist.

Meanwhile, at home his business needed him; and he became convinced that a quiet country life, the regular routine, and the feeling of certainty which she

[34] Letter to Kinkel from Montreux, April 27, 1856, in C.S. MSS., W.H.S.

[35] Letter to Friedrich Althaus from Montreux, March, 1856, *ibid.*

would find in an established existence would be more
beneficial to Mrs. Schurz's health than a continued
quest for a "cure" in Europe.[36]

As for America, he wrote to Kinkel:

> When we shall return to London, is not quite certain;
> probably in the course of May. My affairs in America call me
> there so urgently that I can hardly remain here much longer.
> But nothing is yet fixed, concerning our departure from Europe.
> I cannot deny that in the existing circumstances, I am eager to
> return there. The wish to continue my enterprises there is not
> the only thing. Europe looks at this moment very unpromising.[37]

After reading these letters, one is inclined to give
more credence, rather than less, to his own later account of the view he then took of the European situation. In London, before going to Montreux, he had
had an interview with Kossuth and had seen in him
"the very personification of the defeat suffered by the
revolutionary movement of 1848."[38]

As for Kinkel and the others:

> No part of the European horizon seemed to be illumined
> by a ray of hope to cheer the exiles still living in London.
> There was indeed an international committee of revolutionary
> leaders, to give direction to whatever revolutionary possibility
> might turn up. Whether they could see any such possibilities
> among the hard actualities of the time, it is difficult to say. But,

[36] Letter to Althaus from Montreux, April 12, 1856, in *Lebn.*,
III, 137.

[37] Letter to Kinkel, April 27; *supra,* n. 34. His "enterprises" in
America then included his Watertown farm and real estate project
and the prospect of nomination for the Wisconsin legislature.

[38] C.S., *Rem.*, II, 53.

as a matter of experience, nothing can be more active and fatuous than the imagination, and nothing more eager, boundless, and pathetic than the credulity of the exile. To those whose eyes were open to the real situation, the international committee looked like a gathering of spectres moving about in a graveyard.[39]

Many of the Forty-eighters were, for years after their emigration, so sure of the imminence of another revolution that they paid more attention to European affairs than to American. They were characterized by a German editor, Christian Esselen, who was himself less sanguine about the revolutionary prospect, as "men who begin every sentence with 'when the outbreak comes again' [*Wenn's wieder losgeht*]."[40] Schurz had clearly never been one of these; and any similar hopes which he may have cherished before May of 1856 were pretty well dead by then. From his promise of 1852 to Althaus to be in Europe again "at the proper time,"[41] he had progressed to the prediction that his lot was to be permanently cast in America "unless changes scarcely to be expected should happen" in Europe.[42]

Meanwhile things looked better and better for the family group of the Schurz connection at Watertown. Uncle Jacob Jüssen was found there in 1854 with a

[39] *Ibid.*, p. 50.

[40] Bruncken, "Pol. Act. of Wis. Ger.," p. 210.

[41] Letter of July 12, 1852; *supra*, chap. ii, n. 92, p. 54.

[42] Letter to Althaus from Watertown, November 15, 1856, in *Lebn.*, III, 143.

"prosperous business"[43] in the form of a "new liquor
store."[44] In March, 1856, after the *Watertown
Democrat* had carried for a year his unchanging announcement that he had just received a new shipment
of the choicest brandies, the announcement changed,
whether the stock did or not; and the whole stock and
business were offered for sale. He then bought, re-
modeled, and thereafter operated the Germania Haus.
In the autumn election of 1856, he was an unsuccessful Republican candidate for the office of register of
deeds.[45] Most Republican candidates were unsuccessful in Watertown in those days.

Through the columns of the *Watertown Democrat* in 1855 and 1856, "Miss Antonie Schurz and
sister," Carl's sisters, informed the public that they
were conducting a high-class millinery and dressmak-
ing establishment and that, after their training in the
best houses of Europe and two years' experience in
Philadelphia, they were reliable guides as to the latest
Eastern fashions. But this advertisement, too, disap-
peared when Miss Antonie Schurz married her cousin
Edmund Jüssen and moved to Columbus, in the summer of 1856.

All found the atmosphere of the place hospitable
and congenial and expected to rise to affluence with the

[43] Letter from C.S. to his wife, from Watertown, October 9,
1854, in C.S. MSS., W.H.S.

[44] Advertisement in *Watertown Dem.*

[45] *Ibid.*, October 23, 1856, and the following issues.

rapid growth of the little city. The German immigration into Wisconsin in 1854, according to the estimate of Commissioner of Immigration Fred Horn, himself a German, was 16,000;[46] and Watertown, about as predominantly German as Milwaukee, got a fair share of it. In 1855 it was the second largest city in the state, city and town together claiming by the census figures a population of 10,006, and Madison, city and town combined, 8,296.[47] The following unofficial figures, while perhaps not statistically accurate, at least serve to show a rapid increase in population. In 1850, there are said to have been 1,000 people there;[48] in 1852 there were 3,000;[49] in May of 1853, 4,000.[50] The 1850 figure, here given by Schurz, is probably the least accurate of these, but the census showed a growth of 7,000 in ten years and that the town had more than doubled itself in the past two.[51] That Schurz was credulous and considered the prospect brighter than it was, is a part of the story.

Prices were rising too, in 1855, at a most encouraging rate. The papers were filled with real estate advertisements; and a typical news item was one

[46] Bruncken, "Pol. Act. of Wis. Germans," p. 210.

[47] *Watertown Dem.*, August 2, 1855.

[48] Letter from C.S. to his wife, in C.S., *S.C.&P.P.*, I, 20; *Lebn.*, III, 127.

[49] J. A. Hadley, *Watertown Register*, September 2, 1852.

[50] *Watertown Dem.*, March 1, 1855.

[51] *Ibid.*, September 2, 1855.

showing an 80-acre farm which had been bought for
$700 two years before, sold for $2,200, and still expected to double in value within less than two years.[52]

So it is not surprising that Schurz should have been
hopeful of large profits from the farm, located right
on the edge of the town, which he had bought from
one John Jackson in 1855 and had surveyed for building lots, "so that not a foot of it be wasted."[53] His
optimism, however, led him to pay too much for it—
apparently about $100 per acre; he gave a mortgage
for $8,500 on an 89-acre farm. But he had from the
first been much impressed by the quick prosperity which
he saw others attaining in the West, and had written to
Mrs. Schurz from St. Louis in 1854 that he was confident that they also would "in a couple of years" be
"made people."[54] So in his first summer in Wisconsin,
while he lived with his parents in Watertown in a
house which he had bought for them for $1,000, and
planned for their future there, and while his wife
sought a "cure" in Europe, he wrote to her most optimistically, not only because he wished to brighten, as
much as possible, a prospect which was none too attractive to her, but because he himself just then felt so
hopeful.

Of course, he was consciously making the best of

[52] *Ibid.*, November 15, 1855.

[53] Letters to Mrs. Schurz from Watertown, August 15, 27, and
September 25, 29, 1855. C.S. MSS., W.H.S.

[54] Letter of September 30, 1854; *supra*, n. 22.

things. People came to church in farm wagons drawn by oxen, but people did not mind. Selections from the opera *Norma*, given in Watertown by some members of the Milwaukee Musikverein, had to be given on a bare stage and with only piano accompaniment; but their music was better than he expected, and their director was better paid than those of most German theaters. Some of the country around Watertown was still rather wild, but the scenery was beautiful. A dish of grapes on the table, the gift of a neighbor, gave evidence that Wisconsin was "not so far behind in civilization." Living was plain, but it was cheap. His mother needed but $12 to $14 per month to maintain the household; and he often supplied game for the table by going hunting with Rothe, an old acquaintance from the days of the students' conference at Eisenach. Even the prevalence of chills and fever, particularly among the newly arrived immigrants, living under congested and squalid conditions in the lowlands along the river, where they either went untended or were "poisoned by the doctors with all sorts of devil's-rubbish," was made to appear as an attraction,[55] for it would offer her a fine field for her "favorite activity."[56]

But the same series of letters showed quite clearly that he was not in his element. He wrote that, aside

[55] Series of letters, August to November, 1855, in C.S. MSS., W.H.S.

[56] Mrs. Schurz was interested in social service, and in Watertown, later, founded the first American kindergarten.

from business activity, his life was "pretty empty." Until his land should be sold as building-lots, it must be handled as a farm; and he had all the farmer's trials with rains in haying-time, delays in getting the threshing-machine, and so on. Even when he told himself he was learning something about farming, he ruefully admitted that "when one punishes himself so much with it, he ought to learn something."[57]

At first he found himself "the little pride of the family," and quite popular in Watertown. One of the earliest letters of this series says: "There are many who seek my acquaintance, and from the manner in which I am received, I may conclude that I could easily attain prominence."[58] Later, when his horse fell with him and he was confined to bed for ten days by another injury to one of his long and apparently rather vulnerable legs, he found himself holding "a little court," with sympathetic callers coming early and late in such numbers as seriously to interfere with his reading of

---

[57] While not really happy as a farmer, Schurz was at least less badly misplaced than some of the other Forty-eighters. One group of them took up several hundred acres in Washington County, built a poor sort of house with their own untrained hands, and tried a co-operative experiment. The wife of the one married member of the group was to cook for all. That member was Hans Balatka, formerly of Munich, and later famous in music in Milwaukee, St. Louis, and Chicago. Within less than a year, every man had deserted the group but one, Adolph Jacobson (*Milwaukee Germania Herold*, January 2, 1918).

[58] Letter to Mrs. Schurz, August 6, 1855, in C.S. MSS., W.H.S.; C.S., *S.C.&P.P.*, I, 20; *Lebn.*, 127.

Heine's miscellaneous writings, and Schlosser's *History of the Eighteenth Century;* so that, what with callers and the pain of the injury, these occupied him "whole nights through."

A part of the enforced leisure due to the same injury was used—emulating his patron saint of the period, Thomas Jefferson, in that as in politics—in drawing in detail the plans from which his house was built in the following spring. Far from being consulted about them, Mrs. Schurz could not even be shown them, for one copy must be used for the builders to follow, and his leg got well before he had time to make another.[59]

He did, however, strike off the following description of Watertown:

There is something remarkable about such a place as Watertown. All wealth here is self-made, as it were, right on the spot. There is here almost no imported capital. All the inhabitants here, with perhaps two or three exceptions, have come here without means, and these same people you now see building mills, factories, railroads, gas-works, and great stores, organizing banks, etc. And all that has been produced and done in less than ten years. Everything has been created out of nothing by mere industry, spirit of enterprise, and perseverance. And now you should see the spectacle, as long wagon-trains loaded with wheat, approach the city from all sides, how they are seized upon immediately upon their entrance by the buyers, each eager to get ahead of the other. Then, with filled pockets, the farmers disperse into the stores around the town, the streets stand packed with wagons, and the side-walks are crowded. It is a gay, lively

[59] Letter of October 21, C.S. MSS., W.H.S.

pageant, full of cheerfulness. And here and there you see the rosy cheeks of the newly-arrived, the "green ones," who do not know what it all means, or where to turn. The last weeks have brought us a good number of these pleasing sights, and almost every day I have occasion to go with advice to this or that one, who comes here with the strange plans of the ignorant.[60]

If Schurz had been more of a conformist, he might well have retained his early popularity in Watertown; but he would not have been Carl Schurz. In some respects he was a typical German of his period; in others, a typical Forty-eighter (which is not quite the same); in others, he was typical only of himself. Like the other Germans generally, he strongly opposed the temperance laws then being advocated, and wrote about those of New York with unsympathetic amusement, in phrases that look like an anachronism, antedated by about seventy years.

I had lived in New York two days, already, before I was reminded that the prohibition of liquor is in force. . . . . One drinks just as before, only with the extra pleasure that one discusses the prohibition law over a bottle of wine. A few tavern-keepers lately indulged in a humorous and successful speculation. They engaged Temperance speakers to preach in front of their places, on the street. That was done; of course, a large crowd of people gathered, and the natural consequence was that the bar-rooms of the neighboring tavern-keepers were filled to suffocation with people.

The only good he could find in such a law was that there might be some arrests, followed by fine or im-

[60] Letter to Mrs. Schurz, October 15, 1855, in C.S. MSS., W.H.S.

prisonment, for drunkenness, so that the number of
men "loafing around on the street in a state of intoxi-
cation" would be reduced.[61]

In his opposition to any interference with the fes-
tive German Sunday-afternoon customs, he was in
sympathy with the vast majority of the foreign-born;
and he wrote to his wife with pleasure of a visit with
his parents to a *Lustgarten* in the woods near the city.
But in his expressed fear that that kind of German
Sunday festivity would soon be found only in the West
of America, if in Germany "the abominable high-
handedness of the priestly hierarchy" continued to increase, he appeared more like a free-thinking Forty-
eighter.[62]

But he was too critical of his fellow-Germans
there to continue to be popular with them for long,
even if he had courted popularity with all the devices
of the politician, which he would never do. He objected to their clannishness. As he had condemned the
idea of a German state in America, so he found it
wrong that the Germans of Cincinnati and Indianapolis lived largely in segregated districts and clung too
much to their "distinctive but not very advantageous
old-country customs." He was pleased that the German tongue was heard everywhere, but seemed slightly
embarrassed by the ease with which his "honest fellow-

[61] *Ibid.*, August 8, 1855.

[62] *Ibid.*, August 12, 1855.

countryman" could be recognized, "even without hearing him speak, by his indestructible cap and his decorous
long coat-tails." Milwaukee had "too many Germans."[63]

Then, they failed to learn fast enough for him:

> I cannot refrain from telling you a fact which is not at all
> flattering to our German fellow-countrymen. You would not
> believe how superior the house and the whole domestic organi-
> zation of the American farmer is, in cleanliness and business-
> like management, over the German. When you come into the
> most insignificant log-hut of the American, you at least find
> the walls spotless, all the utensils scoured bright, the windows
> shining, the furniture in order, no farm-tools in the house, and
> all the female inhabitants clothed with a certain degree of taste.
> I have found that, no matter how unexpectedly one enters an
> American farmhouse, the woman never finds it necessary to ab-
> sent herself a while, in order first to make herself presentable
> for the eyes of a stranger, which in a German farm establish-
> ment is almost always the case, if, in fact, the German woman
> considers it necessary to look proper at all. It is the same in the
> practical management, as I find it, that the German farmer has
> an endless lot to learn here.[64]

The German farmer has been so generally and so
properly praised for his industry and thrift, in contrast
with the soil-wasting practices of the American pioneer
farmer, that this notice of the German's stolid conservatism seems to be needed to balance the picture.
The criticism was based, however, upon rather incom-

[63] Letters of 1854 to Mrs. Schurz, *supra.* C.S. MSS., W.H.S.

[64] Letter to Mrs. Schurz from Watertown, September 9, 1855.
C.S. MSS., W.H.S.

plete observation. As a "green" himself, Schurz had probably never seen many of the best of the "grays" or well-established Germans of earlier migrations, nor, at close range, very many of the worst of the native-born pioneer types.

In politics, too, Schurz found the other immigrants exasperatingly slow to change:

> How sad is the contrast which is seen here between the native American, to whatever class he may belong, and the immigrant of German or Irish origin; while the former seizes with ease and clarity upon a new truth and finds at once the means to put it into active practice, the latter through the sheer weight of inertia, sticks anchored fast by stupid prejudices, and it costs him incredible effort to enter into the adventure of a new idea, and to lift himself to some independence of judgment.[65]

Since tact was never, with Schurz, carried to such an extreme as to constitute a deceitful concealment of his opinions, it is not surprising that, as *ein verdammter Republikaner,* he should at times have found himself unpopular in such a Democratic stronghold as Watertown. Dr. W. F. Whyte, in his *Chronicles of Early Watertown,* writes:

> He was even then recognized as a man of extraordinary ability, but he did not escape being assaulted with stale eggs in Watertown because he was "ein verdammter Republikaner." They did not expect anything but contrary opinions from many of the native-born; but that a man of German birth should have the temerity to differ from them was intolerable. The few Re-

---

[65] Letter to Heinrich Meyer from Watertown, November 20, 1856, in C.S. MSS., W.H.S.

publican voters in the sixth ward were in the habit of marching
to the polls in a body for reasons which were strictly prudential.[66]

So Schurz never became the "little pride" of Watertown as one might have supposed, although his ability and personal character always commanded the respect of the respectable. He chose to join the minority.
The choice was made public in October, 1855. A
part of his account of the incident follows:

A few days ago, I was to have been introduced into the domestic politics for the first time. In November, is the choice of
the State governor. The present governor, who would like to
be re-elected, is now traveling around in the state, in order to
start a movement for himself. Yesterday, he was here, and there
was a great gathering. Well, a few days ago, a deputation of
local citizens was at my house, in order to ask me to welcome the
governor, at the assembly, and to recommend him for re-election.
Since, however, the present administration has administered the
finances of the state in an unscrupulous fashion, and is besides in
its political principles at variance with mine, in particular as to
national policy, therefore I refused the request and refused to do
anything for Barstow. However, I have often been asked, already, if I would not participate, as soon as possible, and I am
assured from all sides that I should be chosen to the Legislative
assembly as soon as I permit myself to be put upon the list of
candidates.[67]

[66] *In Wisconsin Magazine of History*, Vol. IV, No. 3 (1921);
also in *Wisconsin State Journal*, August 26, 1923. Several other "old-
timers" also tell the egg story. In 1860 a Democratic attack upon a
Republican torchlight procession in Watertown ended in a riot.

[67] Letter to Mrs. Schurz, October 23, 1855, in C.S. MSS., W.H.S.;
in part, in C.S., *S.C.&P.P.*, I, 23; and in *Lebn.*, III, 132.

It was certainly from no lack of ambition that he refused. Only a month before, stirred by news of the fall of Sebastopol, he had fretted with impatience at being even temporarily barred by his circumstances from an active political career. He had written:

> Why must I sit here—a mere non-entity occupied with miserable plans for making money, although my head is full of ideas and the consciousness of inexhaustible strength—while out there momentous decisions are made and scoundrels and mediocrities crowd the world stage?

It is not quite clear whether the particular "mediocrity" whom he had in mind there was Napoleon III, President Pierce, or someone nearer home; but it is quite clear that he found it difficult to wait even for the easy eligibility laws of Wisconsin to be satisfied by his term of residence and that he would welcome a storm which should "bring new characters and talents to the surface."[68] That hope proved to be more fruitful in the end, than the "miserable plans for making money."

Both before and after his actual entry into public life, he might have been characterized, as well as Bismarck was, by Ludwig's comment: "He is just as little able to carry on a life of affairs without yearning for tranquility as he is able to endure tranquility without a longing for a life of affairs."

His reason for refusing to welcome Barstow was probably very largely just what he said it was—because

[68] C.S., *S.C.&P.P.*, I, 22.

he was Barstow. If he had not refused, his hope of spending a part of the second winter thereafter in Madison[69] would probably have been realized. But he did not belong in the Democratic party.

The statement is often found, used most frequently by writers of the German-American group but occasionally in the newspapers of the period, that Schurz was himself a former Democrat who had "turned Republican."[70] But those who use it are content to make the statement and let it stand; so one is left to judge its truth by weighing a considerable amoun of circumstantial evidence in its favor against a small amount of incomplete but direct evidence against it. It is true that his first political acquaintanceships in Washington were formed with Democrats;[71] in his first years in America they could not well have been with Republicans. It is equally true that he had never had any love for the Whigs. He had associated them, all along, with nativism, and accused them of inconsistency in trying to oppose, at once, both slavery and the influence of the foreigners in politics; for what

[69] Letter of October 23, *supra*, n. 67.

[70] Notably Wilhelm Hense Jensen, *Wisconsin Deutsch-Amerikaner, bis zum Schluss des neunzehnten Jahr-hunderts* (Milwaukee: Verlage der Deutschen Gesellschaft, 1900), I, 176; and Gottlieb Betz, *Die deutsch-amerikanische patriotische Lyrik der Achtundvierziger und ihre historische Grundlage,* "Publications of the University of Pennsylvania," 1916, "Americana Germanica," No. 22, p. 86.

[71] Cf. chap. ii.

was favorable to the rights of foreigners was unfavorable to slavery. But it would have been very inconsistent in himself if he had allied himself actively with a party always sure to be more or less subject to the dictation of the southern, slaveholding portion of its membership, and which he was already calling "the country-gentry" party.[72] If he had, he would have found himself much less in harmony with radical antislavery Hecker than he says he was, in 1854.[73] And he would hardly have written, as he did in 1856, that he was taking an active part in politics "for the first time in seven years."[74]

It seems, therefore, to be more accurate to say that, since the Germans had been so predominantly Democratic up to 1856, and since his associations had been largely with Democrats, he was expected to be one. He had actually been only an observer. When he was in a position to make a public stand, he made it against a gubernatorial candidate who already had behind him a bad record, soon to be made worse by the practice of fraud in the election, and against the party of slavery. Because of the slavery issue, he was compelled to call himself a Republican, though he was one

[72] Letter to Kinkel from Washington, January 23, 1855, in C.S., *S.C.&P.P.*, I, 14.

[73] *Supra*, n. 15.

[74] Letter to Heinrich Meyer, November 20, 1856, in C.S. MSS., W.H.S.; *supra*, n. 65.

of an extreme Jeffersonian wing of that party. He was never a very orthodox Republican, but his adherence to Jeffersonian views in 1856 seems hardly to justify calling him, then or earlier, a Democrat. Politically speaking, either he had not been anything or he had been what he always was afterward, to a greater or less degree—least in 1860 and 1864—an Independent.

CHAPTER V

THE FORTY-EIGHTERS

SOON after his refusal to welcome Barstow to Watertown, Schurz went off, as above narrated, to Philadelphia, London, and Montreux. He returned in the summer of 1856 in time to receive the Republican nomination for the legislature from his district,[1] which in that particular district was just then about as important in its immediate consequences as some of the complimentary nominations given to "favorite sons" in presidential nominating conventions. He was beaten by a vote of more than two to one; and one learns of the incident only through the newspapers, and not from him.[2] But because it marked his active identification with the Republican party, and because in it he was given an opportunity to justify the action of the party leaders who had called him out, the campaign of 1856 was an event of the greatest importance to him and of some significance to the party itself.

His ability as an orator was then unknown. He was a marked man among the Germans as the rescuer

[1] Letter from J. A. Hadley, Watertown, to the *Milwaukee Sentinel*, November 2, 1857.

[2] Chappel (Democrat), 836; Schurz (Republican), 391 (*Watertown Dem.*, November 6, 1856).

of Kinkel,[3] known locally as a tenacious holder of
minority views in politics,[4] and to a few of the native-
born as an educated young German who was opposed
to slavery. On such credentials he was summoned by
the Republican leaders of Wisconsin to do for them
among his fellow-Germans what Hecker, Koerner,
and Hoffman were already doing for the Republicans
of Illinois, and Hassaurek, Rümelin, and Stallo for
those of Ohio.

That the German vote should have needed to be
courted by an antislavery party, and that the Forty-
eighters should have been so prominent in the process,
seems to call at this point for some discussion of the
relationships existing between the Germans and the
political parties and between different groups of Germans up to that time.

Before 1850 the Germans in the United States
had been very largely Democratic, and with very little
question or thought of being anything else. That party
was the first to cultivate their support, and its very
name attracted them. The doctrines of equality
preached by the followers of Jackson would naturally
appeal to an immigrant who had come to this country
to improve his status or to escape from an inferior
position in some country where equality did not prevail. And the slavery question, which later did repel
many of them, had not then become prominent enough
to do so.

[3] Bruncken, "Pol. Act. of Wis. Ger."   [4] C.S., *Rem.*, II, 66.

They were, on the other hand, definitely repelled by the Whig party. Its ultra-governmental tendencies were offensive to men who were definitely looking for less government than they had had at home. The Whig party was suspected by them of being that of the aristocrats and capitalists and of being not simply inhospitable but positively unfriendly to the foreigner. In Wisconsin in particular, the membership of the party was largely of New England origin and was composed to a fairly great extent of the wealthier citizens, natural believers in the protection of vested interests and in strong government. These Old Whigs felt that "there was such a thing as an American nationality, with an individuality and characteristics of its own," which had already been developed and which should be preserved without further great change. They were naturally, also, supporters of New England social customs, a Puritan Sabbath, temperance legislation, and Protestant religious instruction in the public schools. To all of these the Germans were opposed. So when, in 1849, the legislature passed, in spite of the opposition of Horn and other German members, a law holding the vendor of liquor responsible for damage done by his customer while drunk, even to the customer's own wife and children,[5] the membership of the German Whig Club, which was said never to have exceeded "fourteen and

---

[5] Jensen, *Wisconsin Deutsch-Amerikaner*, I, 164–75; Bruncken, *The Germans in Wisconsin Politics*, "Parkman Club Papers," 1896, p. 237.

a half members,"[6] probably shrank to none at all. The
law itself was the cause of a riot in Milwaukee, and
was soon repealed.

To be sure, the Germans were much criticized,
even by many of themselves, later, for making major
issues out of such matters as wine and beer or Sunday
afternoon amusements. Julius Froebel, one of the first
of the Forty-eighters, cited as typical the German vot-
er's answer to an immigrant question, that a democrat
was "a man who voted the Democratic ticket." He
declared that the Germans of the former migrations
had abundantly earned their name of "voting cattle"
by their ignorance and overemphasis of side issues.
But he himself explained why it was natural for the
Calvinist severity of the Old Whigs to be compared
unfavorably with the Catholic and Lutheran tolerance
of pleasure in life (*Lebensgenuss*), which the Democratic party was ready enough to allow.[7] Esselen wrote
bitterly against their losing sight of their principles at
sight of a mug of beer. Rümelin was one of the first
to call even Know-nothingism but a side issue.[8] Schurz
also joined their critics, though he himself had no use

[6] Bruncken, *op. cit.*, p. 237.

[7] Julius Froebel, *Aus Amerika* (2 vols.; Leipzig, 1856, 1857),
Bd. I, Buch III, K. III, IV. Chapter iii deals chiefly with the Democratic and Republican parties, chapter iv with the Whigs, and chapter v
with the Know-nothings—all with reference to the Germans. To him,
only the Republican party was that of progress.

[8] As quoted by G. W. Julian, "First Republican National Convention," *A.H.R.*, IV, 118.

for "blue laws."[9] But until larger issues were presented to them, the Germans continued to be influenced
chiefly by these considerations.

After about 1850, two new elements were in-
jected into the situation, which resulted in complicating
it greatly. These were Know-nothingism and the in-
flux of that group of defeated but still active reformers known as the "Forty-eighters." These men as-
pired to become the leaders of the German element,
and eventually they did; but at first they only scolded
and quarreled with the earlier arrivals. Eventually,
too, they did much to bring the foreign-born and the
native-born into closer and more amicable relation-
ship, but at first their activities only alarmed the conservatives and furnished material upon which the
Know-nothing movement might feed.

The chief reason for the friction between them
and the earlier immigrants, between the "greens" and
the "grays," was their hostility to the churches. Having
found the established ecclesiastical hierarchies in close
alliance with the enemies of reform abroad, these men,
who never knew when their war was ended, continued
in America their fight against the churches.[10] The
Bennet bill in Wisconsin, for example, which would
have repealed the law exempting church property from

[9] Letters of August 8 and 12, 1855, *supra*, chap. iv, nn. 61 and 62.
See also Struve's message to the Germans, *infra*, n. 23.

[10] Channing, *op. cit.*, IV, 127; Morison, *op. cit.*, II, 128; both
cited above in chap. iii, n. 25, p. 70.

payment of taxes, was supported by Forty-eighters and opposed by other Germans.[11] As the earlier immigrants were mostly Catholic or Lutheran, a bitter hostility quickly developed between the groups.[12]

The Forty-eighters further irritated the others by being too strenuous and critical, and seemed opinionated to those who seemed to the Forty-eighters to be slow, stupid, and stubborn. It was also a common criticism of the Forty-eighters that they made the others feel all too plainly their intellectual superiority, and were inclined to associate, wherever possible, with the native-born and to despise the less cultured immigrants from their own country.[13]

If the Forty-eighters aroused such antagonism among their fellow-Germans, the reactions of the native-born were naturally even less favorable. One of the mildest of them was to consider the newcomers meddlesome and presumptuous. "They could not establish the German republic, so they would at least reform the American republic to their own taste."[14] Stronger disapproval was voiced by the *North American Review* in an editorial commenting on two re-

[11] Bruncken, "Pol. Act. of Wis. Ger.," p. 20.

[12] Bruncken, *The Germans in Wisconsin Politics*, p. 230.

[13] Betz, *Die Deutschamerikanische u.s.w.* Gustave Koerner, throughout his *Memoirs,* seems to have held much the same opinion of the group, making an exception of Schurz but finding it easy to differ even with him. He was himself one of an earlier migration.

[14] *Ibid.,* p. 28. Quoting speech of Frederick Hassaurek, himself one of them, from *Der deutscher Pionier,* VII, 114.

cently issued books written about and for Germans in America. It said, in part:

> But among them were also too many of those turbulent, restless, spirits who are always evoked from obscurity by civil commotions. Representatives of every description of German society have been scattered by this last emigration throughout our large cities and the Western States. They are divided into classes that have a deadly hostility to Roman Catholics, and many of them dislike the Lutherans as bitterly. They regard the established churches of Germany as the greatest enemies of civil liberty, and they stamp kingcraft and priestcraft with a common brand of infamy. The great majority of the wealthy and educated are atheists and radicals. They have control of nearly half of the German newspapers in the land. . . . . The irreligious influence of thousands of German infidels must be perceptibly felt by the children who come after them. They grow up as Americans, and it is sad to think of the heavy load that will rest upon their hearts. This is a grave subject for meditation for the Christian patriot.[15]

In so far as the foregoing comment was representative of respectable and intelligent opinion, the attitude of the irresponsible and the prejudiced ignorant would be proportionately less friendly. Know-nothingism, therefore, which without this element would never have been directed primarily or even largely against the Germans, became more and more an object of their fear and hatred. And the Forty-eighters who eventually "very largely bridged over the gap between

---

[15] *N.A.R.*, LXXXII (1856), 266; quoted also by Betz, *op. cit.*, p. 32.

the native American and the newcomer"[16] actually served, in their first five years in the country, to widen the gap perceptibly.

Since the Germans properly associated the Know-nothing movement with the Whig rather than with the Democratic party, their aversion to it was added to their sensitiveness as to laws regulating their personal conduct; and no party connected with it could win their support until Nativism had run its course and wrecked itself. That happened, in 1855, the wreck taking place at the Philadelphia convention of the party on June 5, when it split over slavery, the southern group gaining control. That ended it as a political force, "except as individual actions and attitudes were influenced."[17]

For Schurz that event fulfilled one prophecy and furnished the occasion for another. In the much-quoted letter to Kinkel in January of that year he had written:

> It will not be long before the slave states become the headquarters of the nativistic movement and there it will remain. This will suffice to secure the rights of the foreign elements in the north. I am convinced, moreover, that we have nothing further to fear from the Know-nothings, except the weakening of the anti-slavery movement; this would be all the more deplorable because the movement is already so well under way.[18]

[16] C.S., *Rem.*, II, 45.

[17] Channing, *op. cit.*, VI, 136; see above, chap. iii, n. 25, p. 70.

[18] From Washington, January 23, 1855, in C.S., *S.C.&P.P.*, I, 14.

After the event, but before its significance had become apparent to observers less keen than himself, he wrote to Mrs. Schurz:

As to the Know-nothings, there have begun within this extended party organization, significant, perhaps decisive, changes, and in the same way as I predicted it, already, half a year ago. About two and a half months ago, there was in Philadelphia a great convention of the Know-nothing Party, to which delegates had come from all parts of the Union. Very soon, the slavery problem was discussed, and the Southern Know-nothings, who were in the majority, succeeded in carrying through a resolution favorable to slavery. Immediately, all deputies coming from the north left the convention en masse, and so the Know-nothing party split into two great hostile parts. The next consequence was that the Northern, that is the anti-slavery, Know-nothings approached the foreigners again, and that the slavery question was declared the main question. In this way, the whole Know-nothing movement lost its point, and we see many of their greatest leaders turning back again, saying that not religion and not place of birth, but Republican views are the criterion which determines the fitness of a foreigner for American citizenship. This is the beginning of the end, and it is a question whether the Know-nothing organization will exist until the presidential election in 1856. Here and there, single small parts of the party once more show strength, but the mass of the army is on the retreat.

Thus the political sky here is getting somewhat brighter, and the disagreeable things which have happened will finally be considered as a stirring and beneficial change.[19]

But the great mass of the Germans were much slower than he in recovering from their fear of nativism, and found it more difficult than he to overlook

[19] Letter of August 8, 1855, in C.S. MSS., W.H.S.

the fact that those who thenceforth said that "slavery was the main question" had found their way into the Republican party, along with the Anti-Nebraska Democrats, by way of the Know-nothing lodges. By thus serving to break up the old parties, even the nativist movement was later considered to have worked a "beneficial change," as Schurz had predicted. The fear he expressed to Kinkel, however, was equally well grounded. Because the Republican party fell heir to the evil fruits and the enemies of Whiggism, as well as to many of its members, the bogy of nativism deterred for years the natural enemies of the repeal of the Missouri Compromise from uniting into a solid antislavery party.[20]

In Wisconsin from 1854 to 1858 the partisan press was filled with mutual charges of the parties, each accusing the other of nativism. As an independent political force, nativism died in 1855; but as a prejudice in the minds of the native-born and an obsession in those of many of the Germans, it still lived in 1860. While apparently no more guilty of it than the Democrats, at first the Republicans had all the burden of proof against them; and it was a hard task for Schurz and his colleagues to convince even that fraction of the Germans necessary for victory that it was either non-existent or a non-essential side issue.

The German feeling against slavery naturally

[20] G. W. Julian, "First Republican National Convention," *A.H.R.*, IV, 314.

militated, with them, against the Democratic party. As it was gradually realized that the Kansas-Nebraska Act had not merely failed to get the slavery question out of Congress but had actually spread it all over the country, many of them began to feel uncomfortable about their connection with the party which had opened to slavery territory previously open only to free labor and to such immigrants as themselves. Meanwhile, the Fugitive Slave Law, which Schurz later characterized as "the greatest propagator of abolitionism which Machiavellian ingenuity could have devised,"[21] served as an unpleasant reminder of the realities of an institution which most of them had never seen and which many of them would have been glad to continue to ignore. But as the outcry against the law increased in volume, and its violations in number, so must its supporters strengthen their insistence upon its enforcement. As Schurz further said:

> The binding force of the fugitive-slave law was insisted upon with such exceptional urgency as if the catching of fugitive slaves had become the main constitutional duty of the American citizen. This could not fail to react.[22]

The reaction was the famous Glover case in Wisconsin, "personal liberty" laws in many of the northern states, and a widespread defection of the Germans from the Democratic party.

At least one group of them had never been willing to ignore slavery—the Forty-eighters. How Schurz,

[21] C.S., *Henry Clay*, II, 375.   [22] *Ibid.*, p. 375.

within a month of his arrival, found it the one "false note" and later pledged himself with Hecker to fight it, has already been told. Julius Froebel spent five chapters in discussing it, and either could not or would not stay off the subject elsewhere in his book *Aus Amerika*.

An extreme case was that of Gustave Struve, exiled political leader of the revolt of 1849 in Baden, who issued a sort of manifesto to the Germans, July 18, 1856, pointing out that temperance had nothing to do with presidential elections but that slavery was the big issue. No opponent of despotism could vote for the extension of slavery. His conclusion is most remarkable:

> Which one of us could ever again enter the ranks of Freedom, if he had here advocated the extension of slavery? Every man of freedom would turn his back upon the advocate of slavery, as upon a backslider from our cause.
>
> I myself cannot vote. I am no citizen of America and do not intend to become one, because I have made the struggle against the despots of Europe the principal task of my life. But I wished to say to you how I would have voted, had I become a citizen, for Fremont and Dayton.[23]

Less romantic or theatrical, but probably more significant, was the desertion of the Democratic party in the summer of 1856 by German newspapers. On July 11, the Republican papers displayed the following list of those who had left the ranks of the enemy: *New Orleans Deutsche Zeitung, Louisville Anzeiger,*

[23] *Wisconsin State Journal*, August 1, 1856.

Pittsburgh Courier, Freiheitsfreund, and *Catholic Republikaner*. On August 20, they rejoiced at the desertion of the *Criminal Zeitung,* which claimed the largest general circulation of all the German papers, and at the fact that the only German papers in New York still Democratic were the Catholic *Kirchen-Zeitung* and the dyed-in-the-wool *Staats-Zeitung*.[24]

To see these papers desert from the enemy was something, but it was not enough. The case of the *Watertown Anzeiger* may be typical. In June, 1856, it refused to support Buchanan; but more than a year later it discharged Schurz, after a career of two weeks as editor, as "too Republican."[25] There was still something left at that time of an earlier German trend toward independence in politics. By 1854 the proposal for a German state had been metamorphosed into one for a separate German political party. After it had been seriously discussed by a German debating club in Milwaukee, Bernhard Domschke, one of the earliest and ablest German Republicans, wrote an editorial opposing it on the ground that it would simply throw them into an alliance with the Irish, who, as the strongest supporters of popery, were their worst enemies.[26] But for the few like Rümelin and Domschke,

[24] *Ibid.,* July 11 and August 20, 1856.

[25] Catalogue card, *Watertown Anzeiger,* W.H.S.; *Watertown Dem.,* August 13 and 20, 1857.

[26] In *Wisconsin Demokrat,* August 17, 1854. Quoted by Bruncken, "Pol. Act. of Wis. Ger.," p. 196.

and Wesendonck, who were Democrats whom the action of their party had made Republican, there were many whose attitude was better expressed by the *San Francisco Journal:* "We can fight neither with the slave interests against the nativists nor with the nativists against the slave interests. We fight them both."[27]

Insistent demands were still being made by the German papers in Wisconsin for the official recognition of their language in the legislature, schools, and printing of public documents; and both parties were blackmailed or browbeaten into the awarding of contracts for superfluous printing to German presses. A somewhat similar tone was noticeable wherever else the German element was strong.

The next stage in the development of the Independent-German movement was indicated by a visit paid to Schurz by Wesendonck, of Philadelphia, a one-time member of the Frankfort parliament and a former Democrat turned Republican. The two conferred on matters of business and with regard to a proposed national convention of Germans to be held in Philadelphia. It was their hope to bring the whole body of Germans, so far as possible, into alignment, if not into close affiliation, with the Republican party within the next four years;[28] but the story of that de-

[27] Quoted by Betz, *op. cit.*, p. 48.

[28] Letter to Althaus from Watertown, November 15, 1856, in *Lebn.*, III, 141.

velopment belongs more properly to the history of
the campaign of 1860.

Such, then, were the circumstances under which
Schurz joined Domschke, Roeser, and Wunderley
among the leaders of the German element in the Republican party of Wisconsin; and under somewhat
similar conditions elsewhere—except that, aside from
localized areas like that of St. Louis, the relative importance of the German vote was less great—many
other Forty-eighters joined the Republican party.

Less interested in thoughts of immediate return
to Germany than they had been five years before, and
more concerned about American affairs; less at odds,
though never quite in unison, with either the native-
born or the Germans of earlier migrations; no longer
thinking of themselves simply as Germans, while still
keenly self-conscious as a German-American group,
they were beginning to become Americanized. Incur-
able non-conformists still, it was the party of slavery
with which they found association and conformity most
offensive. They therefore used all the influence they
could win, to defeat at once the inertia and the herd-
instinct which were still holding the more docile Germans to their old affiliations with the Democratic
party[29] (into which the most recent immigrants of

[29] See also statement of Dr. Joseph Schafer to the effect that the
Forty-eighters, because of their superior linguistic training, social adaptability, education, personal desirability, and status, were courted by
both parties, and served the Republicans as "a flying squadron to res-

similar type followed them),[30] and the extreme or Ger-
man-nativist tendencies of the more intractable but
less intelligent ones. Thus, in spite of many objections
to it on their part, they were drawn to the Republican
party by its stand on the slavery question; and they
exerted upon it a real influence, while rendering it and
the cause of freedom invaluable aid.

They therefore abundantly earned both of the following contrasting comments:

> In America, true to their German ideals of unity and lib-
> erty, many of these men were potent factors in preserving the
> Union and in emancipating the negro; they made themselves an
> integral element of a nation which owes in part to them its
> idealism and social stability.[31]

> The influence of the "forty-eighters" at this great critical
> time in our national life [1855–60] was, to my mind, decisive.
> They turned the balance of power in favor of universal lib-
> erty. And if sometimes they were obstinate and difficult mate-
> rial, this very defect was perhaps an outgrowth of their virtues.
> They might not have been the tower of strength they were for
> the Union cause, had they not had the very defects which some-
> times irritated and tired us.[32]

---

cue Germanism from the danger of being permanently enmeshed in
the Democratic party," in "Four Wisconsin Counties," *Wisconsin
Domesday Book*, pp. 153–54.

[30] Letter to Althaus, February 6, 1857, in C.S., *S.C.&P.P.*, I, 28.

[31] George Madison Priest, *Germany since 1740* (New York,
1915), p. 96.

[32] President Edmund James of the University of Illinois, as
quoted by J. H. A. Lacher, *The German Element in Wisconsin*, p. 19.

CHAPTER VI

NEW BEGINNINGS

TO WHAT extent was Carl Schurz, personally and as an early Republican, a typical Forty-eighter? He is probably the man uppermost in the minds of those who comment most favorably upon the men of the group, for he became the most prominent and most influential of them. All of their major virtues—zeal for liberty, hatred of dishonesty as of oppression in government, and personal integrity—he possessed in as high a degree as any of them. In social adaptability and attractiveness, in intellect, and in linguistic ability he surpassed most of them. As an accurate observer and a philosophical student of American institutions, and as an orator capable of making his idealism effective by exerting a real influence over those who heard him, he excelled them all.

He had also the faults of his virtues, though in a less degree than most of the older and more eccentric Forty-eighters. With his independence of judgment, his pride of intellect, and his consciousness of the care and honesty with which his opinions were formed, there went a tendency to regard as insufferable stupidity or deliberate dishonesty the processes by which another came to a different conclusion. When convinced that his opponent on any issue was neither stupid nor dishonest, he could treat him with perfect respect; but it was neither instinctive nor easy for him to do so unless so convinced.

There was always about him, too, what he had recognized in those thoughtful last days at Rastatt as "a certain untamableness." He would not shake hands and slap backs or alter or conceal his views to retain his early popularity in his home town; and if the Americans were not accustomed to such an uncompromising attitude as his on public honesty, "they must get used to it."[1] Many times they found him intransigent, clinging tenaciously to a minority view of party interest, or refusing to consider party interest at all or to compromise. No doubt they found him "difficult."

He has already been shown to have been extremely critical of his fellow-Germans, objecting particularly to their clannishness, the slowness with which many of them became Americanized, and their tendency to act in American affairs as Germans rather than as American citizens. His influence with them was somewhat lessened by the frankness with which he voiced these criticisms and himself acted on the principle implied by them, for he was made to appear to many of them as a snob and a renegade German.

His prominence brought him much bitter criticism, some of which he incurred simply as a Forty-eighter rather than by any public act of his own. In his private correspondence he was frankly anticlerical, but his

[1] Letter to Mrs. Schurz, February 27, 1860. C.S. MSS., W.H.S.

few unfavorable public references to the Catholic church were very scanty evidence on which to base the numerous charges of atheism which were made against him.[2] He was not one of those who warred on the churches; but he had himself renounced Catholicism,[3] and he found no following among the Catholic Germans,[4] to whom the apostate was doubly offensive as a Forty-eighter.

The worst criticism, and one of the most common, voiced against him as against the group, was that they were mere "adventurers" serving the side which offered the highest pay. That they had lost in one adventure is certain; that a few of them, including Schurz, still (in 1856) held themselves subject to recall to Europe by a favorable turn of events, if any such should come,

[2] Compare speech on "True Americanism," Boston, April 18, 1859, and press comment. The real moderation of his views was shown by the small part taken by him in a Watertown school quarrel in 1858. At the insistence of the Catholics, the school board had barred religious instruction from the schools. When asked for his opinion, Schurz said that such action had not been called for by any real abuses and that Protestant instruction might properly have continued to be given in the schools provided that the children of parents unwilling to have them so instructed were excused from it. Over this incident, the radical paper *Wisconsin* called him an infidel and a defamer of religion, unfit for office; but on gaining better information, retracted its accusation (*St. Jour.*, July 23, 1858). He was attacked in the same fashion by the *Appleton Crescent* and defended by the *Fond du Lac Commonwealth* and *State Journal*, July 3.

[3] Chap. i. See also: "There remained, however, within me a strong religious want, a profound respect for religious thought," in C.S., *Rem.*, I, 71.

[4] Schafer, *Four Wisconsin Counties*, p. 157.

is also apparent; but there is no reason for doubting the sincerity of their devotion to the antislavery movement and to the Union. Whatever may have been their mental reservations in the choice between America and Germany, there was no equivocation in their choice of sides on the purely American issues of slavery and the Union.

In spite of the threats of a few of the southern fire-eaters against it, the preservation of the Union was not then recognized as an issue. That the parties did at that time give them a clear choice on the slavery question will be seen by a study of their platforms and of the early Republican conventions, at which it was made the most prominent issue.

At the time of the formation of the Republican state organization in Wisconsin, July 13, 1854, the party was careful to drop the temperance legislation proposals which, two years before, had had the support of the remnants of the Whig and Free-soil parties. Roeser wrote in some exultation that the German leaders had been assured that those proposals would not be taken up again for at least two years and that slavery would be treated as the main question.[5] It was already being so treated by the *Milwaukee Sentinel* and was soon equally stressed by all of the Republican papers.

The attitude of the party as one of protest against the operation of the Fugitive Slave Law and the Kansas-Nebraska Act was further expressed in its state plat-

[5] Bruncken, "Pol. Act. of Wis. Ger.," p. 194.

forms in Ohio and Indiana just a year later. In the former state, the party declared itself in favor of "jealous care of the rights of the several states as independent governments" and further stated: "We will resent the spread of slavery under whatever shape or color it may be attempted." The Indiana platform was similar to that in Ohio.[6]

Both were heartily approved by the *Milwaukee Sentinel*, while the *Wisconsin State Journal* also condemned the Fugitive Slave Law and the extension of slavery into the territories.[7] A particularly strong antislavery editorial in the *Sentinel* was evoked, on July 25, 1855, by the advertisement of five slaves for sale in Nebraska City; and a little later, the same paper presented antislavery quotations from Washington, Madison, Henry Clay, and Thomas Benton.[8]

When the Wisconsin Republicans again met in convention, September 5, 1855, they passed a resolution to the effect that there was no escape from the alternative of freedom or slavery as the dominating policy of the government. Other resolutions advocated the restoration of Kansas and Nebraska to the position of free territories, the repeal and abrogation of the Fugitive Slave Act, the restriction of slavery to the states where it existed, the admission of no more slave states,

[6] *Mil. Sen.*, July 17, 1855.

[7] Comment on call for a Republican state convention. Quoted and indorsed by *Mil. Sen.*, July 14, 1855.

[8] *Mil. Sen.*, August 31, 1855.

and the exclusion of slavery from all territory governed by the United States. It was known that such
a platform would appeal to the Germans; but for fear
that they should be alienated by fear of nativism,
another resolution was added, inviting "all persons,
whether of native or of foreign birth," who were in
favor of the foregoing policies, to join in carrying
them into effect. To clear the party still more convincingly of the charge of nativism, Byron Paine introduced a resolution denouncing secret societies, which
was passed by acclamation. Then, to remove any
doubt still persisting, a delegate named Wood, who
was suspected of being, or of having been, a Know-
nothing, was required to certify that he would vote for
a foreigner if one were nominated by the convention,
before he was permitted to retain his seat. A German
was nominated ("Charles" Roeser being named for
state treasurer),[9] but he was defeated in the election.

By contrast, the Democratic platform, while also
denouncing Know-nothingism on principle but not in
name, upheld "Pierce and Nebraska," the Fugitive
Slave Law, and the interdiction of antislavery agitation.[10]

In the course of the campaign, the speeches of
Seward were given wide circulation. In them he did
much to earn for himself and for his party the name
of "extremists." At Albany he attacked the slaveholders as a privileged aristocracy at variance with the prin-

[9] *Ibid.*, September 7, 1855.   [10] *Ibid.*, October 6, 1855.

ciples of equality on which the government was founded. He also denounced the Fugitive Slave Law and declared:

> Slavery is not and never can be perpetual. It will be overthrown either peacefully and lawfully under this Constitution, or it will work the subversion of the Constitution, together with its own overthrow.[11]

At Buffalo, a week later, he denounced the "dereliction of Congress and the treachery of the President" in the matter of Kansas; and on the more general question of slavery said:

> Slavery was never rightly established anywhere. Nor was it ever established by law. It is in violation of every line of the Declaration of Independence and of the whole summary of personal rights contained in the Constitution. . . . . It is derogatory from the absolute rights of Human Nature, and no human power can subvert those rights.[12]

At the first national convention of the new party, held in Pittsburgh on Washington's birthday, 1856, more radicalism, rather than less, was shown, at least by some of those present, although Horace Greeley advised moderation for fear of alienating possible adherents. In his opening prayer, Owen Lovejoy, who was never notable for restraint in his exercise of that freedom of expression to which his brother was already a martyr, prayed God to enlighten the mind of the President or else to take him away, so that an honest and

[11] Speech at Albany, October 12, 1855, *ibid.*, October 23.

[12] Speech at Buffalo, October 12, 1855, *ibid.*, October 26–27, 1855.

God-fearing man might sit in his place. Later, in an address to the convention, the same speaker declared for "war to the knife, and knife to the hilt, if it must be so," for a free Kansas.[13]

The Germans had at that convention at least one prominent representative. Carl Rümelin of Cincinnati made what Julian called "by far the strongest speech of the convention." Describing himself as a Democrat whom the conduct of his party had made a Republican, he set his countrymen an example by his change of affiliation; and that they might follow it the more consistently, he characterized Know-nothingism as bigotry and intolerance, but as only a mischievous side issue.[14]

The convention was apparently more moved by the extremists than by the moderate leadership of its president, Francis P. Blair, Sr., of Maryland, or by Greeley's warnings as to the necessity for caution. It passed resolutions favoring: the repeal of all laws permitting slavery in the territories, and the passage of no more of them; the support of the free-state movement in Kansas by all lawful means; and the admission of Kansas as a free state. The administration was condemned as a faithless and proslavery one.

According to Julian, the men of that convention did not then anticipate either the Civil War or the

[13] G. W. Julian, "The First Republican National Convention," *A.H.R.*, IV, 315–22.

[14] *Ibid.*

early emancipation of the slaves; and many thought that Greeley was exaggerating again when he predicted that the influence of the convention would be felt for twenty-five years. But "it was the element of uncalculating radicalism which baffled the policy of timidity and hesitation and saved the cause."[15]

The radicalism of Schurz cannot well be called "uncalculating." For a year before the meeting of that convention he had written to Kinkel that such radicalism was more practical than it seemed;[16] and he always maintained that it was more far-sighted policy than conservatism. But both by temperament and by conviction he was properly qualified for membership in such a crusading antislavery party as the Republican promised to be. Until it swung away from its original radical positions more rapidly than he did, he was heartily in accord with it. Meanwhile its managers needed such men as he for work among the Germans, so they offered him the opportunity for which he was none too patiently waiting.

His own story of his actual induction into Wisconsin politics is that L. P. Harvey, of whom he had never heard but who became, and continued until his untimely death to be, one of his most loyal and enthusiastic friends, came to see him in Watertown and invited him to speak at a meeting in Jefferson, Wis-

[15] *Ibid.*

[16] Letter of January 3, 1855, *supra*, chap. iii, n. 33, p. 74.

consin. He had but recently returned from Europe,[17]
was engaged in the completion of his house,[18] and had
had little time in which to acquaint himself with local
issues, so demurred. He accepted an invitation to attend the meeting, however; and there Harvey surprised him, at the conclusion of his own speech, by
introducing him with a reference to his European
career and the announcement that he would then address the Germans present, in their own language. Although extemporaneous, his response, which dealt only
with slavery and the duties of German citizens to their
adopted country, was well received.[19]

The "inside" story of his adoption as a stump
speaker by the party managers is based upon an incident
which apparently followed this one. As told, years
later, by C. C. King[20] and quoted by Bruncken, it was
that Harvey, at a meeting of the state central committee in Madison, mentioned him as a bright young German whom he had met at Watertown, who was engaged in building a house there but who would be
willing to take the stump when it was finished.[21] When

[17] Arrived about July 1 (*Lebn.*, III, 141).

[18] Letter to Heinrich Meyer, August 6, 1856, in C.S. MSS.,
W.H.S.

[19] C.S., *Rem.*, II, 67–69.   [20] *Seebote*, March 27, 1897.

[21] "Pol. Act. of Wis. Ger." This account further says that the
story of Kinkel's rescue was printed at the time as part of a publicity
campaign for him, but it seems to have gained a really wide circulation only in the following year. It and the account of his own escape
from Rastatt were frequently revived for several years thereafter.

once started, he was kept busy during the remainder of the campaign.

His speeches that year were delivered only in German and were not widely reported even in the German papers. They were delivered frequently in small towns, to audiences which were largely hostile, and seem to have created no great sensation. One reason may have been that he was preaching then mostly to sinners and had not in his audiences those large numbers of the saved who in 1860 received him and nearly everything he said with such tremendous outbursts of enthusiasm.

They lacked, too, the element of surprise; there was nothing remarkable about hearing a German make good use of his native tongue. Still, it is a remarkable fact that while he spoke constantly in both languages in subsequent campaigns, all of his greatest oratorical triumphs were achieved in English. Although he states in his *Reminiscences* that he did not use it publicly in this campaign,[22] he wrote to Kinkel, at the end of it, that he already found English, for many things, easier and more effective than German.[23] The making of American political speeches was evidently one of them, after he once began to use it for that purpose.[24]

[22] C.S., *Rem.*, II, 69.

[23] The full letter in C.S. MSS., W.H.S.; most of it in *Lebn.*, II, 145; some of it in C.S., *S.C.&P.P.*, I, 23.

[24] C.S., *Rem.*, II, 13.

Then, too, his speeches lacked the strongly partisan tone which in such cases usually takes the place of
profundity and wins the approval of a partisan press.
The slavery question was the only one then at issue
between the parties in which Schurz was at all vitally
interested. The Glover case had not yet made State
rights an issue. Barstow had not yet furnished the
ammunition for the strongest attacks upon himself and
his party by returning to politics after being ousted
from the governor's chair for proven election frauds;
and the great railroad scandals had not yet occurred;
so that the cry of corruption was less widely raised
then than later. But Schurz was surprised at the bitter and unreasoning—often violent—character of the
partisan opposition, which he considered dangerous to
free institutions.

Those impressions made me shape my speeches so that they
were arguments for my cause, not for a party—or only in so
far for my party as it was a means to further my cause—un-
ceasingly admonishing my hearers not to be mere blind followers of any leadership, whatever its name might be, but to think
for themselves, honestly seeking to discover what was right and
best for the common welfare, not indeed to reject advice, but to
weigh it and then courageously to do that which, according to
their conscientiously formed convictions, would be most apt to
serve the cause of justice and the true interests of the country.
This injunction I repeated in endless variations. Little did I
foresee then what fateful part this way of thinking, which I
then thought was the most natural for a public man, would
play in my political career.[25]

[25] *Ibid.*, p. 71.

He probably did realize, however, that such arguments were admirably designed for the use of a new and proselyting party in its attempt to break up the discipline of an old and established one. The appeal from things as they were and had been to things as they should be could best be made when the rank and file of the defenders of the existing order had ceased to believe in its beneficence or in the omniscient integrity of their leaders. Such disruptive arguments therefore suited the Republicans far better then than after they were themselves established in power; and Schurz was not alone in his failure to realize their ultimate significance.

In his epistolary accounts of the campaign, soon after its conclusion, he wrote with an enthusiasm scarcely equaled by him before. The interest and the hopes aroused in him by it made him write rather condescendingly to his young brother-in-law, Heinrich Meyer:

The last weeks were times when public matters made more demands than ordinarily upon the American citizen. You over there in your decrepit Europe can merely imagine how a great idea can stir up the masses of the people to their depths, and how an enthusiastic struggle for principles can thrust aside for a certain time all other interests, even the materialistic ones. . . . . A general struggle of opinions among a free people has in it something unbelievably imposing; and you never see with greater clearness what a far-reaching influence political freedom exercises upon the development of the masses.[26]

[26] From Watertown, November 20, 1856, in C.S. MSS., W.H.S.

It was because the German immigrants had not benefited, in years past, from the instructive experience of self-government, he said in the same letter, that they compared so unfavorably with the native-born in political intelligence and ability.[27]

Point was lent to that criticism by his subsequent statement that the general Democratic victory of 1856 —(and even in Wisconsin the Republicans had elected but a portion of their ticket)—was principally due to the action of recently arrived European immigrants.[28]

Not only more enthusiasm, but more genuine happiness, showed itself in his letters then than ever before. At last he had a home, and he reveled in the "envious looks" that were cast upon it. Only the presence of his European relatives and friends was lacking—and a piano to play upon. The gaiety of his mood at that period was further shown by his account of an incident in which he figured while on a trip to New York. His host at the Hotel Prescott, learning that he was entertaining the rescuer of Kinkel, set out a bottle of champagne at dinner in his honor. So he wrote: "My fame is nearly seven years old, and in the seventh year it still brings me in a bottle of champagne. Isn't that weighty testimony against the vanity and transitory character of human fame?"[29] The world was his;

[27] *Supra,* chap. iv, n. 65, pp. 115 and 149.

[28] Letter to Friedrich Althaus, February 6, 1857, in C.S., *S.C.&P.P.,* I, 30.

[29] Letter to Mrs. Schurz from New York, March 21, 1857, C.S. MSS., W.H.S. Even the piano was soon supplied. Soon afterward he

and he was tremendously pleased with the small bit of it which he occupied with his family at the moment.

The reasons for such optimism were to be found partly in the fact that he was then enjoying what he always loved but was forced by circumstances much of the time in those early years to forego—a period of almost uninterrupted home life. The rising price of land, which encouraged him to think that they would be financially independent within a few years, contributed.[30] But the real cause of it was the purposeful character of his new and hopeful political status, and the contrast between it and his former detached and disembodied state, as one of the ghosts of 1848. Merely to be a survivor of some great movement or event may suffice to keep an old man satisfied; but a young one of the Carl Schurz type, who insists upon looking forward and not backward, cannot content himself for long with the rôle of professional veteran. He wrote to Kinkel:

> The most contented man cannot deny that he lacks here many things, but the consciousness of existing once more for something, to throw a thought or an action into the scale of common interest, compensates for everything.[31]

---

wrote to her, after hearing Thalberg: "I heard for the first time what piano-playing is; when I come home, I shall show you" (letter, March 24, 1857, in C.S. MSS., W.H.S.).

[30] Letter to Kinkel from Watertown, December 1–17, 1856, in C.S. MSS., W.H.S.; in part, in C.S., *S.C.&P.P.*, I, 26, and in *Lebn.*, III, 145.

[31] Letter to Kinkel, December 1–17, 1856, in C.S. MSS., W.H.S.

In going on, then, to give his correspondent a picture of the political situation, he showed himself to be
so keen an observer as to qualify as a prophet:

There is nothing more strange than both parties after the
campaign, the Democrats, though they have won, discouraged,
depressed, and filled with fear of what may come, the Republican, though beaten, full of strength, full of self-confidence, because of the first results gained, and full of hope for the future.
Fremont is already proposed by several newspapers for 1860;
everywhere the organization is continued; and the agitation
continues as if nothing had happened. The spirit of the party is
what one calls, by an untranslatable expression, "buoyant." It is
said that Buchanan, shaken by the impressive expression of public opinion in the North, will do everything in order to keep
slavery out of Kansas. He may wish such results in secret, but
he will not be able to effect them. He is not his own master.
Chosen by a party the majority of which is in the South, he will
have to follow the policy of this majority in order to hold the
party together, and within it the only support of his administration.

If New York or Boston were the seat of the central government, the northern democracy would have a chance; in
Washington, the southern element rules.

Kansas is likely to be forced into the Union as a slave state,
unless a part of the northern Democrats in Congress become rebellious, or unless the struggle in Kansas can be made a revolutionary one to a great degree. . . . .

From now on, no other party can exist in the Union than a
northern one and a southern one, an Anti-slavery party and a
Pro-slavery one; and already the Democrats up here are only the
outposts of the slavery power in the free states. At last the
slavery issue has become the issue of the day; the time for compromise has passed, and the last chance for a peaceful solution
has come. The next few years will decide the fate of the United

States; in both camps there is firm determination. We have on our side the spirit of the age, a great inspiring idea, and superior ability. The South has unanimity and brutality. I do not know whether this struggle can be decided without powder. I hardly think so. However, should the force of arms be resorted to as a last measure, the result cannot be doubtful, for the material superiority of the North is immense.[32]

He continued to underestimate the military strength of the South until the Civil War was six months old, but he was not alone in that. His prevision of the split in the Democratic party over the Lecompton Constitution, if it was at all general, must have gone a long way toward accounting for the buoyant spirit of the Republicans. In the following February he repeated the prediction: "A rebellion is preparing in the Democratic party, and possibly Buchanan will be the gravestone of the country-gentry, as Fillmore is that of the Whig party."[33]

The more he got into things in America, the more he felt out of things in Europe. To Kinkel, he wrote:

I despair of your finding your way out of dreary England and coming over to the new world, and equally feeble within me is the expectation of events which could bring us into a common activity in Europe. It is so much the more necessary that we should keep in touch with letters, because people like us must not become strangers to each other, any more than the inexorable distance makes necessary.[34]

[32] *Ibid.*

[33] Letter to Friedrich Althaus, from Watertown, February 6, 1857, in C.S., *S.C.&P.P.*, I, 30.

[34] Letter of December 1–17, 1856, *supra*, n. 30.

And to Althaus: "I feel more and more that my lot is cast on this side of the water, unless changes scarcely to be expected happen over there."[35]

In the meanwhile, although national affairs constituted his greatest interest, they were by no means his only one. He was becoming quite active locally. The county seat was moved from Jefferson to Watertown;[36] and Schurz, as commissioner of public improvements, was extremely busy with questions concerning a new courthouse, school buildings, streets, bridges, new sidewalks, etc. He had also been commissioned a notary public, in which capacity he made it his business to handle and invest European and eastern capital.[37] That was probably his most fruitful source of income at that time; for his own real-estate project never paid much profit, and "Karlshuegel"[38] is just as far from the edge of Watertown today as it was when he lived there; whereas his Philadelphia connections were doubtless profitable to him, as a man handling eastern capital. He was also president of an insurance company—of which the Watertown papers took no notice—and was still studying law, with the expecta-

[35] Letter of November 15, 1856, in *Lebn.*, III, 143.

[36] Bill approved by Governor Bashford, October 11, 1856, in *Watertown Dem.*, October 16.

[37] Letter to Kinkel, December 1–17, 1856, *supra*, n. 30.

[38] Name given to the site of the Schurz home by the owners of the modern one which now occupies it, Mr. and Mrs. E. A. Pratt.

tion of soon being admitted to the bar,[39] as he was, in
1858. Not having yet found himself in a professional
way, he showed poor powers of abstention, and went
into too many lines of activity, with the boundless optimism of a boom town.

By March, 1857, he had a partner, C. T. Palme,
and an office in Watertown, where the two, as notaries
public and land agents, offered to "attend promptly to
all business entrusted to their care."[40] In April, in
spite of being a Republican, he was elected alderman
for the fifth ward, and was supervisor for the fifth
and sixth.[41] In May, he resigned as commissioner of
public improvements;[42] but for nearly two years he
continued as a member of the council, attending its
meetings very regularly at first and very irregularly in
the last portion of his term. Associated with him in the
council and on many of its committees was Emil
Rothe, the closest friend of his earliest days in Watertown;[43] but political and personal differences produced
quite a feud between them in the late fifties, as will
appear.[44]

[39] Letters to Althaus, November 15, and Kinkel, December 1–17,
1856, *supra*, nn. 35 and 30.

[40] Advertisement in *Watertown Dem.*, March 5, 1857.

[41] *Ibid.*, April 23, 1857.

[42] *Ibid.*, May 7, 1857.

[43] Reports of bi-weekly meetings of council in *Watertown Dem.*

[44] The two are said by Mr. Otto R. Krueger, the present editor of
the *Watertown Weltburger*, to have reconciled their differences after
1872, when Schurz was less of a Republican and Rothe, perhaps, less

The rapid growth of Watertown, in the decade prior to 1856 has already been described. It was assumed that that growth would continue. The railroad from Milwaukee was completed in the autumn of 1855.[45] In the following year, new ones were projected, via Madison to Prairie du Chien, via Columbus to La Crosse, and via Fond du Lac to Lake Winnebago. Schurz thought Watertown was to become a great railway center;[46] instead, it ceased to be a railway terminus and became merely a railroad crossing.

There was a temporary check in its growth in the spring of 1856; but Schurz, taking his usual broad world-view of things, thought it due only to a fall in grain prices because of the signing of the Paris peace-treaty;[47] and Editor Ballou of the *Watertown Democrat* thought it could be remedied by co-operative measures of the business men.[48] But the vicissitudes of the Watertown Gas Works were probably a fair barograph of the failure of the "boom." The company was formed in 1855. It was in distress in July of 1857, its

---

of a Democrat, and to have revisited the town together, as guests of Mr. D. Blumenfeldt, former editor of the *Weltburger,* by whom Mr. Krueger was then employed.

[45] Letter to Mrs. Schurz, September 16, 1855, in C.S. MSS., W.H.S.; *Watertown Dem.,* November 8, 1855.

[46] Letter .to Heinrich Meyer, August 6, 1856, in C.S. MSS., W.H.S.

[47] *Ibid.*

[48] Editorial, April 17, 1856.

officers claiming that they were losing $4,000 per year and threatening to stop operation unless permitted by the common council to raise the price of gas. The council authorized them to increase their rate from $3.50 to $5.00 per 1,000 cubic feet; and still they could barely pay expenses unless consumption were greatly increased.[49]

Neither water power nor railroads sufficed to make a great city of Watertown; and while the general financial panic of 1857 apparently did not alone kill its growth, it does seem to have given it the *coup de grâce.*

So also perished Schurz's hopes of affluence from the sale of his land. It had all been heavily mortgaged; and when, on account of the financial stringency, payments could not be met either by him or by those to whom a part of the land had been resold by him, much of it was lost by foreclosure. To the bitterness of political defeat, in November, 1857, was added that of financial embarrassment[50] and of having some who had bought from him lose with him.[51] Letters from

[49] *Watertown Dem.,* November 1, 1855; July 27 and August 27, 1857.

[50] Letters from Smith and Salomon, lawyers, December 10, and 18, 1857, in C.S. MSS., L.C.; C.S. to Heinrich Meyer, January 15, 1856, C.S., *S.C.&P.P.,* I, 32; *Lebn.,* III, 52.

[51] Some of these, though Schurz was not legally bound to do so, he later reimbursed. Statement of W. F. Whyte, through whom reimbursement was made to Henry Mulberger, in "Chronicles of Early Watertown," *Wisconsin Magazine of History,* Vol. IV, No. 3 (1921).

Jackson, concerning land payments, followed him even through the campaigns of 1859 and 1860;[52] and lecture fees were ultimately used to meet them. The farm was finally sold in 1867.

The same summer, however, which sealed the fate of his real estate venture, witnessed also his reentrance into another line of work more congenial to him and ultimately, though not immediately, more profitable—that of journalism. He had been doing some writing of political articles before;[53] and in August, 1857, founded a paper of his own, immediately after the close of his above-mentioned extremely short career as editor of the *Watertown Anzeiger*.

Like the *Bonner Zeitung* on which he had made his beginning in that field nine years earlier, the *Watertown Deutsch Volks-Zeitung* was primarily a political paper. In its "salutatory" it announced itself as "independent but not neutral," and proceeded to a statement of views which presumably defined as well as possible the stand which Schurz was then prepared to take on public questions. The editorial advocated: respect for the inherent right of self-government, and a minimum of restriction upon it; uncompromising opposition to slavery; freedom of social life from encroachment on the part of the government, by tem-

[52] C.S. MSS., L.C. Letters also from State Treasurer Hastings, April 30, May 3, and July 7, 1859, *ibid.*

[53] Letters to Althaus and Kinkel, November and December, 1856, *supra*, nn. 35 and 30.

perance laws and the like; an attitude of disapproba-
tion toward financial cupidity and corruption, as a
danger to government. So long as the Republican party adhered to these principles, the paper would be Republican.[54]

The need of a Republican paper in Watertown
was evidently felt much more strongly by Schurz and
other leaders of that party than by the citizens of Watertown. The *Wisconsin State Journal* welcomed the
newcomer to the journalistic order right heartily;[55] the
Watertown Democrat showed less enthusiasm.[56] Unless Schurz could convert a large percentage of the
people of the community to Republicanism, the *Volks-
Zeitung* could never be prosperous; and that never happened. With help from the party leaders it did maintain an artificially stimulated existence at least until
1860.[57] For more than a year it was edited and pub-

[54] *Wisconsin State Journal*, August 31, 1857.

[55] *Ibid.*

[56] *Watertown Dem.*, August 13 and 20, 1857.

[57] Letter from L. P. Harvey, July 20, 1857, in C.S. MSS., L.C.,
concerning subscriptions for its founding, by Senator Doolittle and
others. Letter, C.S. to Horace Rublee, November 11, 1857, in C.S.,
S.C.&P.P., I, 31, declaring himself unable longer to bear without help
the burden of its expense after that of the campaign. Among the many
political newspapers of that period such partisan financial support was
not at all uncommon. In September, 1860, it was the *Milwaukee Atlas*
for which Schurz had indorsed a note, and which was in distress; and
a triangular correspondence was being carried on about it between him
and Potter, and Potter and Doolittle (C.S., *S.C.&P.P.*, I, 77; Jensen,

lished by Schurz himself, later by Herman Lindeman,[58] apparently still more or less under Schurz's
guidance, though the Democratic press was always
more ready to call it his organ and mouthpiece than he
was himself. Its editorial views seem generally to have
coincided with his.

Whether a profitable investment or not from a
purely financial point of view, the paper seems at least
to have served the purpose of getting Schurz known to
the Republicans of Wisconsin, as his participation in
the election campaign of 1856 had helped him to do.
So when he next took the stump, it was not in a second
attempt to secure a seat in the state legislature but as
the candidate of his party for the office of lieutenant-
governor. He continued to serve on the Watertown
common council until 1858, and the home there was
maintained as a place of occasional residence until the
Spanish mission and the Civil War called the family
away from it. But as his interests had never been confined there, his activities likewise extended more and
more broadly beyond the local community, from the
time of that campaign onward.

As for the community, the changing attitude of at
least a considerable portion of it was probably revealed
by the *Watertown Democrat*. While continuing to

Wisconsins Deutsch-Amerikaner, I, 320). Schurz was often asked for
help; e.g., letter from A. Pott, Sheboygan, February 13, 1858, concerning *Niewsbode*, in C.S. MSS., L.C.

[58] *Mil. Sen.*, August 1 and November 9, 1858.

speak most highly of his integrity as a private individual, it lumped him along with the rest of the Republican candidates as "moderately respectable as to
ability," on a ticket composed of names "mostly new
to the public." With apparent reluctance to acknowledge the renegade, it listed him as "Carl Schurz of
Jefferson County"; [59] while the press of the state generally named him "Carl Schurz of Watertown."

[59] *Watertown Dem.*, September 10, 1857.

CHAPTER VII

CARL SCHURZ OF WATERTOWN

ACCORDING to the various reminiscent accounts written by A. M. Thompson,[1] the presentation of the name of Schurz to the Madison nominating convention of September 3, 1857, came as a surprise to most of those present. That it was no surprise to Schurz or to Harvey, whom he afterward credited with the chief responsibility for it, is apparent from a letter to him from Harvey, dated July 20, 1857. In it, he stated that he considered the prospect of Schurz's nomination for that office good, while agreeing with something Schurz had apparently said or written to him to the effect that, for fear of hurting his future prospects, his name should not be brought up at all if there were serious danger of failure. Harvey's own wishes in the matter were entirely friendly to Schurz; but his open usefulness to him in the matter would be limited because of the enmity existing between himself and Governor Bashford.[2]

Whether for that reason or another, the actual nomination was made by the John Wilkes of Wisconsin, Sherman Booth, best known for his radical anti-

---

[1] *Mil. Sen.*, November 11, 1897; April 1, 1900; *Political History of Wisconsin* (Milwaukee: C. N. Caspar Co., 1902).

[2] C.S. MSS., L.C.

slavery views and his connection with the famous
Glover case, of which more must be said later.[3]

Schurz attended the convention as a delegate from
Watertown, a distinction for which there was presumably but little competition. There he was nominated
for lieutenant-governor on the first formal ballot, re-
ceiving 145 votes as against 22 for D. D. Cameron.[4]
In his speech of acceptance he declared his approval of
the platform of the convention (which, as a member
of the committee on resolutions, he had helped to
write)[5] and said that, "as a debt of honor to the old
fatherland and of gratitude to the new," the Germans
must support a party of such principles. As for himself,
he disclaimed any thought that the nomination had
come to him because of his services to the party, but
accepted it as a tribute to the Germans and a recognition of their stand against slavery. Having fought for
liberty in the Old World, he said, he was glad to do
so in the New.[6]

The other side of that picture may be given by
combining the three accounts written at various times
by A. M. Thompson.[7]

Randall had been nominated after a warm contest, and
someone was wanted who would strengthen the ticket. . . . . .
It was thought especially desirable to placate the Germans, who

[3] *Ibid.*; Thompson, in *Mil. Sen.*, April 1, 1900; *St. Jour.*, September 4, 1857.

[4] *Mil. Sen.*, September 4, 1857.

[5] *Mil. Atlas*, September 5.

[6] *St. Jour.*, September 4; *Mil. Sen.*, September 5.   [7] Cf. n. 1.

looked with suspicion on what they regarded as the nativistic tendencies of the new party; . . . . and Carl Schurz seemed to be the only available German to put on the ticket.[8]

The Democrats had long before seen the point of the ancient question, "Doth the ox low that hath fodder?" So, as a counter-attraction it was generally conceded that a German should have a prominent place on the Republican ticket. The nomination for state treasurer had been offered to Schurz, but he had refused to accept any place on the ticket lower than that of lieutenant-governor.[9]

Schurz was presented by Booth as a revolutionist; but as Booth himself was an outstanding figure in a mild form of revolution which the party was then supporting, in its approval of resistance to the Fugitive Slave Law, that would not bar him. Beyond that, little was known of him except that he came from Watertown, that he had "in that hot-bed of Hunker Democracy shown his devotion to Republican principles by working steadily for their success,"[10] and that he had been an effective and zealous speaker for Fremont in 1856.[11]

[8] *Mil. Sen.*, April 1, 1900. Carl Roeser, it will be remembered, was defeated as a candidate for state treasurer two years before. See chap. vi, n. 9.

[9] *St. Jour.*, September 19, 1857.

[10] *Mil. Sen.*, September 4.

[11] *St. Jour.*, September 4. The same article was one of those which claimed him as a convert to Republicanism, stating that he had formerly been a Democrat. Compare conclusion of chap. iv.

Not even that much was known to the delegates generally. With some allowance for exaggeration induced by the lapse of time and by subsequent events, the following account by Mr. Thompson probably describes their state of mind fairly well.

None of us dreamed then that we were dealing with the destiny of one of the highest and most famous German-Americans who ever came to this country. "Who the devil is Carl Schurz?" was the general inquiry among the delegates. Only a few knew him or knew about him.[12]

Then he came forward to make his speech of acceptance. Thompson describes him as tall, angular, and eccentric in appearance (as he always was), and dressed in faded, worn, and ill-fitting clothing.[13]

I believe that nearly every delegate felt as I did that we had made a terrible blunder in nominating him, and we awaited the speech with intense anxiety. We did not have to wait long before our suspense was happily relieved by one of the finest impromptu addresses I have ever heard, which convinced all of us that we had made no mistake, but that the ablest man in the hall was Carl Schurz.[14]

In an earlier account Thompson had written:

The delegates were amazed at his eloquence, and the charm and power of his matchless oratory. When he left the platform he also left the impression upon the mind of everyone present

[12] *Mil. Sen.*, April 1, 1900.

[13] In his more prosperous days he dressed in meticulous fashion. In those early ones, however, his letters sometimes refer to rigidly economical measures in the repair of clothing.

[14] *Mil. Sen.*, April 1, 1900.

that a man of splendid intellectual abilities had appeared among them, challenging their criticism and winning their admiration.[15]

The complete difference in tone noticeable between Thompson's accounts of the reasons which prompted his nomination and of the sensation produced by his speech of acceptance is a sufficient indication that the convention members had found more in the opened package than they had anticipated from the appearance of the wrapper. That they were pleased by the surprise is indicated by the report that "as Mr. Schurz concluded his eloquent remarks, the convention rose as one man and gave three thundering cheers for Carl Schurz."[16]

When the list of nominations was announced, the Republican papers at once bestirred themselves to let the people know who their candidate for the position of presiding officer of the state senate really was; and the stories of his German exploits were widely circulated, in many authorized and unauthorized versions.[17] Both friend and foe made use of them, in fact. The *Milwaukee News* and the *American* soon named him a rebel and traitor "fleeing from the outraged laws" of Germany[18]—an attack which roused resentment among

[15] *Ibid., Mil. Sen.,* November 21, 1897; *ibid.,* in *Political History of Wisconsin,* pp. 141–42.

[16] *Mil. Sen.,* September 5, 1857.

[17] Cf. chap. ii, nn. 37, 38, and 64.

[18] As quoted by *Mil. Sen.,* October 5, 1857.

many of the Germans[19] but may have found some sympathizers among the Catholics and the nativists.

Soon he was attacked even through Kinkel, who was accused of having misappropriated the funds donated for the relief of European refugees, of having wasted a part of it on luxuries paid for from his expense account, and of having invested the remainder in a "farm or brewery" (*sic*) for himself.[20] It was implied that Schurz was guilty, along with Kinkel, of all the offenses of which the latter was accused. Schurz usually refused to answer personal attacks; this one he did answer, but certainly not in a tone designed to placate his hostile critics, even had they wished to be placated, as they did not. In a letter to the *Milwaukee Sentinel* he specifically denied all of the reports against Kinkel which he had heard, and continued:

It is a very significant fact, that partisan editors in this republic surpass the most debased hirelings of European despots in calumniating the characters of men. . . . . As to the charges about me, I have nothing to say. The opinions expressed by the Democratic editors, on the revolutionary movements of 1848, disclose an abyss of ignorance the depth of which it is difficult to measure.[21]

[19] Letter to *Mil. Sen.*, October 7.

[20] *American*, quoted by *Mil. Sen.*, October 10. Kinkel did still have in hand the fund raised for the German loan—or at least, a part of it. Compare letters of Schurz to Kinkel, January 23, 1855, *supra*, chap. iv, n. 13; and of Kinkel to Schurz, August 19, 1860, *supra*, chap. ii, n. 85.

[21] *Mil. Sen.*, October 28.

Schurz was by no means the only victim of violent partisan criticism, of course. The editors of the period exhausted their ingenuity in seeking synonyms for "cheat," "rascal," and "liar." But he did draw more than his proportionate share of comment, both favorable and unfavorable. He would! Men admired and liked him, or men felt the sting of his tongue or the edge of his arguments, and resentment left no room for admiration. But men were never neutral about Carl Schurz.

There being apparently no uniform standard of ethics at all then governing the press, some of the Democratic organs merely went further than others. One even descended to spelling his name "Shirts" in an article naming him as owner of the *Watertown Anzeiger*, which had dismissed him as editor two months before.[22] This was probably due to the fact that the *Anzeiger*, although it had found Schurz "too Republican" in August, had, in October, refused longer to support the Democratic ticket, with the editorial comment that, although it "expected to be ruined financially by the action," it definitely repudiated the party with which it had formerly been associated. It had found that the ballot box was "the only weapon against these leaches"[23] (*sic*). It was eventually united

[22] *American*, quoted by *Mil. Sen.*, October 10. Compare references to the *Anzeiger*, chap. v, n. 25, and chap. vii. The lowest limit was reached by the *American*, when it said, "We really don't know how to spell his name, but in French, it would be *chemise*."

[23] Quoted by *Mil. Sen.*, October 2.

with the *Watertown Weltburger* under the editorship
of Schurz's former friend and local rival, Emil Rothe.

The most far-fetched attack of all, but one that
was to be renewed more than once within the next few
years, was one which charged him with being a Prussian spy, set to watch and to betray his former revolutionary associates. The only basis alleged for it was
that his "considerable wealth" in Germany had not
been confiscated, while that of his fellow-revolution-
ists had. This was immediately answered, but anony-
mously, by someone who claimed to have been a student friend of his at Bonn. This correspondent pointed
out that, as a minor son of poor parents in 1849, he
had owned no property of his own, that his own family
had had to be brought to America because of police
persecution brought upon them by his acts, and that
such property as he did have in Germany belonged to
the family of his wife, whom he had married after the
revolutionary attempt had ended.[24] But these facts
were ignored by the purveyors of the story, both in its
first appearance and in its revivals.

The friends of Schurz and the *Volksfreund* later
accused Rothe of having started the libel. Whether
Schurz believed he had or not, there was certainly
more than any petty jealousy at the bottom of their
enmity during the latter part of the fifties. Rothe was
said to have lost his temper and his head completely,
speaking of Schurz and trying to counteract, by an

[24] *Ibid.*

address in Racine, the effect of a recent one there by
Schurz;[25] while Schurz, even two years later, wrote
home gloatingly about the superiority of his success
over Rothe's in a speaking campaign in Minnesota.[26]
At home, however, Rothe was more popular than he.

A more respectable accusation, but one which
showed an even greater vitality during the campaign
of 1857—after which, of course, it lost its point—
was that Schurz was not a citizen and therefore was
not eligible for office. It was true that at the time of
his nomination he had not yet been a resident of the
country for five years; and he did not at that time
have his final naturalization papers. He was told by
his friends, however, that as he would become eligible
and be able to secure his papers before taking office if
elected, there was nothing to prevent his being a candidate without them.[27]

The opening attack upon his eligibility was made
by the *Watertown Democrat* only a fortnight after the
nominating convention. It stated that he had not secured his naturalization papers (which was true) and
could not get them for some time yet (also true). This
it called a violation of the letter and spirit of the Constitution. That he should do such a thing surprised and

[25] *Mil. Atlas,* October 17. Note action of Racine Germans, September 21, below.

[26] Series of letters to Mrs. Schurz, September, 1859, in C.S. MSS.,
W.H.S.

[27] *C.S., Rem.,* II, 81.

grieved the *Democrat* greatly; for it had numbered him among the "high-minded, honorable, and patriotic citizens" of the town, where he was "justly esteemed in all the social relations of life." A week later, while still objecting to what he called a piece of sharp practice, its editor reported that he had been told by Mr. Schurz that he was entitled to his papers; and he accepted that statement of fact, for "no one who was acquainted with Mr. Schurz would for an instant doubt his statement."[28] Lincoln was not alone in being counted honest by his neighbors.

Other editors, however, were less influenced by knowledge of Schurz and of the facts, or less restrained by decency or regard for truth. When the *Milwaukee Atlas* (German Republican) announced that his papers had been secured and that he was "ready to show any doubter in black and white" that he was a citizen[29]—which was certainly an improvement upon the *Sentinel's* promise that they would "be at the disposal of anyone wishing to see them after he is elected"[30]—the *News*, the *American*, and the *Argus* charged fraud and perjury in the getting of them.[31] While the *Wisconsin State Journal* (Madison, Republican) advanced the date of his landing to August

[28] *Watertown Dem.*, September 17 and 24, 1857. Schurz had landed in the United States, September 17, 1852.

[29] *Mil. Atlas*, October 3.

[30] September 21.

[31] Quoted by *Mil. Sen.*, October 5.

1, 1852, calling him "one of Nature's noblemen, a generous, large-hearted, and tried friend of freedom,"[32] the *Milwaukee News* (Democrat) set it back to May, 1853, and to its previous charges of rebellion and treason in Germany, then repeated, added the somewhat inconsistent one of cowardice for having run away from no real danger.[33]

In all this war of accusations his strongest and steadiest supporters were the oldest and strongest party organ, Rufus King's *Milwaukee Sentinel*, Rublee and Atwood's *Wisconsin Daily State Journal*, and Domschke's German *Milwaukee Atlas*. They followed his activities, reporting his speeches directly or indirectly, and entered the editorial lists so often in his defense that, if all criticism be considered as publicity, he got as much of it in that campaign as all the other members of the ticket combined, including a certain amount of comment in the Chicago and eastern papers. Thereafter, if the question "Who the devil is Carl Schurz?" were asked at all, it was not by a man who had never heard of him but by one who wondered why he had heard so much.

He gave them plenty to talk about. While his attacks upon the Democratic party were of an impersonal nature, directed against their policies and performances and, as in his arguments with Petrasch in student days,

[32] Editorial, October 29, 1857.

[33] October 29; quoted by *Mil. Sen.*, October 30.

dealing in no "extrinsic personalities," they were, none the less, sharp enough. The attacks of the opposition were directed against him with such peculiar bitterness, partly because he was a German and a Forty-eighter and, as such, peculiarly vulnerable, and partly because they felt the effect of his speeches.

He was very active. In October the lists of his speaking engagements showed an average of five per week; the total number must have exceeded thirty.[34] About half of them were made in conjunction with other speakers—Randall, Harvey, or others—on which occasions he usually spoke in German. When appearing alone, he spoke English, and often made two speeches in succession, in English and in German.

A comparison of his speeches with those of the others shows him to have been somewhat more sparing than the rest in the use of the florid and high-sounding but meaningless oratory then common, but more effective in it when he did use it. While his editorial friends constantly complimented him upon the intimate knowledge of state history and conditions revealed by his speeches, those in English seem to the more modern reader to have neglected state and local matters, as well as personalities, almost completely, and to have been devoted very largely to national questions at issue between the parties. He was much more inclined than the others to treat the Wisconsin state election not as an independent enterprise complete in itself but as a

[34] *Mil. Sen.*, October 7 and 28, 1857.

phase in the national struggle between the parties, a sort of opening engagement in the battle of 1860. Just so Lincoln treated the senatorial campaign in Illinois, in the following summer.

His German speeches were of a more informative or instructional sort. In them he undertook to shepherd his German hearers into the fold by tracing for them the histories of the parties on the slavery issue, pointing out to them how their interests were identified with the system of free labor and free-soil territories, in which respect the Democratic party had never served and would never serve them.[35] A response to his activity came from Kansas in the form of a set of resolutions adopted by the German Free-state Club of Wyandotte, published in the *Kansas Zeitung* and sent for publication in English to the *Sentinel* and in German to the *Atlas*. As "friends and admirers of Carl Schurz," these men proclaimed that they considered that the office for which he was a candidate was his due, as a reward for his services to the cause of liberty and to the Republican party. They congratulated the state of Wisconsin upon having such a man among its citizens and recommended him to all voters.[36]

At home the factual character of his German speeches was emphasized in nearly every friendly report of them, the general comment being well sum-

[35] *Ibid.*, October 8, November 2; *St. Jour.*, October 27; *Atlas, et al.*

[36] *Mil. Sen.*, October 3; *Mil. Atlas*, October 3.

marized and typified by one correspondent who described one at Fort Atkinson as "replete with facts and rich in eloquence."[37] In his English speeches he had in his favor that element of surprise which has already been noted as lacking in the German ones of 1856. That an immigrant should know as much about American institutions as he did, and that a German should speak English so well, solved for the reporters their usual difficulty in finding something different to say about a man. Different from what was said about other candidates, at least, whether different from other reports on Schurz or not; for these comments and references to his sacrifices to the cause of liberty abroad were getting shopworn from continuous use before the campaign was half finished. They still did service, however, as late as 1860, but outside of Wisconsin.

The only speech of 1857 which will be here reviewed at any length was an English one at Madison, October 16.[38] It is worthy of study, however, as it was his most significant utterance in that campaign, his first really important effort in English, and on many points the prototype of more famous and more widely reported addresses later. It is most interesting as the earliest indication of the line of his attacks upon slavery and of his persistent hostility to Stephen A. Douglas.

[37] Letter of October 29 from "A Republican" of Fort Atkinson in *Mil. Sen.*

[38] Full report and editorial comment in *St. Jour.*, October 17–20.

W. H. Jensen's comment on Schurz's peculiar position on slavery is, that while other speakers had attacked slavery only from the sentimental or legal and constitutional standpoints, Carl Schurz was the first to seize upon the earliest traditions of the republic and try to get back to its ethical and philosophical fundamental principles.[39] From what has already been said, there appears a possibility that he may have taken lessons in those matters from Seward and suggestions from the editorials of the *Sentinel*. But that the pupil excelled his masters in effectiveness, even if such were the case, will appear from a study of this and later speeches.

Schurz began, almost without introduction, by tracing the history of the Democratic party's attitude toward slavery. So long as the Missouri Compromise appeared as an immediate gain for slavery, he said, they had supported it; as soon as it ceased to appear so, they had thrown it over, by the passage of the Kansas-Nebraska Bill, and in the interest of slavery had been guilty of fraud and violence in Kansas. The antislavery expressions of some northern Democrats, and their claims that popular sovereignty would introduce not slavery but freedom into the territories, he called only a pretense. "If they are opposed to slavery, they love their

[39] Jensen, *Wisconsins Deutsch-Amerikaner*, I, 179. Compare similar comment by A. D. White to Bismarck *(infra)*; and refusal of Schurz, in speech on "The Irrepressible Conflict," Chicago, September 28, 1858, to "talk about the sinfulness of sin, in general" *(infra)*.

enemies more than Christians ought to do." The Dred Scott Decision had declared slavery to be national, and the Democrats had demanded obedience to that decision as to a part of the supreme law of the land.

Schurz denied that slavery was national. Even the constitutional guarantees conceded to it applied only to "persons held to service in the various states under the laws thereof"; so he said that slavery could legally be nothing but a state institution. The Constitution had recognized the existence of slavery as a fact but had evaded recognition of it as a right, and had so stamped it as a local institution.

He came nearer than that to Seward's old appeal to the "higher law" when he said that the Constitution itself could not command respect merely because it was the Constitution, nor even as the work of a group of great men. It was entitled to it only as a bulwark of liberty and of the rights of man. Its real enemies were not those who challenged the Fugitive Slave Law or the Dred Scott Decision, but the Democrats, who had mis-used it and degraded it to the status of a party weapon.

From the Constitution, he worked back to the Declaration of Independence,[40] quoting from the writings of a number of its signers and of Washington, and

[40] He misquoted it, however, by his use of the phrase "all men are created *free and equal*" (author's italics). He frequently did so, even through 1860; but the mistake was such a common one among both speakers and writers of the period that none of his so-keen critics ever seized upon it.

picturing an imaginary repudiation of Stephen A. Douglas by a resurrected Thomas Jefferson.

When on the subject of Douglas, he was always inclined to go to extremes; and while this early attack was less virulent than later ones, it was otherwise no exception. He applied himself particularly to answering a recent speech made by Douglas before the Illinois legislature. In it, Douglas had said that the words "all men," as used in the Declaration, had obviously referred only to white men, not negroes; and that the purpose of the declaration of equality had been merely to justify British subjects in America in a revolt against their home government for rights equal to those of British subjects at home.[41] Schurz objected to such an interpretation, which, he said, would exclude from the meaning of the declaration of equality not only free negroes but people of German, French, and Scandinavian origin as well. (This seems to the reviewer to be rather far-fetched. Surely the colonists of 1776, were all British subjects, regardless of origin.) Such an interpretation would reduce the Declaration of Independence from "a sacred code of rights, written by philosophers and fought for by heroes," to a "hypocritical piece of special pleading, drawn up by a batch of artful pettifoggers." If Douglas was right, then the Declaration was "only a Yankee trick, another

[41] Compare extracts from speeches of Douglas, *Albany Evening Journal* Tracts, 1860.

wooden nutmeg."[42] But so Douglas, Taney, and Buchanan told people to interpret it. Referring to the first of these again, he said that only a prejudiced or a disordered mind could so misunderstand its principles; while the *heart of a villain* (*sic*) was needed so to misrepresent them.

Without going quite to the point of disputing the law with Chief Justice Taney, he did disagree with the jurist's historical assertions about the state of public opinion on the slavery question in 1787, saying that *world* public opinion was then fifty years ahead of all constituted authorities, and pointing out that slavery was very soon abolished elsewhere. In support of his argument he cited judicial opinions against slavery handed down in England as early as 1706 and 1773, and used to the same end his quotations from the writings of the founders of the republic.

The argument better known because of Lincoln's later and better statement of it, in the latter part of his famous remark about the "house divided against itself," was introduced by Schurz following his references to Douglas and Taney. If the Constitution really did recognize the right of property in slaves, it would be impossible permanently to keep slavery out

[42] On exactly such a remark as that, used in precisely the same connection, in Springfield, Massachusetts, in January, 1860, he was picked up by his critics. His denunciation of the Declaration as he said Douglas interpreted it was quoted as his opinion of the thing itself; and he was right roundly berated as God-hater, blasphemer, and defamer of the sacred Declaration and its sainted signers.

of the free states. The barriers to it in the territories had already been broken down in the interest of popular sovereignty; those to the slave trade would be broken down in the interest of free trade. The history of the past generation he traced as that of a long series of encroachments by the slave power upon popular rights. A party which was without principles could not be honest; and by permitting themselves to be "whipped in" by Douglas to support the Kansas-Nebraska Bill and to desert their old antislavery position, the northern Democrats had shown themselves to be unprincipled.

In his peroration, which he afterward characterized as "a somewhat florid piece of oratory," but which "had the honor of being published in some eastern papers,"[43] he spoke once more as an immigrant, saying:

> Americans are the spoiled children of fortune. . . . . You know the curse of despotic rule only by hearsay. . . . . But I have seen despotism and felt its scourge. . . . . You cannot imagine what an electric thrill the word "liberty" sends through the heart of a man whose head is borne down by the weight of oppression. You, perhaps, have never measured the incalculable value of the treasures you possess.

Friend Rublee found no difficulty, next day, in writing favorable comment. He wrote, in part:

[43] C.S., *Rem.*, II, 81. He considered it, at the time, his best speech so far, and sent a copy of it to his brother-in-law in Germany and one to Kinkel. With some pride, but with a charming deference, he wrote that he wished to "lay it at the feet of his teacher" (letter, February 23, 1858, in *Lebn.*, III, 155).

The expectations formed of Mr. Schurz, high as they were, were more than realized in the eloquent, learned, logical, and finished address that followed. He is an easy, fluent speaker, without any of the rant and bluster of the stump orator, but clear, earnest, and eloquent, with the genuine eloquence of thought expressed in language unusually choice and elegant, for an extemporaneous speaker. A slight foreign accent, an occasional idiom, or the use of an unusual word,[44] now and then, are the only evidences that he is not speaking his mother tongue, such is his perfect mastery of our language, and these only heighten the interest of his remarks, as those who have heard or read the speeches of Kossuth will understand.[45]

Three days later, having printed the last of the lengthy speech, he wrote further:

Let its high and manly tone, its clearness of statement, and the irrefragibility of its logic, be contrasted with the personal abuse and rancor, the low gossip and dirty slanders, which are the staple arguments of the opposition.[46]

The contrast was indeed great. No other candidate on either ticket won such extravagant praise or drew such violent attacks. As solace for any wounds the latter may have made, there came the following tribute from the *Oshkosh Democrat:* "The Germans may well feel proud of their fellow-countryman, and Americans may congratulate themselves that our country can induce such specimens of the earth's nobility to make this their home." The writer went on to say

[44] He had described Douglas, for example, as "a little man with rude features and an unwelcome eye."

[45] *St. Jour.*, October 17.

[46] *Ibid.*, October 20.

that he considered it "sad that such a man must stand
up before an American audience and plead with them
not to give up their liberty."[47]

After reading such eulogies, one wonders how such
a candidate can have been defeated; but a perusal of
only the Democratic papers would have left one wondering how such an unprincipled rascal could have been
permitted to remain at large. For any real information
as to his value to the party in the campaign, one must
go to more impersonal or disinterested sources than the
editorial columns of the contemporary press.

He had to serve for one thing as a counterpoise, to
outweigh with the Germans the fact that the most
prominent unsuccessful candidate for first place on the
ticket had been E. D. Holton. Holton was a man of
unexceptionable character and admirable record. He
had been a candidate for the office of governor in 1853
with Free-soil and Whig support, and in 1855 as a
Republican, but both times principally on his record
as a staunch Congregationalist and an ardent prohibi-
tionist. While fully entitled to perfect respect, he was,
none the less, not an asset to his party in its bid for the
support of those Germans who were still inclined to
make major issues out of such minor ones as Sunday
regulations or liquor restrictions.

Something else expected of him was stated with
exactness by H. F. Young, of Glen Haven, Grant
County, in a letter of September 20. He wrote to

[47] Quoted by *Mil. Sen.*, October 24.

Schurz that there was some feeling among the Germans of that county that the Republican party was not free from nativism and that, if it were so, Schurz must prove it so to them or Randall could not be elected.[48] A single instance, which seems fairly typical, must suffice as evidence of the way in which he performed the task. Wherever it was accomplished at all, it was done less by disproving the charge on that issue than by overshadowing it and the above-mentioned side issues with the stress placed on the slavery question. On September 21, shortly after an address there by him, the Germans of Racine published strong antislavery resolutions, which were widely copied by the Republican papers. That county had been theretofore almost entirely Democratic so far as the Germans were concerned, and the men of the group all called themselves former Democrats; but they announced their support of the Republican ticket and their special indorsement of Carl Schurz.[49]

Both then and later, it was generally conceded that more Germans voted the Republican ticket that year than ever before, and that he was entitled to more credit than anyone else for the change. In an editorial many years later, the *Sentinel* said:

The ascendancy of the Republican party in this state may be said to date from the time when the Germans began to cut

[48] C.S. MSS., L.C.

[49] *Racine Advocate; Racine Volksblatt*, September 21; *Mil. Sen.*, September 23; *St. Jour.*, September 28; *Mil. Atlas*, October 3.

adrift from the Democratic party. . . . . The first wedge in
the partition of the German vote was doubtless due to the influence of the political exiles who have come to be known as the
Forty-eighters. One of the most influential of these revolutionists of '48 was Carl Schurz. His influence in turning the drift
of German sentiment toward the Republican party has never
been fully admitted.[50]

Why, then, was he defeated? He had entered the
campaign fully confident of success;[51] and three weeks
after the election, before the final result of the official
canvass had been announced, but while the *Sentinel*
and *Journal* were still claiming a victory for him, he
wrote that he was afraid to believe himself elected, but
revealed that he really did. He was concerned, however, over the reports that only three-fifths of the
eligible vote had been cast and that the Republican majority was evidently going to be less than expected. He
attributed that to the fact that the Republican strength
was mostly in the agricultural districts, and that more
than half of the voters who were kept away from the
polls by excessive solicitude for the welfare of the crops

[50] *Mil. Sen.*, April 1, 1900; C.S. MSS., L.C. "This was . . . .
the first step toward drawing a large class of his fellow-Germans into
the Republican party, without whose support the party would have forever remained in the minority in Wisconsin. He made converts wherever he spoke, and thousands of his nativity were won to the true political faith by his eloquent speeches, and flocked to our standard"
(Thompson, *Political History of Wisconsin*, p. 142). "More Germans voted the Republican ticket than ever before; the falling-off was
due to over-confidence and neglect of the "Old Guard" (*St. Jour.*, November 24).

[51] Letter to Heinrich Meyer, September 20, in C.S. MSS., W.H.S.

and by business worries due to falling prices and money scarcity were Republicans, while the urban vote of the Democrats was more easily manipulable.[52]

The final figures showed his surmise to have been correct. The total Republican vote that year was 21,000 less than in 1856, the Democratic 8,000 less;[53] and only about half of the Republican candidates were elected. The early returns had been very encouraging to Schurz. He had at least won in Watertown, where he had been so badly defeated the year before. He had carried his own ward, 80–21 votes, and the city, 501–484, being the only man on the ticket to do so, 271 votes ahead of Randall there, and about 300 ahead of the average of his ticket.[54] In 1856, Buchanan had had a majority of 450 there. In 1857, Cross, Randall's opponent for the office of governor, had a majority of 254, and Schurz a narrow but significant one of 17.[55] In Jefferson County, he had carried his ticket with him.[56]

When thirty-nine counties had been heard from, Schurz led the Republican ticket in the total number of votes cast; a thousand more votes had been cast for

[52] Letter to Heinrich Meyer, November 25, in C.S. MSS., W.H.S.; *Lebn.*, III, 150. The next year a Republican slogan was, "The potatoes are all dug. No staying away from the polls, this year."

[53] *Mil. Sen.*, December 8.

[54] *Watertown Dem.*, November 5. Watertown defeated the Republican candidates in succeeding years as regularly and decisively as ever. Files of the *Democrat*.

[55] *St. Jour.*, November 7.   [56] *Mil. Sen.*, November 6.

the two candidates for the office of lieutenant-governor
than for any of their fellow-candidates.[57] So all the
campaign publicity had accomplished that much at
least; but as his opponent, D. D. Cameron, mayor of
La Crosse, also ran ahead of his ticket, his relative
standing was but little improved thereby. On the late
returns he lost. The *Sentinel* gave the figure as 104
against him;[58] he himself, as 107.[59]

Eventually he was very philosophical about his
defeat and could say, both as a consolation and as a
warning to himself, that his popularity had been due in
part simply to the novelty of his peculiar combination
of qualities and experience and had come too quickly
to be permanent;[60] but at the time he called it a "dis-
grace to the state of Wisconsin"[61] and an "obvious
fraud." What fraud he suspected, he did not say. A
natural first guess at what he had in mind would be
that he suspected that the bears had been voting again,
as they were said to have done in the fraudulent Bar-
stow-Bashford election of 1855, or that somehow there
had been more votes cast than there were voters. That
had happened two years before, and returns had been
sent in from towns which did not exist. Though he

[57] *Ibid.*, November 30.

[58] *Ibid.*, December 8.   [59] C.S., *Rem.*, II, 82.

[60] *Ibid.*; letter to Kinkel, February 15, 1858, in C.S. MSS.,
W.H.S.; *Lebn.*, III, 153; in part, in C.S., *S.C.&P.P.*, I, 33.

[61] Letter to Horace Rublee, November 11, 1857, in C.S.,
S.C.&P.P., I, 31.

suspected fraud, he "could not bear the expense of proving it." But if this was what he had in mind, it leaves unexplained why he thought that he, and not the state, should have borne the expense of proving the fraud. Perhaps he feared he would be less fortunate than Governor Bashford had been, in securing compensation for the expense of initiating action.[62]

A second guess would be that he referred to the action of the Jefferson County board of canvassers in throwing out the vote of the "five towns" of Jefferson County because of a state supreme court decision declaring illegal their recent transfer from Dodge to Jefferson County. In those towns Schurz had run 233 votes ahead of Randall and 195 ahead of the Republican average; but as Cameron, his opponent, had still led him by 86 votes, to have counted the votes of those counties would merely have diminished Randall's majority, without winning one for Schurz.[63]

Harvey probably came nearer to the truth when he attributed his friend's defeat to "disaffection in the locality of a rival for the nomination, and the unreasoning prejudice here and there of a vagabond native whose prejudices were stronger than his principles."[64]

[62] Letter to Heinrich Meyer, January 15, 1858, *ibid.*, I, 32; *Lebn.*, III, 152. Legislative appropriations had subsequently paid $9,000 for the ousting of Barstow by Bashford (*Assembly Journal*, 1857, pp. 417, 639).

[63] *Watertown Dem.*, December 3, 1857, in C.S. MSS., L.C.

[64] Letter to Schurz, December 20, 1857, in C.S. MSS., L.C.

Certainly, a very small percentage of the absentee Republican vote, which outnumbered the absentee Democratic vote almost two to one, would have sufficed to elect him. But what really irked him, and led to coolness amounting to something like enmity between him and Randall, was the obvious fact that, while numerous Germans had doubtless scratched their ballots in favor of Schurz, an even greater number, presumably native Americans, who voted for Randall had scratched theirs against him. He suspected Randall of failure to support him loyally, among his own friends, or as enthusiastically as he should have done, in his speeches.[65]

His friends remained loyal to him. Rublee wrote of his defeat with "poignant regret" and repeated that "a truer, nobler-hearted man was never presented for the suffrages of the people";[66] while the *Sheboygan Times* called his defeat "a reproach to the people of the state."[67]

Even the *Milwaukee News* shed crocodile tears over him:

Where is the eloquent and patriotic Carl Schurz, who evinced more talent and performed more effective service during the campaign than all the other candidates of the Black Republican party? Large numbers of his countrymen were induced, through their admiration of his excellent qualities, to

[65] See also, Thompson, *Political History of Wisconsin*, p. 144.

[66] *St. Jour.*, December 10 and 17.

[67] Quoted in *St. Jour.*, December 2.

vote for him; and yet, despite all this, he has fallen a victim of that intolerant spirit which pervades the party to which he, in an evil hour, attached himself.[68]

But of course, its sincerity was more than merely "open to question"; it was non-existent.

Once he was safely defeated, the editor of the *Watertown Democrat* also felt safe in speaking kindly of him once more. In congratulating him upon the "handsome compliment" paid him by the Republican members of the state senate in unanimously offering him the clerkship of that body (which he had naturally declined, as he still considered himself its rightful president), Ballou himself paid a high compliment to his "acknowledged talent, cultivated tastes, and ripe scholarship." While, politically, the paper could not regret his defeat but only wished more of his friends had shared it, it did consider that he had been "the ablest and most eloquent speaker, either in German or in English," in the recent election campaign, and that he had "deserved success, if he did not achieve it."[69]

The last and best consolation came from Harvey, who had been active and who said that he had even been "officious" in securing the nomination for him in the first place. He expressed himself as chagrined, mortified, and indignant over his friend's defeat, but assured him that:

[68] Quoted in *Mil. Sen.*, November 23.

[69] *Watertown Dem.*, January 14, 1858; *St. Jour.*, January 16.

The substitution of any other name for yours would have brought the defeat of the whole ticket. . . . . You have laid the Republican Party under the strongest debt of gratitude to you. Then you have borne yourself nobly in the canvass, and have won for yourself the confidence and regard of the true, working Republicans of the state, as few have the talent or opportunity to do.[70]

With thoughts such as those just suggested, Schurz was soon able to console himself for the loss of an office which would very soon have palled upon him if he had got it. Still, he did not enjoy the experience of losing it; and the defeat, combined with the heavy injury done him by the economic depression, made 1857 seem, just then, to have been "an abominable year."[71] His ultimate gain from it was in the reputation he had won; his immediate profit came from the lecture fees which the prominence he attained in politics, with its attendant publicity, enabled him to earn. Lecturing and political stump-speaking dovetailed together for him for years, thereafter, each contributing to his success in the other.

This is the more significant when viewed in connection with the fact that in the canvasses of 1858, 1859, and 1860, in which he had opportunity so greatly to enhance his reputation as an orator, public speaking played a part relatively much greater than former-

[70] Letter of December 20, in C.S. MSS., L.C. *Supra*, n. 64, and chap. i, n. 28, p. 13.

[71] Letter to Heinrich Meyer, January 15, 1858, in C.S., *S.C.&P.P.*, I, 32. *Supra*, n. 62.

ly, in comparison with the use of newspapers and other printed material.[72] To anyone who has read the mass of contradictory editorial comment on the Wisconsin election of 1857 which is reviewed in this chapter, it is not surprising that it should have been so. While the standard of many of the speeches may have been but little better, the stuff printed in the contest of eulogy and denunciation, here reviewed as typical of that which went on around Schurz as a center through four successive campaigns, must have ceased to be convincing to anyone.

With the decline of editorial influence, there began the real heyday of the political orator. In that field none excelled, if any equaled, the man who soon came to be nationally known as "Carl Schurz of Wisconsin."

[72] McMaster, *A History of the People of the United States*, VIII, 459–61; Rhodes, *History of the United States*, II, 484.

CHAPTER VIII

CARL SCHURZ OF WISCONSIN

EARLY in 1858 the plan announced by Schurz to Althaus and Adolph Meyer before his migration to America, at last came to fruition.[1] While in France, he had made a special study of the great French Revolution and of conditions during the period of the Second Republic, and during his first half-year in America he had written a German study of the modern history of France.[2] His whole career had served to indoctrinate him with the ideas of democracy, while he had found despotism in France more arbitrary and annoying, in the petty manner of its administration, than in Germany. His ideas had been colored somewhat, perhaps, by those experiences; but they were affected much more by the bitterness of the disappointment felt by him when France failed to lead Europe once more into revolution in the interest of liberal reform. So it was very natural that his first offering on the American lecture platform, which then offered a lucrative field of activity for a number of the leading intellectuals, and a priceless opportunity for adult education to the people, was "Democracy and

[1] To earn money by lecturing. Cf. p. 53.

[2] Letter to Kinkel, April 12, 1853 in C.S. MSS., W.H.S.

Despotism in France."[3] Just at the period when he was writing to Kinkel that he was less interested in the latter's account of European affairs than in that of the Kinkel family,[4] he was capitalizing his knowledge of European history on the lecture platform. The viewpoint of the cosmopolitan was also that from which his second lyceum paper was written, on "American Civilization," as were later ones on "Germany" and "Germany and France."

Not content with alternating between the mutually helpful and complementary activities of the popular lecturer and the political speaker, Schurz showed in his early lectures a certain tendency to combine the two. Just as he seems to have assumed that his wife would not be bored by his lengthy disquisitions upon political subjects in his letters to her—and apparently quite correctly, for she seems to have been genuinely and intelligently interested—so he rightly judged that his best work as a lecturer would be done on a historical subject and that the logical conclusion of such an address would be the application of its lessons to American politics.

It was also in keeping with the seriously educational and cultural tone at that time characteristic of the lecture courses that he aimed at making his lectures instructive. But if he assumed that Americans wished

[3] MS. in L.C.

[4] February 15, 1858, in C.S. MSS., W.H.S. Not included in portion printed in C.S., *S.C.&P.P.*, I, 33; *Lebn.*, III, 153.

to be instructed as to the lessons to be drawn from American conditions, as well as to those prevalent in France, he reckoned without his first host, at least.

On the lyceum platform, as in so many other less-profitable lines of business, he got his start in Watertown. With really notable skill, which causes one to conclude that one of the known results of the events of 1848 was that some German university was deprived of a right good professor of history, he reviewed the history of France under its three monarchies and two republics during the lifetime of the American republic. But to the historian's presentation of facts was added the ingrained liberal's interpretation of them, so that the account became a restrained but sorry tale of the loss of liberties through the apathy of the people which had permitted a pernicious growth of centralization in government. The conclusion, applying the lessons of French history to American conditions, was doctrinaire rather than partisan.

But it was considered partisan by the Watertown *Democrat*, and as such, was roundly condemned. Editor Ballou, for one, was less willing than Mrs. Schurz to listen to the expounding of those political views which seemed so profound to her but were so repugnant to him. So after conceding the literary and scholarly merits of the paper generously enough, the *Democrat* concluded with a rather ungenerous comment to the effect that Schurz had not quite recovered from his experience of getting all ready to climb upstairs and then seeing the stairs fall flat before him. It described him as a man ill at ease because of "the restless consciousness that somehow he ought to fill a place which he does not." But it virtually conceded the reality of the basis for such a feeling, in the action (or failure to act) of the "potato-diggers" who had let him down in the recent election.[5]

The stairs which would have led him to a temporary eminence in the not very exalted position of lieutenant-governor had indeed fallen flat before him. But it is perhaps well that they did. His real future lay in the field of national, not state, politics. A less direct but really quicker rise to fame was achieved by the individual activity from which the holding of a state office would not necessarily have barred him, but for which he was left more free, and into which he was in a sense driven by his failure to get the office. In the next state campaign, it was against some of his own conflicting impulses, and against the advice of many of his friends, that he sought the nomination for the office of governor; for it was felt by them that his national career would be hurt more than it would be helped by his getting it.[6]

Back to Watertown he came, then, but only for a

[5] *Watertown Dem.*, January 20, 1858. See also references to absentee rural vote, chap. vii.

[6] Letters from James Sunderland, June 2, from L. P. Harvey, June 21, from J. W. Hoyt, August 19, from George W. Tenney, August 19, 1859, in C.S. MSS., L.C.; from Schurz to Doolittle, August 18, 1859, in *Milwaukee* (evening) *Wisconsin*, May 17, 1906.

fresh start. From January to May Watertown saw
very little of him; he was absent from nearly all meetings of the common council during that period, and
very inactive when in attendance.[7] In the charter election of April 4 he was defeated by Philip Piper in the
election of a supervisor for the fifth and sixth wards,
but he continued as alderman.[8] He failed to attend
either the last meeting of the old council or the first
one of the new; but was named chairman of the committees on schools and education in the reorganized
body.[9] From May to July he was once more fairly
regular in attendance.

His attendance seems to have been fairly indicative
of his interest, which was going beyond Watertown to
an even greater extent than before. During the first
months of the year he was lecturing in Janesville[10]
(twice), in Madison[11] (tickets twenty-five cents at the
door), in Racine,[12] and elsewhere.

The comments of Rublee and Rufus King were
more favorable, of course, than that of Ballou, although based upon the same lecture. A more neutral

[7] Clerk's reports of meetings, *Watertown Dem.*

[8] *Ibid.*, April 15, 1858.

[9] *Ibid.*, April 22, 1858.

[10] *Janesville Standard*, as quoted in *Mil. Sen.*, February 1, and
again *St. Jour.*, February 2.

[11] *St. Jour.*, February 6; *Madison Democrat* and *Madison Patriot* quoted by *Mil. Sen.*, February 9.

[12] Letter from A. Winter, March 27, 1858, in C.S. MSS., L.C.

and more typical one than any of them was that of the *Madison Patriot:* "The disinterestedness of Carl Schurz as a politician has gained him many friends, as his literary excellence has gained him admirers."[13]

The word "read," used often with reference to his lectures, was used advisedly. It was his own, derived probably from the English word "lecture" by way of Latin and the German; his usual report to Mrs. Schurz was *"Ich lass. . . . ."* The newspapers describe his reading of lectures as restrained and quiet, with some show of repressed feeling but with no oratorical flights. He was the academic scholar whose aim was instruction, when lecturing, and not the crusader or the avenger into which he was converted on the campaign platform.

At the time of the charter election which cost him the office of supervisor, he was absent on a business trip to Philadelphia.[14] He returned, however, just in time to participate in a lively series of popular assemblies and sessions of the common council, at which State Senator Chappell, Democrat, of Watertown, was strongly censured, disowned by his party, and requested to resign because of his guilty participation in the La Crosse railroad scandal then being revealed. Chappell had been the successful candidate against Schurz in 1856.[15] No record is left to show that there was any

---

[13] *Mil. Sen.,* February 9, 1858.

[14] *St. Jour.,* April 21 and 22, 1858.

[15] Cf. chap. v, nn. 1 and 2.

special satisfaction for him in the discomfiture of his
rival, nor that his strictures against Chappell were even
as severe as against the partners of his guilt; but it is
of record that Chappell was still present in the state
senate in the following February to make an unsuccessful attempt to prevent Schurz's election to the board of
regents of the University of Wisconsin by a bitter and
violent attack upon him.[16]

From the teapot tempest over the misconduct of
the state senator from the Fourteenth District, Schurz
went out from Watertown again in mid-summer of
1858 to enter upon what was in many respects the happiest of his many relationships, that with the colleges
and universities. He was neither a born revolutionist
nor a natural politician. Just as he was driven against
his natural impulses into further revolutionary activity after the collapse of the attack on the Siegburg
arsenal, by the thought that he was irretrievably compromised already and that return was impossible, so he
was constantly driven on in politics by his insistent ambition at once to improve his own position and to exert
the most potent influence possible upon the course of
events, and by the thought that he could best do that
through political action. Where he was most perfectly
at home was in the realm of ideas, and among young
men not yet quite blinded by partisan or parochial prejudices, where theory, philosophy, idealism, and love of
beauty might have a chance. There he was happiest.

[16] *Assembly Journal*, 1859, p. 198.

Speculation may be idle, but it is interesting. One is tempted to think that if Schurz had succeeded sooner than he did in becoming financially independent, and if a professorship of history and government had been open to him which was big enough to offer fair scope for his ambition, he would have arrived sooner than he did at his decision that his influence could be exerted as effectively from outside official circles as from within. Then, occupied in a combination of teaching and occasional outside lectures and editorial-writing, or even with a few campaign speeches, he would have found his greatest peace and happiness in the quiet of academic surroundings. His fondness for, and courtesy to, young men, and his love of decorum and quiet were always notable;[17] while the disrespectful indignities of political campaigning, although they roused him to thrust and parry with the rest, were always extremely distasteful to him. Despite all his democratic theories, the only offices for which he was temperamentally fitted were those of patriarch in a university or a life-membership in the United States Senate, free from the necessity of exposing himself to the processes of election.

It was before the Archaean Society of Beloit that

[17] Compare the letter to Mrs. Schurz, from New York, March 12, 1858, in which he expressed his dislike for, and melancholy in, the din and confusion of New York, and longed for his "western freedom" and the quiet of his home: "Und das ich mich jetzt schon herzlich nach unsern stillen Hause im Westen zurücksehne, ist gewiss (C.S. MSS., W.H.S.).

his first important college address was given, July 13,
1858. It was, "by common consent, assigned first place
among the many addresses that made the week a feast"
—the only unfavorable criticism, in striking contrast
with his political oratory, being that its delivery was
"not sufficiently forceful."[18]

Like the Madison address of the year before, it is
interesting as an early example of his use of English.
It shows a bold and colorful style, marked by occasional awkwardness of grammar or oddity of phrase,
with here and there a slightly mixed metaphor like that
describing the German barbarians as having invaded the
Roman Empire and "grasped the ideas of Christianity
with a bloody but firm hand." But it was characterized
also by a beauty and classical accuracy of diction that
would have been notable at any time or place and
would have done credit to the most formal public func-
tion of any university.

His subject was "Americanism"; his viewpoint
that of the cosmopolite. Much of the same material
was used in later addresses on the same subject; and
this one fathered the better-known Faneuil Hall speech
in Boston nearly a year later, in much the same fashion
as that in which the Madison one did the Springfield,
Massachusetts, philippic against Douglas.[19]

He began with an artistically beautiful description
of the region of his birthplace, followed by a well-told

[18] Correspondent of *St. Jour.*, July 11.

[19] Both of the latter will be reviewed briefly, below.

tale of his boyhood, of his seeing a train of emigrants starting off for America, and of his youthful dreams of the land to which they were bound; then of the up-risings of 1848, the failure of which had left America "the last depository of the hopes of all friends of hu-manity." In a swift summary the whole history of civilization in Europe was called upon to yield the story of the growth of the concept of democracy, the Ger-man conscience in the Protestant revolt and the Anglo-Saxon capacity for action and for the practical conver-sion of ideas into institutions being presented as the most potent factors in the process, no French contribu-tion being much emphasized. True Americanism, he said, must be the product of the best thought of Europe —but an improvement upon it. It must be a productive cosmopolitanism.

Fundamental principles upon which it should be based were natural equality, with no special privileges to any class; reciprocity; and a general solidarity of interests. With such principles the "American move-ment" was incompatible. He called it wrong in prin-ciple and mistaken in policy. It was wrong, he said, to make a natural right appear as a man-made privilege; it was bad policy to give a group the right to revolt by denying them the right of self-government.

Liberty was another fundamental principle. Peo-ple must learn self-government by practice; they had never been successfully taught it, without; and democratic institutions would survive the mistakes of democracy better than the abuses of bureaucracy.

Tolerance was another. It was not presented as a moral duty or as something of sentimental virtue only, but as the best defense against radicalism or fanaticism of any sort.[20]

Slavery was naturally in direct conflict with his conception of democracy; and no one except Lincoln, whose ideas and expressions on the subject were often almost identical with his, could state that conflict so clearly or convincingly. Differences in training and temperament caused, or enabled, Lincoln to reduce their kindred thoughts to simpler terms; but otherwise it might have been Lincoln who said at Beloit:

> The oppressive spirit of the master is no less inconsistent with true democracy than the oppressed spirit of the slave. . . . . The struggle that is going on about that system concerns the vitality of our democratic system of government, and the decision of that struggle will decide of the stability of this republic.

Reasoning by "the logic of things and events," he predicted a speedy end of slavery.

Applying the principles of Americanism to practice and policy he gave it as his opinion that they could be followed best by the avoidance of centralization in government, whereby the people might be governed as little as possible and left to manage all the details of government for themselves. No aggressive wars could

[20] Compare quotation on censorship, chap. ii, n. 17, p. 24.

consistently be waged, nor forcible annexations be made.[21]

Coming, at length, to the matter of education, he pointed out that it, too, should be democratic, the leaders of thought being careful not to lose touch with the people, as too great a diversity between the intellectual standards of different classes would destroy the unity which should exist between them. Both practical and cultural studies should be pursued, but the latter received his strongest support.

As to the purposes of education, it was his view that "in all educational institutions of a higher order, the development of the ideal nature of man should be a principal object," and that toward such a purpose, the study of classical languages and literature would contribute by their "harmonious beauty of form" as well as in other ways. The ultimate and most essential object should be to bring the people up to the level of their rights, to make "of the cosmopolitan nation organized in the republic of equal rights, ... the representative people of the modern age."

His conclusion was a stirring defense of idealism. Ideals were likened to stars; they could not be reached, perhaps, but they could be used as guides for one's course; and their guidance could be accepted as right. One of the greatest dangers to true Americanism he saw in the prevalent tendency to concede to corruption,

[21] The Democratic party was at that period frankly one of expansion; the Republican, strongly anti-imperialistic.

dishonesty, coarseness, prejudice, and indifference the *right* to exist just because they *did* exist. Students and other young men should keep alive the ambition to rise, in their ideal nature, above the level of such thinking.[22]

A fortnight later, the same address, in substance, was delivered before the Literary Society of the University of Wisconsin.[23] Both addresses, being of a non-political nature and being delivered in the brief season of truce occasionally allowed between the frequent elections in Wisconsin, escaped the outbursts of destructive criticism which usually awaited those of a more debatable nature. There was an abundance of praise from the faithful Republican papers of Madison and Milwaukee,[24] and either favorable notice or none from those of the opposing faith.

The *Press* and *Tribune* of Chicago, the city which was soon to be the scene of a more sensational and therefore better-known, though no more worthy, effort, found in him someone quite different from the other "mouthpieces of democracy," and ended its report of the address with the following comment: "Mr. Schurz not only showed that he was well read in universal history, but that he had *considered* the same and

[22] Miscellaneous pamphlets, Beloit College, W.H.S.

[23] Two days after that, he was nominated in a meeting of the board of regents for a professorship of modern languages, and five weeks later given a temporary appointment to the board itself by Governor Randall.

[24] *St. Jour.*, July 19, 21, 28; *Mil. Sen.*, July 20, 21.

generalized upon its great facts until they had crystal-
lized into broad forms of universal truth in his mind."
He had "been over the whole ground," and amazed his
hearers by the wide range and accuracy of his knowledge. "He spoke like a statesman and a man," present-
ing to his hearers "gems of thought expressed in words
that would not have dishonored the lips of Bacon." He
had won their enthusiastic admiration by his "spirit,
genius, learning, and great ideas."[25]

Before re-entering the political arena with him, by
taking up the Chicago speech of September, 1858, on
the "Irrepressible Conflict," it seems justifiable to do
violence to the time element in his story and to maintain, rather, the continuity of his connection with the
institutions of higher learning, by completing the account of his relations with the University of Wisconsin.

On August 31, 1858, on the resignation of Professor E. S. Carr from the board of regents, Schurz
was appointed by Governor Randall to fill out the un-
expired portion of his term; but in the following
February he had to be re-elected by the legislature, to
succeed himself. The re-election was won, but only
by what appears to have been a strict party vote, the
parties having agreed beforehand upon other nominees
but having been divided upon him.[26] At least two

[25] *Chicago Press and Tribune; Mil. Sen.,* July 20, 1858.

[26] Schurz, 63; Metz, 49. See *Assembly Journal,* 1859, p. 198;
also Bruncken, "Pol. Act. of Wis. Ger.," p. 207.

reasons for his being thus singled out for opposition were revealed. One was in the protest of the *Madison Argus* against the "abolitionizing of the University";[27] the other, in the feeling which Chappell doubtless had against him as a result of the events of the preceding summer in Watertown. His support was partially attributable, no doubt, to his position in his party, no matter whether the choice of a man for such a position ought to have been so based or not; but there was more than his own wish to prompt him to think, as he did, that the speech on Americanism had won it for him.[28]

On the board of regents, his record was as notable for regularity of attendance as that of his second year on the Watertown common council was for irregularity. One of his activities was to secure the appointment of Dr. J. P. Fuchs to a professorship of modern languages, for which he had himself been considered at the last meeting before he became a member of the board, in the summer of 1858, and which he offered to Althaus in November, 1858.[29] The idea of bringing Kinkel there was also considered, raised in correspondence, and dropped.[30] He was active on committees dealing with the subjects to be taught, the number and

[27] January 28, 1859; compare editorial opposing partisanship in such matters, *St. Jour.*, January 20, 1859.

[28] Letter to Adolph Meyer, October 18, 1858, in C.S. MSS., W.H.S.

[29] Letter to Althaus, November 5, 1858, in C.S., *S.C.&P.P.*, I, 37.

[30] Letter, Kinkel to Schurz, August 19, 1860, in C.S. MSS., W.H.S.

compensation of instructors, the reorganization of the
university after the inauguration of Dr. Barnard as
chancellor, and the organization of preparatory, normal, and scientific departments.[31] His relations with
Chancellor Barnard seem to have been amicable and
pleasant.[32]

His public reception of Barnard was certainly cordial enough. He was chosen by the board of regents to
deliver the address of welcome to the new chancellor
on their behalf on the occasion of the chancellor's
formal inauguration, July 27, 1859. Two days later,
the board passed a resolution to the effect that his address, with those of Julius T. Clark and the Honorable
Henry Barnard on the same occasion, should be printed
in pamphlet form, the number of copies to be deter-
 ---ed by the executive committee. This motion was
      ved by a second one by Mr. Hobart, soon to be
      emocratic candidate for the office of governor
      appear in two joint meetings with his fellow-
      Schurz, to the effect that the secretary should
      synopsis of the proceedings and use his own
      t as to what portion should be published and
      omitted.[33] This proved to be a means of sup-

[31] *Record of Board of Regents, University of Wisconsin,* pp.
215–58; *St. Jour.,* January 19, 1859.

[32] Letters from Barnard, June 25, 1859, asking him to speak at
commencement, and from Mrs. Barnard, June 29, 1860, in C.S.
MSS., L.C.

[33] *Board Record,* B, p. 224 (July 29, 1859).

pressing it entirely; for the speech delivered by Schurz
was not included in the formal records of the University.[34] His being a Republican was no crime in the eyes
of Rublee, however, and the *State Journal* carried its
usual full account of it.[35]

His introduction, as always, was brief. It consisted
of a reference to the Indian traditions of the hill on
which the University buildings stood, and to the triumph of western enterprise which was represented by
the institution itself.

Results like these mark the geographical expansion of civilization. While flattering our pride, they must stimulate our
ambition, for this result is very far from being the ultimate end
to be attained. It is a mere frame to be filled, an arable field to
be cultivated. . . . .

He referred to the fact that almost all the people
then residents of Wisconsin had migrated there for
purpose of improving their condition, and to the en
boldness, and steady application to the hard wo
subduing the wilderness and harnessing its
which had been necessary to build up the co
wealth so rapidly. Such purposes and such w
called the mechanical arts and sciences into service
large extent, and with admirable success.

But here we arrive at the dark side of the picture; for it
cannot be denied that the spirit of materialism has almost exclu-

[34] Statement of Mr. M. B. Olbrich, Madison, member of the
board of regents.

[35] July 27, 1859.

sively presided over our councils and impressed its mark on the character of society. What I shall say on this point is not intended to be a reproach, for this tendency of our pursuits was natural in our circumstances and almost unavoidable. But in candidly criticizing the condition of things I mean to point out the dangers we have to obviate and the duties which devolve upon us. For, when speaking of the generation to which we belong we ought not to forget that up grows another, for which we are responsible.

The pursuit of gain exercises indeed a strengthening influence on the understanding. It stirs up our inventive genius, it sharpens our faculty of calculation, it keeps awake our caution, it electrifies our energy. But I think that people who devote their whole attention to the practical occupations and concentrate their whole mental activity on material pursuits, must in the course of time become low in their feelings. Dealing always with the actualities, basing all their calculations upon facts as they are, and all their hopes upon their calculations, they will by the force of habit become inclined to forget that a great many things are not what they ought to be. It being the principal object of their ambition to surmount the obstacles which stand in the way of their material ends, they become apt to regard even scruples of conscience as mere obstacles to be overcome. When the pursuit of gain has once taken exclusive possession of a human soul, it may make a man prudent and energetic, but it will rarely develop his higher attributes.

It breeds that peculiar class of men who call themselves practical par excellence. Priding themselves upon the small and not always glorious successes of their material pursuits, they treat with contempt all ideal views which address themselves to the nobler interests of human nature, and sneer at everything that rises above the dusty level of every-day notions.

These are the worshippers of success, regardless of the means by which success may have been achieved. They acquiesce in every thing that is, because it stands there with the brutal force of reality. They concede even to a manifest wrong *the right* to exist, because it *does* exist. Such men have a dangerous influence upon the tone and character of society. Successful in attaining their material ends, they often appear wise, when they are only sly, efficient when they are only trickish, smart when only base. They often succeed in palming off for the true wisdom of life, what is only the mean shrewdness of selfishness. When such men succeed in determining and controlling the current of public opinion and in fixing the standard of honor and morals, they will soon corrupt the principles, lower the feelings and emasculate the ambition of the popular heart. Incapable of grasping broad and generous ideas, unwilling to acknowledge the relation between practical occupation and the higher ends of society, they will view everything from the stand-point of immediate expediency. Appreciating only what is immediately useful and profitable, they will reduce even the destinies of a great people to the small dimensions of a mercantile speculation.

It is but natural that a tendency like this should have left its mark on the character of a social organization which like ours was founded on the basis of material interest.—This is the point where a higher order of popular education has to interpose its ennobling influence. . . . .

As at Beloit, he defined the primary purpose of education as being the development of the characters of men, based upon intellectual training but going far beyond the point of merely imparting to them a mental technique. That was necessary in elementary and vocational schools, and in the university as well; but it was not enough, there.

And again, as at Beloit, he spoke a word for the classics.

They lead us irresistibly to an ideal view of men and things. In the literature of antiquity, man is magnified beyond his natural dimensions. We see him mostly divested of the common cares of life and occupied with great things only, whether absorbed in meditative contemplation or active in the great affairs of State. The misty distance which separates us from him like an airy vision lends grandeur to all his motions and attitudes; and this spectacle of human life on the grandest scale transports us above the common level of every-day sentiments. —This is not all. Classical literature excels all other in the harmonious chastity of form. In a democratic organization of society like ours, we become apt to forget what influence the beauty of form exercises upon the mind. It imparts to us a sensitiveness of feeling which often, almost imperceptibly, determines the current of our thoughts. . . . . In my opinion, the stronger we lean to the side of the material, the more it is necessary that we should promote, by education, the culture of the ideal. In cultivating the noble and beautiful along with the useful, we should evade that onesidedness of character which may make a people for a while rich but not good, powerful but not great.

The effects of this kind of education will not be confined to those who have enjoyed its immediate benefits. Where men live in a state of social and political equality, they will educate each other by mutual influence. As a scientific and aesthetic education gives tone to the mind and even to the character of an individual, so a great number of men so educated will give tone to society and what comparatively few have acquired by individual efforts will in varied and multiplied form be transmitted to many by daily social intercourse. For it is the instinctive desire of man to improve himself, and he will choose his models above and not below his level. In this manner, a higher order of education will become a common good, and its ennobling and refining influence will gradually pervade all classes of society.

Such are the ends to be accomplished by the University. It has to educate not individuals only, but the people. . . . .

Such were the views on education of a man who combined in himself a student's taste for reading, a musician's feeling for harmony, an artist's love of beauty, and a scholar's zeal for truth. As a member of a university faculty he would have served the cause of education well. But long before the occasion of the address above quoted, political life had again claimed him.

As one of the results of the Beloit address he was invited to take part in the political campaign in the autumn of 1858 in the state of New York, but declined, as he had already promised to spend a week in the Lincoln-Douglas campaign in Illinois and to do some work in his own Congressional district.[36]

It was easy for him to support Lincoln against Douglas, as Lincoln's views on slavery were so nearly identical with his own, and as Douglas was always a *bête noire* to him. Both he and Lincoln found it difficult to understand how anyone outside the plantation belt could honestly befriend slavery; and a sympathetic response must have been roused in him by Lincoln's statement that he had always hated slavery, he thought, as much as any abolitionist, and that he had kept quiet about it until the Kansas-Nebraska agitation came up, only because he had "always believed that everybody was against it, and that it was on the way of ultimate extinction."[37]

[36] Letter to Gerrit Smith, C.S., *S.C.&P.P.*, I, 35.
[37] *Chicago Press and Tribune*, July 10, 1858.

As for Douglas, Schurz was entirely unable to agree to Greeley's suggestion that since he had opposed the Lecompton Constitution in Congress, and in the hope that popular sovereignty would exclude slavery in the territories, Douglas should be unopposed in Illinois. There is nothing in his letters now available to show that he had any knowledge that Greeley was not alone in his support of that suggestion.

In a letter to Theodore Parker, September 20, 1858, William H. Herndon claimed to have positive knowledge that in October, 1857, Greeley, Seward, and Thurlow Weed had met Douglas in Chicago and promised to support him for the Senate in 1858, with the understanding that he should give way to Seward as a presidential candidate in 1860 and wait for his own turn at that office later.[38] It is apparently upon that letter or upon a similar belief that Newton's statement is based that some such indorsement of Douglas was proposed "as the only means of breaking the hold of the Southern oligarchy upon the Northwest,"[39] and Channing's that "it may well be that Lincoln entered into the fray to prevent a coalition between Douglas

---

[38] Newton, *Lincoln and Herndon* (Cedar Rapids, Iowa: The Torch Press, 1910), p. 215. Ex-Senator Beveridge (*Abraham Lincoln* [2 vols.; Houghton Mifflin Co., 1928]), entirely discredits the story of this meeting, and puts down its acceptance by Herndon and others to the remarkable credulity induced by the partisan excitement of the period. II, 558, 592, 624, 639.

[39] *Ibid.*, pp. 147–48; W. E. Dodd, "The Fight for the Northwest in 1860," *A.H.R.*, XVI, 776.

and the Republicans, more especially those of the Northeastern States."[40]

One of the northeastern Republicans who was for a time actively friendly to the idea was Henry Wilson, of Massachusetts,[41] who became the political friend of Schurz, as for some years Seward was his political idol. Schurz's writings do not disclose that he suspected either of them of complicity in a scheme which, as coming from Greeley, he later condemned as an "unholy alliance" and "a revolting idea to the class of men to which I [he] instinctively belonged."[42] They do reveal that he keenly enjoyed seeing Lincoln cut, "with the sword of his logic," through the "adroit sophistries" by which Douglas tried to wriggle out of the dilemma in which he was placed by the conflict between his own doctrine of popular sovereignty and the Dred Scott Decision.[43]

His most significant performance in the Lincoln-Douglas campaign was the delivery, in Chicago, of the speech which was afterward widely circulated under the name of "The Irrepressible Conflict." It was delivered four weeks before that of Seward which, by virtue of Seward's greater prominence as a presidential possibility and his reputation as a radical antislav-

---

[40] Channing, *op. cit.*, VI, 229; *Chicago Press and Tribune,* November 9, 1858.

[41] Letter, Wilson to Parker, February 28, 1858; Newton, *op. cit.*, 147–48.

[42] C.S., *Rem.*, II, 88.   [43] *Ibid.*, p. 86.

ery leader of years' standing, as well as of the character of the phrase itself, put those words into such
wide circulation. It anticipates every idea in Seward's
Rochester speech of October 25, 1858; but, for that
matter, so had Seward himself, and others, often
done.[44] Only that single suggestive phrase and the ear
of the nation, which he soon won but which Seward
already had, were lacking.

Speaking at a large mass meeting held for the
purpose of ratifying the Republican state nominations,
Schurz neglected the nominations almost entirely and
plunged at once into a new presentation of his favorite
antislavery theme.

A democratic system of government, although it may overcome local and temporary inconveniences, cannot bear a direct
contradiction between political principles on the one and social
institutions on the other side. Such inconsistencies will and must
bring forth questions and conflicts involving the very foundations of popular liberty. They may appear in different shapes;
but when once they have taken possession of the political arena
they will overshadow all other issues. Everything also will be
subordinate to them; they will form the only legitimate line of
distinction between parties, and all attempts to divert public attention from them or to palliate them with compromises or sec-

[44] Substantially the same doctrine had been stated before, by
Seward at Cleveland in 1848 and at Auburn in 1856, by the *Albany
Evening Journal* in 1850, by Benjamin Wade in the United States Senate, and by Henry Ward Beecher in 1854, by the Richmond *Enquirer*
in 1856, by Lincoln in June and Carl Schurz in September of 1858
(Frederic Bancroft, *Life of William H. Seward* [2 vols.; New York
and London: Harper & Bros., 1900], I, 462).

ondary issues, will prove futile and abortive. Their final decision, one way or the other, will decide the practical existence of
a people. . . . .

With the explanation that he would refrain from
talking about the sufferings of slaves or "the sinfulness
of sin in general," he proceeded to a consideration of
the effect of slavery on republican governmental institutions.

Such a contradiction is that between liberty, founded upon
the rights of man, and slavery, founded upon usurpation; between Democracy, which is the life-element of our Federal Constitution, and Privilege, which is the life-element of the slaveholding system and of Southern society. . . . . When in a
democratic community there is a powerful individual or an association or a class of men, whose claims and pretensions are in
conflict with the natural rights of man in general or with the
legitimate claims of individuals, and who deem their own particular interests above all other considerations, we may well say
that the liberties of the people are in danger. When such an individual or class of men find that their claims and pretensions
cannot stand before a free criticism, they will spare no effort to
impose silence upon the organs of public opinion; they will use
force, if argument is of no avail.

Absolute monarchies manacled the press to prevent
opposition to tyranny, he said. An aristocracy or
association of great merchants and planters might do the same.
. . . . To such an interest the people will have to submit, or
against such an interest the people will have to fight. There will
be a struggle, and there must be a victory, final and conclusive.

The slaveholding interest, he said, constituted just
such a menace to the peace of the republic, having al-

ready destroyed all liberty, even for whites, in the South, and dictated the policy of the Democrats in the North.

Shall we sacrifice our liberties to that institution, or that institution to our liberties? *I hold that no interest which is incompatible with a free expression of public opinion can have a right to exist in a democratic organization of society.* . . . . Your standard bearer [Lincoln] is right. A house divided against itself cannot stand. It must fall unless it cease to be divided. . . . . We must either abandon the principle of equal rights even among white men. . . . . [and] formally recognize slavery as the ruling interest in our national policy, or we must deny it the recognition of any national right, and confine it to a merely local existence under positive state legislation. This is the alternative.

He said that Douglas was inconsistent with his own Senate record, not to see the issue. "Perhaps it does [did] not suit him" to see it. After numerous "final settlements" the slavery question had arisen again, "like Banquo's ghost"; but he blamed the slaveholders for the renewed agitation.

Slavery can never live unless it rules, and it can never keep peace, unless it dies. . . . . There is and will be war in the Cabinet of the President, war in both houses of Congress, war in every state legislature, war in the smallest log-hamlet in the west, aye, war in every heart, until that all-absorbing conflict is settled. . . . .

Then he came again to Douglas and, after a wickedly sarcastic slash at the latter's notable "refinement of style," denounced popular sovereignty as a counterfeit—"merely another embodiment of the old contra-

diction between political and social institutions." He
called it a wild delusion—

if not an imposition and a lie. . . . . The Dred Scott decision is
the most logical construction of the Kansas-Nebraska Bill, and
acknowledged to be such by Mr. Douglas himself, and his quib-
bles between his squatter sovereignty and that decision are the
most contemptible subterfuges by which ever a pettifogger made
himself ridiculous. Thus Mr. Douglas's popular sovereignty is
based upon a presumption *in favor of slavery,* upon the presumption that slavery exists *of right* where it is not prohibited
by positive legislation!

The founders of the Republic, he said, had considered slavery a local institution, allowed it to exist
only on sufferance, and barred it where they could—in
the Northwest Territory.

The manifest tendency was to remove the contradiction
between the fundamental principles of our government and a
social institution by sacrificing the latter.[45] The Nebraska Bill,
in opening the national territories to slavery, elevated slavery
from the rank of a mere obnoxious fact to the rank of a national principle. . . . . What is nonsense in theory you will
never make sense in practice. . . . . [Friction is certain] when
the construction of ambiguous measures is put into the hands of
conflicting interests.

Slavery must expand, to survive; so pen it up! If the slave
power cannot rule unless you lie prostrate on your knees,—rise!
. . . . If they will call this revolutionary, let them call it so.
It is the Revolutionary spirit to which this country owes its existence.

He continued in a tone equally aggressive and uncompromising: "And now let us hear no more of the

[45] Compare with Lincoln's Cooper Union speech of 1860.

fanatics of the North disturbing the poor slave-holders in their meek philanthropic intentions." The "bragging cavaliers" of the South were warned that the Roundheads of the North, reinforced by a solid column of Germans and Scandinavians who knew "how to handle a musket," stood ready for them.

But his conclusion was more conciliatory. He predicted that if the designs of the slaveholders were resisted, the voice of reason would slowly prevail in the South and slavery be gradually eliminated by action of the South itself, with happy results for the nation.

When slavery ceases to be a power, it will cease to exercise its demoralizing influence upon our national polity. No anti-democratic tendency will any longer rule the government of this country. The people will no longer be distracted and confused by the conflict of antagonistic principles. Our foreign policy will no longer be subservient to the grasping appetites of the slave aristocracy, but to the real interests of the whole country. Our influence with foreign nations will rise in the same measure as they have reason to believe in the sincerity of our democratic professions. The policy of our national parties will no longer be determined by a sectional minority, and the most venal of our politicians no longer sell themselves to an anti-democratic interest, which has waxed to be a ruling political power.

The South, he thought, had no reason to fear actual interference with slavery in the states where it existed; and he saw no real danger of disunion. "And yet, there is one great and real danger to the Union: It is, that by abandoning the great principles of the

Revolution, it might miss the very aims and ends for which it has been instituted."[46]

In 1865, when the Civil War had given him another estimate of the strength and spirit of the South, he still thought that

a properly firm stand by the North against secession talk would have deterred Southern leaders from making the movement, or the people from following them, and the Northern Democrats from encouraging them to think that the North would not fight to preserve the Union.

Secession had come, he thought, because such statements as his were not believed in the South.

If the threat of disunion had from the beginning been treated by every Northern man with becoming indignation and contempt, and if the South had been made to understand the North on that matter, no secession movement would have taken place. Slavery would have been gradually reduced and extinguished, as designed by the statesmen of the Revolutionary period.[47]

The speech made a great sensation. The "gifted German" had been brought to Chicago because of his

[46] Delivered at Mechanics' Hall, Chicago, September 28, 1858. Printed in full by *Chicago Press and Tribune, Chicago Journal, Quincy* (Illinois) *Republican, St. Jour., Mil. Sen., New York Tribune,* and others. Not in Bancroft edition, C.S., *S.C.&P.P.;* included in C.S., *Speeches* (Lippincott [1865] edition); also in numerous campaign pamphlets. Schurz wrote to his German friend Althaus that a million copies had been made. Letter of November 5, 1858, in C.S., *S.C.&P.P.*, I, 37.

[47] Footnote by Schurz, in *Speeches* (Lippincott edition), pp. 29–31.

Wisconsin reputation, to speak first in English and to address the Germans of Chicago in their own language on the following night, which he did with good effect. But the address above reviewed represented the greatest step he had yet taken toward gaining national renown. When it was printed in full by the widely read *New York Tribune*, with the following favorable comment, he was a "made" man, as an orator. The influential eastern organ called the address "certainly one of the ablest and clearest expositions yet made of the chief political questions to be settled in the coming elections," and of Schurz himself said: "He speaks with an eloquence, force, and intelligence which prove him an invaluable acquisition to his adopted country."[48]

To the copy of the foregoing, and to its own previous encomiums, the *Wisconsin State Journal* added the following: "His political sentiments are not mere matters of convenience and expediency, but the earnest convictions of an enlightened mind and a noble heart." It is submitted that, while such praises sound extravagant, they appear from the record to have been very well merited.

Subsequent speeches were made by him in both English and German, in Quincy and Peoria, Illinois. The former of these was set for the evening of the day on which the Lincoln-Douglas debate was held in that city. That arrangement was responsible for his first meeting with Lincoln, and the incident marked

[48] Quoted by *Mil. Sen.*, and *St. Jour.*, October 21, 1858.

the beginning of a very cordial friendship which endured and grew, in spite of occasional differences of
opinion, until Lincoln's death. To it we are also indebted for the best description of a Lincoln-Douglas
debate by an eyewitness, that of Schurz in his *Reminiscences.*[49]

Aside from a surprised and wondering sort of admiration for Lincoln, and an intensification of his dislike for Douglas, the most dominant impression carried away from the Illinois campaign by him was that
party regimentation had been carried to the point where
it had become a serious evil. Of course, it was also an
obstacle in the way of the younger and still proselyting
party. People who felt that, because they had always
belonged to the Democratic party, they were in duty
bound to follow it, needed to be encouraged to break
away from such party discipline. In this case, with
Schurz, expediency and principle pointed in the same
direction; but it would be unjust, and contradictory
to his record, to say that expediency pointed the way
for principle.

In all his speaking, he urged independence of
thought and judgment upon his hearers;[50] while his

[49] C.S., *Rem.*, II, 90–94. In Quincy and Peoria, both of which
were Democratic strongholds, the Republican vote was greatly increased that year, a victory being won in the former and a defeat suffered in the latter, by a very narrow margin. The gain was largely
German, but it would be hard to evaluate Schurz's share of the credit.
Cf. *Chicago Press and Tribune,* November 9.

[50] C.S., *Rem.*, II, 100.

own creed as an Independent was fully laid down in an address in Milwaukee in November, 1858, on "Political Morals."[51] But that occurred at a meeting held in celebration of a victory which he had helped to win; so a return to Wisconsin politics must precede it.

In contrast with the German Republicans of Illinois, who, under the leadership of Koerner, Schneider, Butz, Hecker, Hoffman, and Schurz, were winning the gratitude of the Republican press[52] by doing a large share toward piling up Lincoln's futile majority over Douglas,[53] those of Wisconsin were none too well pleased with their affiliations. There had been widespread resentment among them because of the defeat of Schurz in the preceding year; and the malcontents were led by one who had been among the first to join the new party and who had himself suffered a similar fate in 1855—Carl Roeser.[54]

As early as February, 1858, Roeser had complained, editorially, that Germans were appointed by the Republicans only to such positions as those of

[51] *Infra.*

[52] Cf. *Chicago Press and Tribune,* October 26 and November 9, 1858.

[53] The total vote cast for Lincoln men was 190,000, that for Douglas men, 174,000. Yet the state house of representatives stood 35 to 40, and the state senate 7 to 8, in favor of Douglas. Seven hundred and fifty-four votes in "Egypt" offset 1,000 in "Canaan." "The Democratic vote showed an increase over 1856 not accounted for by increase in population" (Allen Johnson, *Stephen A. Douglas,* pp. 391–92; Newton, *op. cit.,* p. 223).

[54] *Supra,* chap. vi, n. 9, and chap. vii, n. 8, pp. 142 and 164.

watchmen, messengers, firemen, and the like, or at
most made sergeant-at-arms, and that even such appointments as those were to be gained only through
Carl Schurz, "their Catholic patron saint, to whom
Germans must turn to secure the granting of their de-
vout requests from the Omnipotence of Republicanism."[55] That many of them did so is attested by Schurz
in his *Reminiscences* and by a considerable number of
letters in the manuscript collection in the Library of
Congress, from Germans scattered from coast to
coast.[56]

On August 21 a conference of German Republican editors was held in Milwaukee, Schurz being present as editor, still, of the *Watertown Volks-Zeitung;*
and a manifesto was issued over his name, with those of
Cordier, Lindeman, Domschke, Winter, Ritchie, and
Roeser, reproving the party for what they considered
its incomplete and insincere repudiation of Bashford
and his associates, and demanding that the morals of
the party be improved and its principles clarified if it
were to have their continued support.[57]

That the Germans of both parties were dissatisfied
at that period is further indicated by an editorial in the

[55] *Manitowoc Pilot,* quoted in *Madison Demokrat* (German,
Democratic), February 16, which confessed that the attitude of the
other party was not very different.

[56] E.g., letters from Louis Markgraff, Fort Bridger, W.T., August 20, 1857, and one Weltzenstein, of New York, November 21,
1857, in C.S. MSS., L.C.

[57] *Mil. Sen.,* August 30; *Madison Demokrat,* September 3.

Madison Demokrat after the election[58] and by a letter from Judge Timothy Howe of Green Bay to Schurz, telling him that many of the Germans there, formerly Democratic, had left that party in anger because of the printing of the Prussian-spy libel against him and because of slurring remarks about his "gift of gab" by the local papers[59] and by the *Beaver Dam Democrat*.[60]

Despite all this dissatisfaction, Schurz worked with the party during the entire campaign. He was present at the party convention of the Third Congressional District, September 7 and 8, and served on the committees on credentials and resolutions.[61]

At the state convention in Madison, October 5, he was again, as usual, on the committee on resolutions, and as its chairman, made its report.[62] He was also a member of the committee appointed to prepare an address to the voters for general circulation.[63]

In his address on behalf of the committee on reso-

[58] December 31.

[59] Letter of December 29, 1858, in C.S. MSS., L.C. In the light of subsequent events, the conclusion of that letter is doubly interesting: "I do not know what your plans are, for the future, but do not doubt they are worthy of you and of the Republican cause. Being so, I shall be very glad to promote them."

[60] December 22, *Mil. Sen.*, December 29. Schurz was defended as vigorously as ever by Dr. Otto Stannis, the *Sentinel, Journal, Volksfreund,* and many others.

[61] *Oshkosh Democrat*, quoted by *Mil. Sen.*, September 9.

[62] *Mil. Sen.*, October 8.

[63] *Ibid.*

lutions he anticipated his own action in the conventions of 1860 by stressing the importance of the party's sticking to its principles instead of trying to attract Douglas men by broadening or lowering them. Although it was ostensibly directed at the Democrats, it was possible to suspect that he intended a double application to be made of his denunciation of party disciplinarians who would "drive and dog men like sheep, turn them to pasture like sheep between elections, and fleece them like sheep."[64]

Both the platform and the address to the voters, in the writing of which it is fair to assume that he took an influential part, denounced corruption in both parties, as well as the action of Congress regarding Kansas, and declared their opposition to the acquisition of further territory by the United States, along with their support of the Union and of the rights of the individual states.[65]

Although the convention as a whole was a stormy one,[66] Schurz had at least the satisfaction of securing, from the party, declarations in accordance with his views. After his return from the Illinois campaign, he was active in that of Wisconsin until the election, his most important effort being made at a meeting in Mil-

[64] *St. Jour.*, October 5.

[65] *Mil. Sen.*, October 14.

[66] The *Madison Demokrat* (German, Democratic) reported (October 8) that Sherman Booth was twice thrown out and twice readmitted.

waukee in conjunction with his friend and confidant of the next two years, Congressman John F. Potter.[67]

Following the election, the Republicans had an opportunity to celebrate that rare thing, a victory in the Milwaukee district. At the celebration meeting, the principal address was delivered by Schurz; and in it, he practically served notice upon the party that he served it as an Independent. He was still as strongly opposed as ever to the idea of a separate German party, thinking it best that Germans in America should act only as American citizens, but he was willing to use them as the nucleus of the larger group of independent citizens who might hold the balance between the parties and tip the scale in favor of the one which conformed most closely to their principles. In their rivalry for the support of such a group, both parties must raise the standard of their political morals.

"Barstow and the balance" being still apparently in good standing with the Democrats, while the Republican corruptionists had been pretty generally repudiated, it was still possible, without incongruity, for a respectable Republican to call the Democratic party "corrupt." To these circumstances, Schurz referred in the following paragraphs:

We have, indeed, achieved a surprising success in this city. But, glorious as it was, I warn my Republican friends not to mistake its meaning. It was, indeed, a most hearty endorsement

[67] *Mil. Sen.*, October 1, 2; *Chicago Press and Tribune*, November 6, 1858.

of our noble representative in Congress, and a crushing verdict against the corrupt party organization which so long has ruled the destinies of this district; but the glorious majority we gained was not a mere partisan majority; the victory we achieved was not a mere partisan victory. It was the victory of political honesty over corruption; was the victory of moral independence over moral servitude, of manhood over servile partisanship. Glory enough for the Republicans that the voice of political independence spoke in their favor.

I know, and you all know, how this great result has been obtained. It was the German vote that defeated you so often; it is the German vote that gives us now so brilliant a victory. . . . .

But now, having preached the true principles of American liberty to the Germans, you must allow me to explain the true feelings of my countrymen to the Americans. I entreat you, let not your victory lead you into the dangerous decision, that the Germans, after having shaken off the yoke of one party despotism, are ready to take upon their necks the yoke of another. After having raised the banner of independence today, they are certainly not prepared to surrender it tomorrow. They will follow the lead of political honesty, so long as it is true honesty that leads them. . . . . But I tell you, my Republican friends, and I speak with the full earnestness of my heart, I sincerely hope that my countrymen who have emancipated themselves from party despotism, will never again consent to be made use of in corrupt combinations and political tricks, that they will never again be parties to dirty political trades and corrupt bargains, *on whatever side they may be attempted.* And I do not hesitate to prophesy, that if the Republican party should be unfortunate enough to entangle itself in the same network of corruption with which the Democracy is choking itself to death, the people will strike it down with the same crushing verdict under which Hunkerism is sinking now. And in that case, I confess my heart would behold with grief and sorrow its degradation, but would have no tears for its defeat. . . . .

Great principles, he said, could be defended only by an honest party. So if the liberties of the people were to be safe, the standard of political morals of the parties, as such, must be kept high, while the political action of the masses must be dictated by their consciences. To their ideas of expediency and party discipline he attributed the numerous and inconsistent changes of the northern Democrats on the slavery question, which he traced at length.

How is this? Is it probable that a man should have been truly and deeply convinced of the truth of any one of those principles, if he was always ready to abandon it for another? Is it possible that those who changed leading doctrines as easily as they changed their clothes, should have cared for principle at all? Could it be that true conviction ruled them? And if it was not conviction that ruled them, what concern could their conscience have in their politics?

They were ruled, he said, by blind devotion to party:

But what feelings have our hearts, what designation has our language, for those who in a free country like this, unfettered by any kind of despotism, with no terror to over-awe and no force to coerce them, sacrifice their convictions and their consciences to a moral tyranny of their own making? And those we find in our midst. Do not try to disguise the fact. . . . . How many are there who immolate their consciences, their convictions, all their moral independence, on the altar of a savage idol, whose name is Party! How many submit to a thraldom, which is the more shameful as it is unsupported by force, and rests only on the slavish propensities of its devotee! . . . .

He refused to accept even the split between the Douglas and Buchanan groups of Democrats as evidence of moral independence on the part of either, but called their leaders only two rival pretenders, each aspiring to be dictator of "the party."

He stated that the indifference of the voters bred the worst evils:

It is said that there are but few men who, however honest otherwise, can withstand the seductions of power. If this is true, what effect must it have on leaders, when they see that, in point of principle and political doctrine, they can do with the masses whatever they please? When they find out that they will be obeyed and applauded, no matter what their commands may be? That there is no somerset [sic] so glaring, no sophistry so absurd, and no doctrine so atrocious, but that the rank and file will accept them? That they may sell themselves, and sell others, without being rebuked? That they may even squander the money and rob the treasury of the people, without being held to account? Nay, that their very depravity gives them a claim to the protection of their party? Let me tell you, that not only the politicians debauch the consciences of the people by contempt of principle, but that the masses demoralize the politicians by culpable indulgence. . . . .

Where this course would lead, if the masses persevered in it, I do not know. But I do know that there is no remedy, unless we put an axe to the roots of the evil, and I consider this one of the most important parts of the mission of Republicanism.

It must be our principal object, not only to catch the people's votes for our candidates, but to enlist in our cause the people's conscience. We must encourage moral independence in politics; we must admonish every man to think and reason for himself, to form his own convictions, and to stand by them; we must entreat him never to accept, unseen and uninvestigated, the principles and opinions of others, even if they be our own. Let those who follow your lead believe in your words because what you say is true, and not because you say it. Do not object that this will loosen the party organization and destroy its efficiency. For our cause is great, and the principles of Republicanism stand on the firm ground of the rights of man. The more they are investigated, the clearer they stand in the open light of day, the more invincible they are. If what you say is true, you need no tricks and no deception in order to make people believe. Address yourselves to their moral nature, and their conscience will enlighten their understanding. Then you will organize the party of independent men. This independence will keep the rank and file vigilant, and this vigilance will keep the leaders upright and honest. . . . .

I have no faith in the wisdom of that policy of expediency which consists in forming alliances with heterogeneous elements, and in compromising leading principles for the sake of gaining numerical strength. Temporary successes may indeed be achieved by such operations, and short-sighted men who consider themselves eminently practical, may glory in their exploits. But they are only too apt to forget that serious moral defeats have sometimes been suffered in apparent victories, and moral victories have been won in apparent defeats. . . . .

Our true strength consists in the honest confidence of the people. . . . . I believe that even in politics honesty is the best policy. I believe in the possibility of reforming our political life. . . . .

Republicans, if you claim the right to be severe on your opponents, you must be no less severe against yourselves. Let the Republican organization be a permanent investigating committee, watching its own members, and let it be understood that, if it is not sufficient excuse for a scoundrel to be a Democrat, a scoundrel is, in your eyes, ten thousand times more damnable if he pretends to be a Republican. . . . .

He closed with an expression of his pleasure at seeing the close combination then being formed be-

tween the "honest and liberty-loving Germans" and
the Americans of like mind, and an exhortation to
them to realize and to safeguard their identical interests.[68]

Again he went almost unscathed by hostile comment. He had a reputation as an orator by then, and it
was generally conceded that he had lived up to it. Numerous laudatory editorials were written, from which
but a single sentence will be quoted: "Whether you
hear him or read him, the lightning leaps along your
veins."[69]

But the full import of what he said was not then
realized, or else many of those who then praised him
so highly chose to overlook it, so long as he supported
the party—unless, indeed, they thought him insincere.
If they had understood and believed him, or paid any
real attention to his record in the two years then ending, Republicans need never, in later years, have been
surprised to find him an Independent, an inexorable
enemy of corruption and dishonesty in every form, an
anti-imperialist, an advocate of civil service reform, a
quickener of the public mind, and a practical idealist.
Nor could charges of party treason have been so freely

[68] Delivered at Albany Hall, Milwaukee, November 18, 1858.
Printed in Lippincott edition but not in Bancroft edition of *Speeches;*
also in contemporary newspapers; *Mil. Sen.,* November 20, 27; *St.
Jour.,* November 22.

[69] *Fond du Lac Commonwealth,* quoted by *Mil. Sen.,* November 27.

preferred against a man who had taken no oath of allegiance, save to principles and his own honest mind and conscience.

In the time allowed by another brief cessation of political activity, Schurz turned again to plans for his private establishment. Immediately after his Chicago address in September he had been urged to set up a law office there, and attractive prospects had offered themselves. But all such inducements were at once matched by Milwaukee business men; and as his success as a lawyer would be expedited by the *ziemlich bedeutende* reputation which he already had in Wisconsin, he chose Milwaukee.[70] An added attraction of that city was that, so long as he was unable to sell out, in Watertown, Mrs. Schurz and the children might continue to live there, at least during the summers, and he could return there frequently by train. In winter they found quarters in Milwaukee.[71]

On January 1, 1859, he entered into a law partnership with Halbert E. Paine;[72] but it must be said that his law business never fulfilled his sanguine expec-

[70] Letters, C.S. to Adolph Meyer, October 18, 1858, in C.S. MSS., W.H.S.; and James Abrams, Milwaukee, to C.S., December 7, 1858, in C.S. MSS., L.C.

[71] Letters, C.S. to Althaus, November 5, 1858, in *Lebn.*, III, 157; E. L. Buttrick, Milwaukee, to C.S., September 15, 1861, in C.S. MSS., L.C.

[72] Original letter of agreement, in C.S. MSS., L.C.

tations.[73] It never had a chance. Within less than a
year, the "business card" of Schurz and Paine disap-
peared from the *Sentinel* column which it had headed;
in 1860 the office served only as political headquarters
for Schurz,[74] a sort of point of departure and return;
and in 1861 both men went off to national service.
That their friendship was lasting, cordial, and affec-
tionate, and that Schurz was encouraged by his partner
to follow his fortune in lyceum work and in politics, is
attested not only by Schurz in his *Reminiscences*[75] but
by the Paine letters.[76]

While not at all steadily occupied as a lawyer,
Schurz was busy enough otherwise. A radical must,
apparently, always be active; and he was then one of
the radical wing of the Republican party—made so,
very largely, by his views on slavery. As early as February, 1858, he had written to Kinkel: "All things
disappear before the overshadowing magnitude of the
question of slavery, and all efforts to conceal it are of
no avail."[77] In November, in a letter to Althaus, he

[73] Letter to Meyer, October 18, 1858, *supra*, n. 70.

[74] He was president of one of the three German Republican clubs
of Milwaukee (*Mil. Sen.*, January 11, 1859).

[75] C.S., *Rem.*, II, 104–5.

[76] C.S. MSS., L.C. Schurz wished to take Paine to Madrid with
him as Secretary of Legation, in 1861, and when Secretary of the
Interior to have him as Assistant Secretary; but each time, Paine
found a bigger job—a colonel's (later brigadier general's) commission in the first case, and the Commissionership of Patents in the second. Paine's permanent post-war residence was in Washington.

[77] February 15, 1858, in C.S., *S.C.&P.P.*, I, 34.

had expressed the fear that the Republican party would not be wise enough in its policies to hold the ground it had gained.[78] In December, in one to Potter, he protested strongly against any proposal to consolidate with the "American" party, or to compromise with the idea of popular sovereignty, which he called "the same humbug that it was two years ago . . . . [and] the very same principle against which our party was originally organized."[79]

The slavery question did, with him, so overshadow and dominate all others that his hatred for that institution, and for the Fugitive Slave Law which supported it, somewhat emotionalized his thinking on the constitutional question of State rights, and led him to take a position on that question which he afterward conceded to have been an extreme and a wrong one, and which materially affected his position in Wisconsin politics.

He afterward said that it was moral sentiment which had so colored his constitutional views:

Indeed, it was the prevailing moral sentiment in the North, not that it would be sinful to violate that [the Fugitive Slave] law, but rather that it would be sinful to obey it. And nothing can be more futile, unstatesmanlike, as well as inhuman, under a popular government, than the enactment of laws that are offensive to a moral sense springing from an intuitive conception of justice and the natural sympathies of the human heart.[80]

[78] November 5, 1858, *ibid.*, p. 36; *Lebn.*, III, 156.

[79] To Congressman John F. Potter, December 24, 1858, in C.S., *S.C.&P.P.*, I, 38; *Mil. Sen.*, April 1, 1900; Jensen, *Wisconsins Deutschamerikaner*, I, 317.

[80] C.S., *Rem.*, II, 110.

The general opposition to the law in Wisconsin greatly heightened the excitement over the various developments of the Glover case, which arose from one of its violations. In 1854, a certain Joshua Glover, a negro laborer in Racine, had been seized as an escaped slave by federal officers and a man who claimed to be his owner. As the party passed through Milwaukee, the negro was released by a mob, headed by Sherman Booth, and shipped to Canada. Booth was arrested on a federal warrant but released on a writ of habeas corpus issued by Judge Abram D. Smith, of the Wisconsin supreme court, on the ground that the Fugitive Slave Law of 1850 was, in the judge's mind, unconstitutional. His opinion was upheld by the supreme court of Wisconsin, which claimed the right, in a habeas proceeding, to pass on the constitutionality of a federal law. That decision, however, was reversed by the United States Supreme Court in a decision written by Chief Justice Taney, in which the court conceded that a state court could issue a writ of habeas corpus in such a case, but held that a federal deputy was not bound to recognize it except by showing his warrant as cause for the arrest.[81]

The battle of writ against warrant continued, and Booth was intermittently in and out of custody until March, 1860, when warrant finally won. By that time, Booth had so alienated Schurz and other respectable men by his scandalous personal conduct, that his

[81] *Ibid.*, II, 107–113; files of *St. Jour.* and *Mil. Sen.*

cause was supported by them only for the sake of the principle involved in the case;[82] and the state court had lost its unity, as men realized the danger to the Union involved in their former nullification doctrines.[83]

When the case was finally dropped, Schurz was still connected with it, having been chosen to plead for a new writ of habeas corpus before the state supreme court—a duty from which, because of the personal aversion he had come to feel for the man who had placed his name before the 1857 convention, he was glad to be relieved.

In March, 1859, however, before Booth had given him cause for such feelings, and while the only personality involved was that of the admirable and attractive Byron Paine, Schurz had gone with zeal into the campaign for the election of a supreme court justice, advocating the choice of Byron Paine, who had been Booth's counsel.

The enemies of the Fugitive Slave Law naturally, unless deterred by scruples against defiance or nullification of a federal law, wished to see the election of a judge who would continue to uphold the Smith deci-

[82] Letters, C.S. to Mrs. Schurz, March 2, in C.S., *S.C.&P.P.*, I, 108; *Lebn.*, III, 174; March 14, 1860, in C.S. MSS, W.H.S.; and Brisbane to C.S. April 4, 1859, in C.S. MSS., L.C. Accounts of criminal trial of Sherman Booth on a statutory charge in Milwaukee, in contemporary newspapers, March 21, 1859, and following dates.

[83] The conservative group was led by Judge Timothy Howe and Supreme Court Justice Dixon, who was re-elected in April, 1860.

sion, declaring it unconstitutional. That Byron Paine
did after election; but, like Schurz and H. E. Paine,
when the cotton states had carried that doctrine to its
logical conclusion by secession, he joined the army to
uphold the Union.[84]

On March 23, 1859, Schurz delivered his fateful
speech on "State Rights and Byron Paine." It was less
a direct attack upon the federal courts and the federal
law in question than an elaborate and spirited defense
of those who defied the one and nullified the other. It
is unnecessary to review it in detail. It was a brilliant
piece of debating. Federal district judges were dubbed
"petty proconsuls." The principle of "government by
consent of the governed" appeared as a statement that
it was "better that the Union be 'a rope of sand' around
those who are willing to stay together, than a rope of
hemp around the neck of Liberty." But his theory of
democratization through decentralization was as old as
the Union, and his fear of the abuse of the judicial
power to construe the constitution as old as constitutional government, though incited by new applications
of it in the cases of Dred Scott and Sherman Booth. As
for the nullification which he advocated, it had changed
its essence as little since 1832 as he himself said popular sovereignty had since 1856.[85]

His conclusion is of personal interest, for the reader at once brings Schurz into mind instead of Paine,
when reading his argument that Paine's youth need

[84] C.S., *Rem.*, II, 115.   [85] Cf. n. 79.

not be considered as a disqualification for the office. Schurz called it folly to judge a man's wisdom or his experience by his years, a folly of which few would be guilty save those who, even with years, would never gain experience.[86] (He was himself then almost a month less than thirty years of age.)

The radical, or State-rights, wing of the party being still the dominant one, the address was well received, generally. Byron Painc won the contest by a majority of 10,000;[87] and Schurz enjoyed the rare experience of seeing his arguments, rather than himself, attacked by the opposition. A rather wild attack was made by the *Milwaukee News,* dealing only with trivialities;[88] while a very able and closely reasoned one appeared in the German *Madison Demokrat.*[89]

The criticism which counted, however, was not public, and came in letters, not to him but to his friends. Timothy Howe, who three months before would have been "very glad to promote" the plans of Schurz, they being worthy of him and of the party,[90] found in his views, as expressed in that speech, a danger to the party. He wrote to Rublee:

[86] Speech printed in *Mil. Sen.,* March 24; German translation in Jensen, *op. cit., supra,* n. 79 (Fünfter Anhang), I, 334.

[87] *Mil. Sen.,* April 11.

[88] *Mil. News,* March 25, quoted and answered in *Mil. Sen.,* March 26.

[89] April 1, 1858.

[90] Letter to C.S., December 29, 1858, in C.S. MSS., L.C., *supra,* n. 59.

It is a splendid thing, but he has struck the cause of Republicanism the hardest blow it ever received. Hitherto, it has only been denounced as fanatical. Hereafter, it will be stigmatized as traitorous and disloyal.[91]

In two letters to John H. Tweedy in April, Judge Howe expressed his fear that the Republican party would go to extremes on a doctrine which Calhoun had been unable to get the American people to accept, and which seemed to him no more acceptable when presented by A. D. Smith or Carl Schurz. Schurz could count upon Howe's opposition to the movement already on foot, to make him governor, in the election of that year.[92]

Howe was, at least, consistent in the matter. He adhered to his belief in the subordination of state courts to national law, at a time when it was extremely unpopular and cost him a long postponement of his election to the United States senatorship. He and Schurz were always personally friendly, but they opposed one another steadily on the State-rights question through 1859 and the February convention of 1860. He also led a strong opposition to the candidacy of Schurz for the Republican nomination for the office of Governor, on the same grounds.

The immediate results of the speech in support of Byron Paine, however, were much more pleasant. His

[91] Letter to Rublee, March 27, 1859, in *Mil. Sen.*, December 15, 1889.

[92] Letters of April 11 and 17, 1859, Howe to Tweedy; quoted by Jensen, *op. cit.*, I, 177, 315.

reputation as a speaker was enhanced; and to his already fairly numerous lecture engagements[93] was added an invitation to appear as the spokesman of the Northwest on the State-rights question at a Jefferson Day dinner in Boston.[94] Opposition to the Fugitive Slave Law was particularly strong there, and had given the State-rights theory a popularity in that section of the country such as it had not enjoyed since the days of the Hartford Convention.

It was hoped that he might be used, also, in the intramural fight in the Republican party over the proposed Two-year Amendment, which provided that, in addition to the requirements for United States citizenship, a naturalized citizen must be for two more years a resident of the state before being permitted to vote in state elections.

The measure was aimed chiefly against the Irish, who presented a peculiar problem in Massachusetts, where they were especially numerous. Family feeling being strong among them, Irish immigrants brought with them the aged and infirm members of their fam-

[93] Indicated by letters from E. M. Randall, Waukesha, January 1, and H. G. Lachmund, Sauk City, January 14, in C.S. MSS., L.C.; *Racine Advocate*, January 7; *Watertown Dem.*, March 3, 1859; etc.

[94] Copy of his reply to E. L. Pierce in C.S. MSS., L.C. Unless his expenses were paid—$100 at least—he would be unable to go, "having been bled to a considerable amount in our own judicial canvass, here." He said he considered it a sacrifice, even then, to go, and would be willing to do so only if Pierce thought he could "do a great deal of good there." Pierce apparently did, both before and after the event.

ilies, to be supported by the able-bodied, who were usually poor and ignorant. Hence there was much pauperism among them. It was perhaps partly due to their hardships and strange surroundings that a proportionately large number of them were soon to be found in penal institutions and insane asylums. As voters, they were nearly all Democratic and easily manipulated.[95]

So much in explanation of the apparently reactionary policy of the majority. Some of the more liberal Republicans, however, among them E. L. Pierce and Henry Wilson, opposed it; and under their management, and with their indorsement, Schurz spoke twice more against it, at Faneuil Hall, Boston, April 18, and at Worcester, April 20.

At the Jefferson Day dinner, the doctrines presented by him were strictly and appropriately Jeffersonian—equality, self-government, limited powers of the central government, protection by habeas corpus against "anything not law."[96] The great effort of the series was made in his address in Faneuil Hall on "True Americanism," which need not be reviewed here at length, as it resembled very closely that delivered before the Archaean Society of Beloit College in the preceding summer, with changes made only in its special application to the circumstances under which it was delivered. Hospitality, cosmopolitanism, democ-

---

[95] Channing, *op. cit.*, VI, 129.

[96] *Boston Daily Advertiser,* April 14, 1859; *Boston Journal,* account copied in *St. Jour.,* April 18. Verbatim account from *Boston Courier* in *Advertiser* of April 15.

racy, equality, solidarity of interests, and toleration
were presented as the attributes of true Americanism;
and his hearers were warned that liberty could never
be safeguarded by despotic measures which were at
variance with those attributes.[97]

In the speech at Worcester he quickly reviewed
the arguments of the Faneuil Hall address, and passed
on to a discussion of the part to be played by the Northwest in national politics, warning the party that without the Northwest the Republicans could never elect a
president and that, among the potential voters of that
region, a not inconsiderable element was composed of
Germans, who were likely to be alienated by proscriptive legislation against foreigners.[98]

The *Boston Courier* called both of the last two
speeches "presumptuous";[99] the *Madison Demokrat*
scolded him for not speaking more boldly for the Germans in the first two, and for his "blind threats" in the
third. Pierce wrote to him: "You introduced a new
element into our civilization. Everywhere and by all
classes, except by the *Atlas and Bee,* your efforts have
been applauded."[100] It is no exaggeration to say that
the speeches attracted wide attention throughout the

[97] C.S., *S.C.&P.P.,* I, 48–68; *Boston Journal,* April 19, copied
by *St. Jour.,* April 27; *New York Tribune,* copied by *Mil. Sen.,* May 5.

[98] *Mil. Sen.,* May 2; *Madison Demokrat,* May 6.

[99] Quoted by *Boston Advertiser.*

[100] Letter from E. L. Pierce, Boston, April 28, 1859, in C.S.
MSS., L.C.

Northwest and that "Carl Schurz of Wisconsin" had become a name of significance.[101]

On his return to Milwaukee a perfect storm of editorial criticism arose. The *Chicago Times* and *Milwaukee News* attacked him for having failed to denounce the proscription of foreigners, while the *Cincinnati Commercial* and *Milwaukee Sentinel* praised him for having done so with such spirit and effect (although the amendment was adopted).[102] The *Madison Argus, Madison Patriot,* and *Janesville Times* denounced him for "joining in jubilee with those who had just deprived his countrymen of rights they gave to negroes"; while the *Boston Liberator* called his speech, "with one or two exceptions, the most eloquent address that has ever been made in Faneuil Hall for fifty years."[103] Schurz, who had written home from the East about the pleasures and rigors of "the lion business,"[104] wrote back East, from home, that he found himself "the best abused man in America."[105]

For him, personally, the venture into New Eng-

[101] The Faneuil Hall address was printed, in full or in summary, in papers of New England, New York, Philadelphia, Cincinnati, Chicago, Madison, Milwaukee, and elsewhere, and extensively commented upon.

[102] *Mil. Sen.,* April 26.

[103] *Ibid.,* April 27.

[104] Letter to Mrs. Schurz, from New York, April 21, C.S. MSS., W.H.S.

[105] Letter to E. L. Pierce, from Milwaukee, in C.S., *S.C.&P.P.,* I, 73.

land politics brought some immediate unpleasantness, as has been seen. It also brought its compensations, for he had won favor with the intellectuals there and made friends among them. He had won the praise of Josiah Quincy, Sr.[106] He had dined with Longfellow and Holmes.[107] Sumner, Longfellow, Charles Francis Adams, and others would assure him plenty of lecture engagements in New England.[108] He had also established personal contacts with the eastern Republicans Greeley, Weed, and Seward, in addition to those already named.[109]

He had, furthermore, come to be considered as the spokesman of the Northwest in the councils of the party as a whole,[110] and of the Germans in those of the West, even though some of them did choose to consider him a renegade and to repudiate him.[111]

[106] Letter from Pierce, May 5, 1859: "Your speeches have been praised beyond measure by all thinking men. On Monday evening, I met Josiah Quincy, Sr., of whom you have heard much. He said to me that the speech of Mr. Schurz was a remarkable one, very original, [and] that he had laid it aside carefully and wished he had a pamphlet copy" (C.S. MSS., L.C.).

[107] Letter to Mrs. Schurz, April 13–15, in C.S., *S.C.&P.P.*, I, 46–8; April 19, in C.S. MSS., W.H.S.

[108] Letter to Mrs. Schurz, April 21, in C.S. MSS., W.H.S.

[109] Letter to E. L. Pierce, April 22, in C.S., *S.C.&P.P.*, I, 72.

[110] Cf. editorial, *Boston Advertiser*, April 20.

[111] Letter to Pierce, May 12, in C.S., *S.C.&P.P.*, I, 75, asking Pierce to do something to clear him of blame for passage of the Massachusetts amendment, and expressing fear of loss of Wisconsin by the party in 1860; editorials of *Madison Demokrat* and others.

The national significance of the whole incident was best sensed by the *Philadelphia Press,* then Democratic, which wrote, in part:

> Politicians of all parties must not omit to notice the fermentation going on in the German mind of the United States, especially among the foreign-born Germans. The speech of Carl Schurz of Wisconsin, ... in Faneuil Hall, Boston, was a signal of the prevailing sentiment among those composing his nationality, as well as of their earnest determination for the future. He gave his hearers pretty distinctly to understand that under no circumstances would they operate with any party who did not oppose native-Americanism doctrines, and earnestly advocate civil and religious equality. . . . . Such leaders as Carl Schurz of Wisconsin, able and fearless men as they are, will submit to no compromise by which their particular opinions are to be subordinated in order to please another section of the opposition party.[112]

Such widespread resentment was, in fact, roused among the Germans by the Massachusetts amendment that it was necessary for it to be expressly repudiated by the Republican national convention of 1860, and for Schurz and others who remained loyal to put forth tremendous exertions in order to neutralize its effect and to win over a sufficient number of German voters to make a national victory possible. For he had spoken the truth at Worcester: without the Northwest the party could not elect a president; and without the foreign vote, which they so nearly threw away in spite of his warning, they could not have won the Northwest.

[112] Quoted by *Mil. Sen.,* April 30.

On his return from the East, in April, 1859, Schurz plunged into a voluminous correspondence, which is of greater interest to the student of his life than any of his other activities until the state convention in August. Some of it dealt with mortgage, interest, and tax payments and a patent deed for his land.[113] In other letters, arrangements were made for a number of lectures in Wisconsin, and for a series in New England in the following November and December, which were more lucrative than his earlier ones, paying a hundred dollars at Boston, where he was to be sandwiched between Henry Ward Beecher and Bayard Taylor, and predicting an average of fifty dollars for repetitions elsewhere.[114] By these and subsequent similar tours, the debts which burdened him so seriously, after 1857, were eventually lifted; but it took him several more years to free himself from them.

But the bulk of his correspondence in the early summer of 1859 was concerned with the prospect of his nomination for the office of governor. He professed to be lukewarm toward the project but was apparently willing to be persuaded. The manuscript collection in the Library of Congress contains only letters to him, in that period, and the other collection nothing

[113] Letters from Samuel Hastings, state treasurer, April 30, May 3, and July 7, and from John Jackson, May 13, July 19, in C.S. MSS., L.C.

[114] C.S. MSS., L.C. Letters from Charles W. Slack and others. Edward Everett was able to contribute $25,000 to the Mount Vernon fund exclusively from his earnings on the lecture platform.

at all; but three of his letters on the subject are available elsewhere. On December 24, 1858, he had asked Congressman Potter for advice as to whether he should, or should not, try to muzzle Roeser and others, who were already demanding his nomination. As reasons why he did not care for the office, he stated that it was not the object of his ambition; his political standing was such that he could do without official position; he cared only for a position of influence over the German vote in the northern states that would "tell in 1860." Further, he did not wish to stand in Harvey's way, and he had not the money for a campaign.[115] In August he asked Potter whether he could count upon the support of Doolittle;[116] but before he could possibly have received an answer, he was writing to Doolittle that the office would not satisfy any political ambition of his or be of advantage to him financially or politically.[117] He would value it only as evidence that the party was really free from Know-nothingism. As he "could not help taking a comprehensive view" of politics, he felt that, except for its importance in the next national campaign, a defeat would be a good thing for the Wis-

[115] C.S., *S.C.&P.P.*, I, 39; *Mil. Sen.*, April 1, 1900; Jensen, *op. cit.*, I, 319; C.S., *Rem.*, II, 132.

[116] Letter of August 12, in C.S., *S.C.&P.P.*, I, 77.

[117] The governor's legal salary was fixed by the constitution at $1,250. Randall had refused, as contrary to the spirit of the constitution, an indirect increase, which would have paid him an additional $2,000, as an expense account for visiting state institutions (*St. Jour.*, April 15, 1858).

consin Republican party, which needed to be whipped out of its petty sordidness.[118]

He seems actually to have been waiting for the party to draft him, supposing that they would consider it necessary to nominate some German for some state office. He would himself accept no position on the ticket save the first; nor would he suggest any other German for any other nomination.

His friends, taken all together, were as equivocal as he. Both Potter and Doolittle were then, and continued to be, very friendly to him;[119] but he was told that Potter favored Randall.[120] Many of his best friends hoped he would not be nominated, for fear that a defeat in the election, or the storms of criticism and factionalism which always beat around the governor, would ruin his chances for a national office, when he should be eligible for one. Harvey assured him that many considered him "the leading mind of the party" but the man whose future it could least afford to hazard.[121] Hoyt and Cover wrote in similar vein, while Tenney urged him to pay no attention to such talk, which was only meant to sidetrack him and make way for a placeman. His Republican fellow-regents

[118] *The Milwaukee Wisconsin*, May 17, 1906.

[119] Letter, Doolittle to Potter, September 10, 1859, in C.S., *S.C.&P.P.*, I, 79.

[120] Letter from J. W. Hoyt, August 19, in C.S. MSS., L.C.

[121] Letter of June 21, in C.S. MSS., L.C.

thought Randall would be defeated, even if nominated.[122]

But the friends from whom Schurz really needed deliverance were those of the group headed by Roeser, who demanded that he be nominated, "not because he is a German, but because we demand of the Republican party that through a public, distinctive action, namely the nomination of a foreign-born citizen, who has won for himself respect and consideration over the whole United States, it shall condemn the proscription of foreign-born citizens."[123] This expression of a German nativism, in the dictatorial form of a demand, was extremely irritating to the native-born Republicans and did great injury to the cause it was meant to serve.[124]

The party finally went before the people without a German on its ticket. The convention met on August 31, and Randall was renominated on the first ballot.[125] The defeat of Schurz may be attributed to five causes: Randall was in office and had made a very respectable record. There was strong opposition to Schurz, headed by Judge Timothy Howe, because of his extreme views on the State-rights question. There

[122] Letters from William Henry Brisbane, April 4; H. H. Davis, June 19, J. C. Cover, August 15; George W. Tenney, J. W. Hoyt, August 19; Henry Cordier, Watson, and others, in C.S. MSS., L.C.

[123] *Manitowoc Pilot*; Jensen, *op. cit.*, I, 176.

[124] Cf. editorial, *St. Jour.*, June 30, July 28.

[125] *St. Jour.*, August 31.

was still some reluctance to vote for a German. The bullying attitude of much of the German press, enraged by the Massachusetts amendment, alienated many who might have supported him. And many of his best friends wanted to "save" him from the nomination, for the sake of his future in national politics.

He was again offered the second place on the ticket, which he rather curtly declined.[126] While Roeser and a few others made his defeat the reason of a refusal to support the ticket,[127] Schurz told the convention that his reasons for supporting the Republican policies were larger than personal considerations, and that his loyalty could be depended upon. On his return to Milwaukee, the Republicans of that city, who had supported him strongly for the nomination, gave him an ovation as if he were a conquering hero—one doubly impressive, as being clearly a personal tribute to him, unsullied by sycophancy. In his response, he recognized the right of the convention to name whom it chose, spoke well of Randall's record, and showed resentment only at the offer of a lower place on the ticket than that which he had sought. He was hurt, he said, only to find that the party could still suppose that he belonged to "that class of politicians who will take *anything* in order to have

[126] *Mil. Sen.*, September 3.

[127] *St. Jour.*, January 30, 1860. It was ten days after the convention that Doolittle wrote to Potter that they must save Schurz, who was in danger of being "destroyed between German Know-nothingism and American Know-nothingism" (C.S., *S.C.&P.P.*, I, 79).

something." The greatest disinterestedness, he said, was "not devoid of a certain kind of pride."

As other Forty-eighters were doing all over the country, he urged his hearers not to generalize upon injuries of a local or personal character but to be guided, in making their choice between parties, by unbiased consideration of the greater essentials.

It is significant, too, to see the man who was, many years later, to leave the party in order to support Cleveland, saying: "I look upon the offices of our government not as wages to be paid for services rendered, but as an opportunity given for services to be rendered."[128]

He did serve the party, even in that campaign, but not immediately. Arrangements had already been made for a stump-speaking tour in Minnesota; and his help had been requested also in Illinois and Iowa,[129] where he was unable to give it. The Minnesota tour was one of triumph in the large towns and of novel frontier experiences in the small ones. The story of it is admirably told in his *Reminiscences*,[130] and still better in another of those remarkable series of letters to Mrs. Schurz.[131] He traveled 600 miles, made thirty-one speeches,[132] and was given a large share of the

[128] *Mil. Sen.*, September 7, 8; *Manitowoc Tribune*, September 10.

[129] Letters from H. A. Wiltse, Dubuque, August 17, October 5; and Daniel Rohrer, St. Paul, September 5, in C.S. MSS., L.C.

[130] C.S. MSS., II, 143–56.

[131] C.S. MSS., W.H.S.

[132] *St. Jour.*, October 20.

credit for the Republican victory there;[133] while his enemies in Wisconsin rejoiced that the "vagrant foreigner," having "exhausted his stock of vagaries" in his home state, had gone to vend them secondhand, elsewhere.[134]

By the middle of October he was back again in Wisconsin, where "the magic of his name" was sufficient to fill the largest hall to capacity on twenty-four hours' notice.[135] He was active until the election, the chief item of personal interest in the campaign being his joint appearances with Hobart, the Democratic gubernatorial candidate, at Sheboygan and Manitowoc. Of them the reporters wrote that "the feeling possessed them in the first ten minutes of Mr. Schurz's speech, that Hobart had the hand of a giant upon him, as upon a pygmy."[136] It appears from the full press reports of these two meetings that, in them, he really let his cleverness more or less run away with him. His speeches fairly blazed with wit, and with irony and satire of a scorching sort. Hobart having been forced to repudiate Barstow, he excoriated him for not having done it sooner, then wrote to Mrs. Schurz in wicked glee that

[133] *St. Paul Times*, September 27, *St. Paul Minnesotian*, October 14, correspondence from St. Paul, October 1, letter from Anoka, Minnesota, to *Janesville Gazette*, all quoted by *Mil. Sen.* through October.

[134] *Manitowoc Tribune*, September 21.

[135] Letter from correspondent at Sauk City, October 27, to *St. Jour.*

[136] Correspondence of *St. Jour.*, November 2.

he had been told that no one had ever been more completely "flayed, roasted, and cut up" than his fellow-
regent then was.[137] He said he had done it all good-
naturedly, and seems to have done it partly for fun. He
made no mention, even in the letter to Mrs. Schurz, of
the suppression of his address of welcome to Chancellor Barnard;[138] but if Hobart had been responsible for
that, it was amply avenged.

That year,[139] for the first time in their history, the
Republicans carried their whole state ticket; and
Schurz went off at once to New England to lecture on
Louis Napoleon and France.[140]

His intimate connection with Wisconsin politics
was almost at an end. But at the same convention
which sent him to Chicago as delegate-at-large and
chairman of the Wisconsin delegation to the Republican national convention, and thereby properly launched
him into national politics, there transpired also a fight
of his own making, which showed at once the strength
of his influence and the use he meant to make of it.

By the death of Chief Justice Whiton, another

[137] From Milwaukee, November 5, C.S. MSS., W.H.S.

[138] *Supra*, nn. 33 and 34.

[139] In 1855 the governor only had been a Republican; in 1857,
governor, state treasurer, and prison commissioner had been Republican, with the five other state officials Democratic (*Mil. Sen.*, November 12, 1859).

[140] Letter, E. L. Pierce to C. F. Adams, December 1, 1859. Copy
in C.S. MSS., L.C.

vacancy had been left in the state supreme court.
Neither of the two most prominent candidates for the
place suited Schurz—Dixon, because he was known, by
his record on the court, to be willing to concede the
right of the federal court to review the action of a
state court in a case involving the rights of a man accused under the Fugitive Slave Law; and A. D. Smith
for what the *State Journal* called "reasons satisfactory
to the convention."[141] Schurz put it more plainly, as
being because he "took the La Crosse bonds."[142]

That situation led him into a course which would
seem strange in him, unless viewed in the light of the
existing circumstances. He insisted upon a party nomination for a justice of the supreme court. This was a
new manifestation of his tendency to subordinate party
to other interests. He had constantly preached, but not
yet practiced, the abandonment of party for principle;
now he proposed to use the party organization to prevent the election of either an upright jurist who would
concede to the federal court the right of appellate juris-
diction in the Glover case, or a corruptionist who had
already denied it.

He had known beforehand that he would be al-

[141] *St. Jour.*, March 5; *Chicago Press and Tribune*, March 8.

[142] Letter to Mrs. Schurz, February 23, 1860, in C.S. MSS.,
W.H.S.; *Appendix to Assembly Journal, 1858*, and *Reports of Com-
mittees, State of Wisconsin, 1858*, pp. 8–10, quoted by Bessie Sara
Winn in *The Wisconsin Railroad Scandals of 1856*. He had found
$10,000 in bonds on his desk, "suspected" their source, and put them
into a bank, where he said they still were at the time of his testimony.
The report was made by the committee May 13, 1858.

most alone in his insistence on that point, but had written to Mrs. Schurz:

> I hear that the party of A. D. Smith is fairly strong. But I shall not depart from the principles which guide me in my political life, even if I should have to fight the whole Republican party. Be assured that you will have no need to be ashamed of your husband. I am going to convince the Republicans that my declaration of war against corruption was seriously meant, and that in this fight there is no quarter. The Republicans are not used to that, but if they want to have the Germans under my leadership, then they will have to get used to it.[143]

While he did not have to fight quite the whole party, he did stand alone in a long and spirited debate in the convention, against Timothy O. and James H. Howe, J. P. McGregor, and Giles, all of whom wished that no nomination be made and that the voters be left to choose between the two men who could then be counted upon to run as Independent candidates, Smith and Dixon. He won his immediate objective and secured the nomination of A. Scott Sloan; but in the course of the debate he was forced, by the insistence of T. O. Howe, to make the concession that he did not consider the State-rights doctrine an essential element of Republicanism.[144]

In the triangular contest which followed, Dixon gained steadily in strength as the electorate came to realize that the doctrine of State rights was a danger-

[143] Letter to Mrs. Schurz from Milwaukee, February 27, 1860, in C.S. MSS., W.H.S.

[144] *St. Jour.*, March 1–5; *Mil. Sen.*, March 1–5.

ous one. Even Roeser had written that it was a two-edged sword, more useful to the slavery party than to that opposed to slavery.[145] Then Sloan alienated some of his own potential support by his "Dear-brother" letter, which he permitted to be published, stating that he would have considered it an act of bad faith to accept the nomination except as an upholder of the Smith decision.[146] The letter was, of course, pounced upon by the Democratic press;[147] while many Republicans, Schurz included, considered the letter improper, as giving in advance his opinion on a case likely to come before him as judge. Schurz had advised him to publish nothing of the sort, but he wrote that the advice had come too late.[148] Sloan was defeated.

But even before Dixon's re-election, the Wisconsin State-rights movement was dead and the famous Glover case had come to a rather sudden end. In sharp contrast with the conduct of the Sloan brothers, in permitting the publication of the above-mentioned letter, Judge Byron Paine refused to sit on the case at all when Booth's final appeal for a writ of habeas corpus came before the court, because of his previous active identification with the case as Booth's counsel. Dixon

[145] *Manitowoc Demokrat,* quoted by *St. Jour.,* January 31.

[146] A.C. to I. S. Sloan, dated March 6, 1860, printed March 15, and following editions, in *St. Jour.* and others.

[147] *Madison Demokrat,* March 16.

[148] Letter, C.S. to Potter, April 12, in C.S., *S.C.&P.P.,* I, 111; Jensen, *op. cit.,* I, 322.

and Cole disagreed; the appeal went by default;[149] and Schurz, as already noted, was glad to be relieved of the necessity of completing the argument for the writ, already begun by his partner, H. E. Paine.[150]

His last prominent participation in Wisconsin state politics, as such, was fairly typical of his whole career —creditable to him personally, unprofitable to him politically, and just sufficiently unsuccessful to nourish the deprecatory charge that he was "impractical." Adhering still, with but slight change of views, to the rather radical doctrines which had been those of the party and had won his allegiance, three years before, he was reprobated by the centralists for his failure to swing away from those doctrines as rapidly as the majority.[151] Alienated from many of his fellow-radicals of the extreme anti-slavery and de-centralist groups, by his repulsion for the private misconduct of a Booth and the public malfeasance of an A. D. Smith, he was ostracized by them, as well.[152]

He was named spokesman for the state delegation without contest; but yet, in a sense, "Carl Schurz of Wisconsin" went to the national convention, and into national politics, alone.

[149] *Chicago Press and Tribune,* March 8.

[150] Letter to Mrs. Schurz, March 14, in C.S. MSS., W.H.S.; *supra,* n. 82.

[151] Letters from F. A. Ryan, April 18 and 30, 1860, in C.S. MSS., L.C.; *Madison Demokrat,* March 30, 1860.

[152] Speech of A. D. Smith, March 22, in *St. Jour.,* March 24.

CHAPTER IX

THE LINCOLN CAMPAIGN

THE great campaign of 1860 really began for Schurz in 1856. That for Fremont had never ended. His view of citizenship, as indicated in his Milwaukee speech on "Political Morals," entailed a continuous, active, vigilant interest in government on the part of the whole electorate; while that at Madison in the Wisconsin canvass of 1857 is a fair illustration of his manner of treating state elections, even those in which he himself was an actual or potential candidate, as entirely subsidiary to the greater national issues. His first invasion of the enemy camp, in Massachusetts, in the very heart of the district where the "American" movement was strongest, was no mere quixotic crusade for the relief of the Catholic Irish, though it was illustrative of his tendency to go where the opposition was strongest. It was rather an attempt to prevent state action which might hinder the national movement hoped for in 1860.

In January, 1860, he was again in New England, lecturing; and at the suggestion of Samuel Bowles, editor of the *Springfield* (Massachusetts) *Republican*, turned aside from France and Napoleon III to devote another entire evening to "Douglas and Popular Sovereignty." He could well hope for a better reception of that speech by the people of that section than of those of the previous year on Americanism; and from Bowles he could expect favorable publicity which would be useful to himself and to the cause with which he was identified. In neither of these anticipations was he disappointed.

In fact, it even won the approval of Jefferson Davis in spite of its antislavery tone, as having "silenced the charlatanry of Douglas."[1] However, it did not silence Douglas—nothing could do that. But the remark of Davis is an admirable indication of the attitude of the sections. The Republicans paid very little attention in 1860 to the extreme, or southern, wing of the Democrats, except to state the slaveholders' program with their own interpretation and to combat it openly but respectfully. To a certain extent the same was true of the southern Democrats in their attitude toward the Republicans. But Douglas, in spite of all efforts to hold together a party composed of both southern and northern elements, was the object of the bitterest attacks of both.[2] Considered as a traitor by one party and a moral renegade by the other, he had "put the sword of logic into the hands of his opponents, and

[1] C.S., *Rem.*, II, 163.

[2] Compare speech of Judah P. Benjamin in the United States Senate, May 29, 1860, expressing a preference for Lincoln rather than Douglas—if either must be accepted—on the ground that Lincoln was not much more unfriendly to slavery than Douglas and was at least sincere and honest. Quoted and indorsed by *Memphis Avalanche*, June 5.

tried to defend himself with the empty scabbard."[3] None wielded that sword more industriously than Schurz; and none, save Lincoln, so effectively.

The actual record of Douglas laid him open to attack. At Springfield Schurz began with a discussion of the legal basis of slavery much as he had done in his speeches in Madison and Chicago in 1857 and 1858. He maintained that a slave was held under the laws of a state and not under the Constitution or laws of the United States, that slavery therefore existed only by virtue of local law of a positive or municipal character, and that it had no foundation in the law of nature or the unwritten or the common law. Then he dwelt at length on the inconsistency of Douglas, who had said in a *Harper's Magazine* article, that slavery was "the creature of local law" but, in a New Orleans speech, that it had the protection of the Constitution just as any other property.

For such lack of logic, Schurz said

we might indeed feel tempted to pity him, if we had not to reserve that generous emotion of our hearts for those who are wrong by mistake and unfortunate without guilt. . . . . Dealing with slavery only as a matter of fact, and treating the natural rights of man and the relation between slavery and republican institutions as a matter of complete indifference, he is

[3] C.S., speech on "Douglas and Popular Sovereignty," Springfield, Massachusetts, January 4, 1860, in C.S., *S.C.&P.P.*, I, 79. First printed in *Springfield Republican*, January 12. Republican campaign pamphlet, in German and English, from February onward.

bound to demonstrate that slavery never was seriously deemed inconsistent with liberty, and that the black never was seriously supposed to possess any rights which the white man was bound to respect. [The Declaration of Independence and Ordinance of 1787 should have made that impossible.] But as Mr. Douglas had no logic to guide him in his theories, so he had no conscience to restrain him in his historical constructions.

He then proceeded to an exposé of Douglas's interpretation of the Declaration of Independence, which resembled that made in "The Irrepressible Conflict" even in its misquotation of the Declaration, with some rather shaky history thrown in, showing Washington participating in an imaginatively reconstructed debate on its adoption.

As for the intentions of the founders, he found them stated in the Ordinance of 1787.[4] "There it stands in characters of light. Only a blind man cannot see; only a fool can misunderstand it; only a knave can wilfully misinterpret it."

The Douglas doctrine was "unable to stop the war of principle and interests,[5] because it was at war with itself."

His peroration was devoted to the failure of Douglas to take a definite moral stand as to whether slavery was right or wrong:

[4] Again compare with Lincoln's Cooper Union address, delivered two months later: "As the fathers marked it, so let it be again marked, as an evil not to be extended, but to be tolerated and protected only because and so far as its actual presence among us makes that toleration and protection a necessity."

[5] Compare the speech on "The Irrepressible Conflict."

But one thing he does tell you: *"I do not care whether slavery be voted up or down."* . . . . Today, in the midst of the nineteenth century, in a republic whose program was laid down in the Declaration of Independence, there comes a man to you, and tells you with cynical coolness he does not care! And *because* he does not care, he pretends to be the representative statesman of the age.

Sir, I always thought that he can be no true statesman whose ideas and conceptions are not founded upon profound moral convictions of right and wrong. What, then, shall we say of him who boastingly parades his indifference as a virtue? May we not drop the discussion of his statesmanship, and ask, what is he worth as a man? Yes, he mistakes the motive power which shapes the events of history. . . . .

"There is the slavery question: not a mere occasional quarrel between the two sections of the country, divided by a geographical line; not a mere contest between two economic interests for the preponderance; not a mere wrangle between two political parties for power and spoils; but the great struggle between two antagonistic systems of social organization; between advancing civilization and retreating barbarism; between the human conscience and a burning wrong. . . . .

But as long as the moral vitality of this nation is not entirely exhausted, Mr. Douglas and men like him will in vain endeavor to reduce the people to that disgusting state of moral indifference which he himself is not ashamed to boast of. I solemnly protest that the American people are not to be measured by Mr. Douglas's self-made moral standard. However degraded some of our politicians may be, the progress of the struggle will show that the popular conscience is still alive, and that the people DO CARE.

Lincoln put all that more simply. He recognized a difference of opinion as to whether the slaveholder possessed the right (not specifically stated in the Constitution) to possess slaves as property in a territory. The framers of the government, he said, had purposely refrained from affirming any such right; and the Dred Scott Decision, which did so, had been arrived at only "in a sort of way," by a bare majority of judges, and was subject to change.

But Lincoln, too, could thrust the "sword of logic" through the gaping joints of the Douglas armor as readily as Schurz. The Republicans, he said, could afford to leave slavery alone where it was; but if their sense of duty forbade them to permit it to spread into the territories, then:

> Let us stand by our duty fearlessly and effectively. Let us be diverted by none of those sophistical contrivances wherewith we are so industriously plied and belabored,—contrivances such as groping for some middle ground between the right and the wrong, vain as the search for a man who would be neither a living man nor a dead man,—such as a policy of "don't care" about a policy about which all true men do care,—such as Union appeals beseeching true Union men to yield to Disunionists, reversing the divine rule and calling not the sinners, but the righteous, to repentance,—such as invocations to Washington, imploring men to unsay what Washington said, and undo what Washington did.[6]

In the hands of Schurz, the sword flashed more and was swung in more sweeping flourishes; in Lincoln's hands, it found its mark no more unerringly but

[6] Part of peroration of Lincoln's Cooper Union speech, February 27, 1860.

with more deadly effect. It is unfair to Schurz, in a way, to use his Douglas speeches as the basis of comparison with Lincoln, unless one remembers that in them he was seduced by his contempt for intellectual and moral obliquity into excesses not characteristic of his treatment of other subjects. But it should be noted that in essentials these very dissimilar men were in complete accord—they even worked together. A fortnight before the delivery of his own address, above quoted, Lincoln wrote to Schurz that he envied him because of the one it so closely resembled;[7] and another[8] got most of its teeth from a studious use of a "Douglas scrapbook" compiled by Lincoln and lent by him to Schurz.[9]

The identity of views existing between Schurz and Lincoln, both before and after 1860, was more marked than any differences between them. Such differences as were to be noticed were the product of contrasting temperaments and were rather those of expression than those of idea—differences which one would expect to find between two men both characterized by keenness and clarity of thought, whose expressions were marked alike by accuracy but those of one by brilliance and those of the other by simple clarity. No one realized the fundamental elements of the questions then at issue as did those two; and only the greater sim-

[7] Letter from C.S. to Mrs. Schurz, February 23, in C.S. MSS., W.H.S.; *Lebn.*, II, 173; C.S., *S.C.&P.P.*, I, 161, n. 1.

[8] "The Bill of Indictment," September 13, 1860, *infra*.

[9] Letter from Lincoln to C.S., July 28, 1860, in C.S. MSS., L.C.

plicity of his nature and his closer natural sympathy with the common people of America enabled the greatest product of American conditions to surpass their ablest student in his interpretation of them.

To the foregoing statements, a study of the speeches of the great Seward impels the reviewer to make no exception. In experience of public life, there was an enormous disparity between Seward and Schurz or Lincoln; but he was inferior to them in open-eyed observation of life. He perceived more political considerations than they did, but was less far-sighted or clear of vision than they in his interpretation of what he saw. He lacked their ability to grasp the results of his own philosophical analysis of public questions quite firmly enough to present them as clearly and convincingly as they; and he lacked both the unshakable tenacity of Schurz and the rugged sturdiness of Lincoln, which held them steadier than he.

Perhaps Seward, like Douglas, suffered at one period from what Schurz called "presidential fever" (to which Schurz himself, being foreign-born, was fortunately immune) and, at a later period, from its effects. At any rate, the modern reader finds his speeches, which were reported all too fully by an admiring northwestern press and in the tracts of the family paper, the *Albany Evening Journal,* good but not great. They were filled with padding—the weather, the scenery, the natural resources, and the local history of the communities in which he spoke. He was never successful in his attempts to talk down to his auditors, and did not find the way to lift them to his own level. He was inconsistent in denouncing the expansion proposals of the slaveholders, while talking casually in Kansas about the conquest of Canada as something certain soon to occur, and was excessively polite but insincere in assuring each audience that it was composed of the most intelligent, the bravest, and the most virtuous people in the United States.[10]

Still, at the Chicago national convention, Schurz was a willing spokesman for his state in favor of Seward in preference to Lincoln. His admiration for Seward as leader of the antislavery movement dated back to his first visits to Washington;[11] he had known Lincoln less than two years. He was, moreover, a man of the sort least prone to be affected by those prudential considerations which played so prominent a part in the choice of a supposedly "safe" man as the new standard-bearer for the party.

Seward was, in fact, neither his first nor his ultimate choice. A year earlier, in common with William Henry Brisbane[12] and Edward L. Pierce,[13] he had favored Chase; but in March he wrote:

[10] Series of speeches of 1860, *Albany Evening Journal Tracts*, Republican campaign documents of 1860, and contemporary press reports, 1855 onward, some cited above.

[11] Cf. chap. III.

[12] Letter, Brisbane to C.S., April 4, 1859, in C.S. MSS., L.C.

[13] Letter, Pierce to C.S., May 18, 1859, in C.S. MSS., L.C.

If Douglas is not nominated in Charleston, I consider it most probable that Seward will get the nomination in Chicago. If Douglas is nominated, Lincoln will probably be the man for our side. I shall be very well satisfied with either.[14]

Shortly afterward, with characteristic frankness, he voiced much the same opinion to Chase himself. From a lecture engagement in Cincinnati[15] he went to Columbus on invitation of Governor Chase;[16] and while there, was asked point-blank by his host (another victim of presidential fever) for his opinion as to the chance of his (Chase's) nomination. To so direct a question, he replied: "Governor, if the Republicans at Chicago have the courage to nominate an anti-slavery man, they will nominate Seward; if not, they will not nominate you."[17]

In April, shortly after his tour through Illinois, Indiana, and Ohio, where, as he went from place to place lecturing, he also busied himself with an attempt to establish a widespread system of correspondence, he wrote to Potter and Doolittle that he considered Seward's chances best. Bates could not get the foreign vote; but neither did he think Bates could be nominated. He himself felt a certain fondness for Wade

[14] Letter to Mrs. Schurz, March 9, 1860, in C.S., *S.C.&P.P.*, I, 111; *Lebn.*, III, 177.

[15] *Cincinnati Commercial*, March 19, 1860; *Mil. Sen.*, March, 26.

[16] Letter to Mrs. Schurz, March 14, in C.S. MSS., W.H.S.

[17] Bancroft, *Seward*, I, 526. Based on a statement made by Mr. Schurz personally to Dr. Bancroft. Duplicated in C.S., *Rem.*, II, 171.

but was sure that Lincoln would be stronger than Wade in the convention.[18]

It is clear, then, that Schurz had little fear of being disappointed in the candidate, but he was seriously concerned about the platform. In the Wisconsin convention of February 29 which sent him to Chicago, there had been little difficulty, except that already discussed, over the nomination of Sloan. He had receded from his old, extreme, position on State rights, and no pronouncement on that subject was made in the platform; instead, the party pledged itself to the integrity and maintenance of the Union. But the items which would be most attractive to the Germans were there—a protest against the Massachusetts two-year amendment, and a declaration in favor of the distribution of public lands in limited quantities on equal terms to actual settlers.[19]

Of the party as a whole, however, he felt less sure. It had ceased to be quite the crusading organization it had started out to be, and its control was passing into the hands of a seasoned and weatherwise group of managers of greater skill than its earlier ones—or of greater practical experience than formerly, in the case of those who had themselves been among the early leaders. A much more marked tendency was shown than former-

[18] Letters to Potter, March 17, from Columbus, and April 12, to Potter and Doolittle, from Milwaukee, in C.S., *S.C.&PP.*, I, 107, 113, 114.

[19] *Chicago Press & Tribune*, March 5, 1860.

ly, to appeal to economic interest by proposed tariff and homestead legislation, and to drop their high-sounding but incendiary references to natural equality and the rights of man, along with their customary references to the Declaration of Independence.

Realizing the tremendous advantage given them by the divided state of their enemies, the more practical of the party managers were not disposed to throw it away by an explicit avowal of adherence to the Declaration of Independence which might cost them the support of moderate men by making them seem dangerously radical. To many, the revolutionary philosophy did seem dangerous.

> By endowing men with inalienable rights superior to those of positive law, it was a standing invitation to insurrection and a persistent cause of anarchy. . . . . Friends of the Human Race were rarely to be found. Humanity was commonly abandoned to its own devices.[20]

John Brown's raid, and the almost universal repudiation of it, as well as the general moderation which marked Republican platforms of 1860 in comparison with those of 1856, may serve as examples.

With such conceptions of public opinion, many of the party managers thought that they saw their chances of success diminishing, especially in the doubtful and critical states, and that the cause of the loss was the radicalism of 1858 (which had then been opposed by

[20] Carl Becker, *The Declaration of Independence* (New York, 1922), pp. 257, 279.

Seward, Greeley, and others who had at that time favored Douglas).[21] There was a fairly strong feeling that it would be expedient so to word the platform as to make easy a fusion with other party elements; and even the usual references to the Declaration of Independence would have been omitted but for the bold insistence of Joshua Giddings and George William Curtis, a friend of Schurz from that day onward.

But there were others who opposed any such compromise. Lincoln was already on record against it.[22] Schurz, in accepting the nomination as delegate, had promised, in Madison, to oppose any lowering of the Republican platform, done for the purpose of "picking up the ancient mariners of shipwrecked parties, who might still be clinging to the remnants of their shattered crafts." Such action, he said, would be ultimately inexpedient, for it would lose for the party the honest enthusiasm of the people and, while making some doubtful states sure, would "make some sure states doubtful."[23]

At Chicago, just prior to the national convention, a special meeting of the German delegates had been held. That was contrary to the judgment of Schurz, who had all along insisted that as Americans and as Republicans they might demand what they would of the party, but

[21] W. E. Dodd, "The Fight for the Northwest in 1860," *A.H.R.*, XVI, 788.

[22] Newton, *Lincoln and Herndon*, p. 256.

[23] *Mil. Sen.*, March 3.

that as Germans they had no right to demand anything.[24] At the meeting he was one of the most conservative, opposing extreme measures or action.[25] Resolutions were adopted and circulated in English among
the delegates, urging upon the party as a whole that it
pledge itself to equality of rights by a repudiation of
the Massachusetts amendment, and to the passage of
the Homestead bill and the admission of Kansas as a
free state, and that it nominate a candidate who had
not opposed the Republican platform or candidate in
1856.[26]

Given a choice between the German vote and the
Whig, Know-nothing, and Anti-Nebraska Democratic
fragments whom they might have hoped to pick up, the
party wisely chose to retain the Germans and to try to
win more of them. But the pre-convention action of
the Germans probably exerted less influence upon the
actual platform than their leaders who helped to write
it—Schurz and Koerner.

Schurz himself wrote the fourteenth resolution,
against any change in the naturalization laws or any
state legislation abridging or impairing rights of citizenship previously accorded to immigrants; and he and
Hassaurek, by spirited short speeches, preserved it from
partial deletion by the convention, on motion of Wil-

[24] Compare editorials, *Watertown Volks-zeitung,* quoted by *Milwaukee Atlas,* May 7, and *Criminal Zeitung, ibid.,* May 28.

[25] Milwaukee *Banner und Volksfreund,* May 18.

[26] *Ibid.*

mot—Schurz avowing that it was aimed at the Massachusetts amendment,[27] and Boutwell and Koerner holding Andrew (later Governor) of Massachusetts down in his chair, while the unamended resolution was adopted.[28] Schurz also shared in the writing of the antislavery declaration of the platform and in that on the homestead question.[29]

While he had opposed the preconvention meeting of the Germans, he chose a strategic moment to make their weight felt on the floor of the convention. While speaking for the retention of the fourteenth resolution unamended, though the danger of its amendment was already past, he went further, and said:

> I wish that the resolution would be passed without opposition. The German Republicans of the northern states have given you 300,000 votes; and I wish that they should find it consistent with their honor and safety to give you 300,000 more. . . . . Let me tell you one thing, that the votes you get by truckling to the prejudices of people will never be safe; while those votes you get by recognizing constitutional rights may every time be counted upon.[30]

The nomination of a presidential candidate had not yet been made; the Germans were known to be insisting upon the nomination of a "real Republican"

---

[27] Murat Halstead, *History of the National Political Conventions* (Columbus, 1860), p. 137.

[28] Gustave Koerner, *Memoirs*, p. 87.

[29] C.S., *Rem.*, II, 189; speech at Milwaukee ratification meeting, May 26.

[30] *Mil. Sen.*, May 19.

and the elimination of Bates; and men were reminded of their 300,000 votes and their further potentialities. That may have been borne in mind by some when Curtis and Lane declared that their states, whose votes would have elected Fremont, if they had been given to him,[31] could not be carried with Seward at the head of the ticket, and when Lincoln and Bates appeared as the most logical alternative candidates.[32] Many Germans preferred Lincoln, even to Seward;[33] while others, like Schurz, while not choosing him, would be satisfied with him. But not with Bates, whom Greeley had favored as a candidate likely to conciliate the conservatives on the slavery question and as a means of defeating Seward, to whom Greeley was strongly opposed.[34]

So the field was narrowed to Lincoln and Seward; and the candidate who was radical enough to win the opponents of Bates and not radical enough to repel those of Seward was chosen.

Lincoln was more "available" than Seward and could summarize, in a single penciled comment on a

---

[31] Betz, *Die Deutschamerikanische u.s.w.*

[32] James Ford Rhodes, *History of the United States, from the Compromise of 1850* (8 vols.; New York, 1910–13), II, 366.

[33] Compare editorial from *Baltimore Turnzeitung*, official paper of the *Turners' Bund*, quoted by *Chicago Press and Tribune*, May 2; Newton, *Lincoln and Herndon*, p. 256.

[34] C.S., *Rem.*, II, 175; *New York Tribune*, May 14, letter, Dr. Wisz, Baltimore, to C.S., reprinted from *Turnzeitung* in *St. Jour.*, June 5.

marked copy of a speech of Seward's, the doctrinal difference between them. "I agree with Seward's 'irrepressible conflict,' but do not agree with his 'higher law'
doctrine."[35]

No one was more surprised than Seward, who not
only had expected the nomination but had practically
demanded it as his right, threatened to retire from public life if he did not get it, and scolded Medill of the
Chicago Press and Tribune for his editorial preferring
"that prairie lawyer" to him.[36] Thurlow Weed had
overdone his work for once; and while that did not
decide Seward's fate, it helped his supporters, like
Schurz, to reconcile themselves to it.[37]

Lincoln's managers were more adroit. Despite his
explicit and repeated instructions to the effect that he
had authorized no bargains and would be bound by
none, they secretly came to an understanding with the
Cameron and Chase delegations;[38] and so the contest
was decided.

Schurz had every reason, later, to be glad that it
was decided in Lincoln's favor. At the time, when sec-
onding the motion of Evarts of New York, making
the nomination unanimous—as he had previously seconded that which placed Seward's name before the

[35] Carl Sandburg, *Abraham Lincoln* (New York, 1926), II, "The
Prairie Years," 341.

[36] Letter, Joseph Medill to Frederic Bancroft, February 18,
1896, in Bancroft, *Seward*, I, 530.

[37] C.S., *Rem.*, II, 176–79.

[38] Sandburg, *op. cit.*, II, 341, 342, 351.

convention—he frankly admitted his disappointment; but then and always later he urged whole-hearted support of Lincoln.[39]

He soon had the opportunity to voice to Lincoln, in person, his satisfaction with the convention's choice, as he was chosen as a member of the committee sent to Springfield to carry to him the official notice of his nomination and to receive his oral acceptance. Less than a week later he did so again, in a letter from Watertown, in which he explained that he had supported Seward steadily in the convention, in accordance with the wishes of his constituents and as "a debt of honor to the old chieftain of the anti-slavery movement," but that he was ready to "do the work of a hundred men" for Lincoln.[40]

Along with Governor Morgan of New York, George G. Fogg, John Z. Goodrich, Gideon Welles, Denning Duer, and Norman B. Judd, he had been named a member of the Republican National Executive Committee.[41] He was considered by the committee as being in charge of the "foreign department" of its work. He outlined to Lincoln his plan of campaign,

[39] Reported in *Chicago Press and Tribune*, May 20, and *St. Jour.*, May 22; contrasting comments in Halstead, *Conventions of 1860*, p. 150, and Koerner, *Memoirs*, II, 91.

[40] Letter to Lincoln, May 22, 1860, in C.S., *S.C.&P.P.*, I, 116.

[41] Letter-head, L.C.; *Mil. Sen.*, May 26. The German Democratic papers commented bitterly on the "very special distinction" with which he was treated throughout the convention. Cf. *Mil. Sen.*; *Banner und Volksfreund*, May 20.

which was that he should organize squads of speakers
and a system of correspondence among the Germans,
Scandinavians, and Hollanders. In addition to super-
vising the work of the others, he was to "go to all principal points and do the heavy work" himself, confining
his own personal activities, however, almost exclusively
to the doubtful states. He would devote all of his time
to it until election day, and hoped that Indiana, Pennsylvania, and New York might so be carried.[42]

To those suggestions, Lincoln sent a delayed but
sufficiently cordial reply, approving the plan, and assuring him of his regard and that he cherished no ill feeling because of his steady support of Seward.[43]

The "heavy work" started on May 26, at a meeting in Milwaukee, called for the ostensible purpose of
ratifying the nominations made in Chicago. As returning chairman of the state delegation, Schurz gave an
account of his stewardship by describing the conflict of
opinions there as to policy, and the part taken in it by
the Wisconsin delegation for the preservation of "the
peculiar character of the party."

As for the candidates, Schurz said that Seward
had been popular with his friends and had had the support of the Wisconsin delegation but that he had been
hurt, as a candidate, by the positiveness of his public
declarations. If Seward had not been in the field, he

[42] Letter to Lincoln, *supra*, n. 40.

[43] Letter from Lincoln, June 18, in C.S., *S.C.&P.P.*, I, 118; MS.
in L.C.

said, Lincoln would probably have been the choice of Wisconsin. He gave Lincoln his hearty personal indorsement; with him, "all those great qualities would return to the White House, which make republican government what it ought to be,—a government founded on virtue." An eastern delegate, who had voted against Lincoln in the convention but who had gone with the committee to Springfield, had later said to Schurz: "We might have done a more daring thing; but we certainly could not have done a better thing."[44]

He then passed to a comparison of party platforms, pronouncing that of the Republicans the only one of them which was straightforward, unequivocal, and consistent. Disappointment (such as had been voiced by many papers) with such a platform and such candidates, he professed to find scarcely credible (though visibly subject to it, himself, in Chicago).

He closed with an exhortation to unity, such as would have pleased the most orthodox had it not been made with the typical Schurz reservations:

I do not plead the cause of party discipline. That is not one of the deities at whose shrine I worship. It never will be. But must I, born in a foreign land, speak to you of the best interest of your country? Must I entreat you to sacrifice the small whim of a personal preference to the greatest cause of the age? . . . .[45]

[44] Kelley, of Pennsylvania. Cf. C.S., *Rem.*, II, 188.

[45] C.S., *Speeches* (Lippincott, 1865), p. 105; Republican campaign pamphlet; widely copied in newspapers.

The *Buffalo Express* said that Schurz had "expressed the animating spirit of the Chicago convention with greater justice and eloquence than any other"; and his friends King and Rublee, still running a sort of press-bureau for him, had their hands full and their columns crowded with enthusiastic comment quoted from the eastern papers.

However, the weakest point in the speech, the quickness with which he had recovered from his disappointment over Seward's defeat, was promptly seized upon by the hostile press as a point of attack, and made the basis of another charge that he had "sold out." It was no mere expense account which he was said to have received, this time, either. Paying him the indirect compliment of an implication that he could deliver it, they charged that, as the price of the German vote, he had extorted from Lincoln the promise that Seward would be made Secretary of State.[46]

The charges were vigorously denied, of course, by the *New York Tribune*, the Wisconsin Republican papers, and the *Chicago Press and Tribune*. If the editorial of the last-named journal was written by Medill, it was a beautiful example of the art of conveying a misleading idea by a perfectly accurate statement of facts. It was Medill who, in violation of Lincoln's instructions, had promised Carter of Ohio that Chase could have anything he wanted, in return for support

[46] *Mil. News,* quoted in *Mil. Sen.,* May 29.

of Lincoln.[47] The writer of the editorial claimed that he had seen Lincoln's reply to a note (of Dubois) suggesting the necessity of negotiating for support, and that Lincoln had "absolutely refused to make any pledge or promise, in order to win the nomination"— every word of which was probably perfectly true, as far as it went.[48]

That the conversion of Schurz from Seward to Lincoln was less sudden than it appeared has already been shown; that it was more sincere than his enemies supposed is indicated by his March letter to Mrs. Schurz saying that he would be satisfied with either, and by a letter to Sumner in which, after alluding to the temporary feeling of disappointment in Wisconsin, he said:

> I know Mr. Lincoln, and I am sure that his administration will very favorably disappoint those who look upon him as a "conservative" man. His impulses are in the right direction, and I think he has courage enough to follow them.[49]

The Seward forces themselves, having decided to make the best of the situation and support the ticket, found solace in the remarks of Schurz. The *Milwaukee Evening Journal* praised him and his speech in the highest terms[50] and Weed vied with Greeley in the distribution of pamphlet copies of it.

Requests for pamphlet copies of practically every

[47] Sandburg, *op. cit.*, II, 351; *supra*, n. 46.

[48] *Chicago Press and Tribune*, May 28.

[49] Dated June 8. Copy in C.S. MSS., L.C.

[50] June 7; quoted by *Mil. Sen.*, June 11.

speech he had ever made, and urgent invitations to speak at political meetings, literally poured in upon him from all parts of the North. Republican young men's and Wide-awake clubs were quickly formed everywhere; and their harassed secretaries, hard pressed to secure the best speakers they could, used every device of cajolery and flattery to convince him that the fate of nations hung upon his making a speech in Dubuque or St. Paul, Boston, Easton, or Evansville. A very small percentage of the assurances of his unique importance which reached him in every mail, if believed, would have turned the head of almost any man.[51] While not entirely unaffected by them, Carl Schurz, aged thirty-one, kept his balance remarkably well.

The requests which were most urgent, and with which he tried hardest to comply, were those coming from districts where the Germans were most numerous and doubtful, or where Douglas seemed to be particularly dangerous. His refusal to go to districts not doubtful was as proud, and as arrogant, as the statement of the French Chasseurs Alpins in the World War, "We do not *hold* trenches." But even so, human strength could hardly have endured exertions greater than those which he made.

By the beginning of July he was well into his work. Its strenuous nature is well illustrated by one week's program, sketched in a letter to Mrs. Schurz written in New York. He had just come from a meet-

[51] Numerous letters in C.S. MSS., L.C.

ing of the national executive committee. Next day, on
Mrs. Barnard's invitation, he was going to Hartford
to see Chancellor Barnard. On Thursday financial
questions, which were later to cause him some annoyance, were to be taken up with the national committee.
The next day he was to go to Philadelphia and thence
to Pittsburgh, Curtin conferring with him on the train
regarding plans for the Pennsylvania campaign. On
Monday he was to speak in Cleveland.[52]

In the same 'etter there appears the following significant passage:

> In the committee, the question came up as to what would
> follow upon the election of Lincoln. That I should go on a
> mission to Europe was treated as if it were a matter of course.
> [Wie eine sich vonselbst verstehende Sache.]

The subject of a reward for his services was again
mentioned, three weeks later, after a long and intimate interview with Lincoln in Springfield on July 24.
He had been lying down in his room at the hotel, he
said, when Lincoln came to see him. Lincoln insisted
that he should continue to recline while his caller sat;
and they talked for two hours about the campaign.
Lincoln predicted that undeserving office-seekers would
find him, if elected, "a tough customer to deal with";
but he assured Schurz that he might depend upon him

[52] Letter to Mrs. Schurz, from New York, July 1, in C.S. MSS.,
W.H.S. On the sixth, he was in Philadelphia, and on the ninth the
Cleveland papers reported his meeting there, of the night before.
Cleveland Herald, quoted by *Mil. Sen.*, July 14.

to know "how to distinguish deserving men from drones."—"Alright, Old Abe, thought I."[53]

These two letters reveal one of the extremely few inaccuracies in the *Reminiscences*. There Schurz wrote that, while he was easily convinced, after the election was over, that a good appointment was his due, the idea of reward had not entered his mind during the campaign.[54] It would have been very remarkable if it had not—more particularly in view of the fact that years must yet elapse before he would be eligible for election to Congress; and his correspondence shows no evidence of a continued interest in any state office.[55]

On the evening of his day in Springfield he had supper in Lincoln's home, where he found his host genial, simple, and attractive.[56] On the other members of the family, he later wrote to Mrs. Schurz the following observations:

The Madame was very nicely dressed up, and is already quite skilful in handling her fan. She chats fairly well, and

[53] Letter to Mrs. Schurz, from Alton, Illinois, July 24, 1860, in *S.C.&P.P.*, I, 119; *Lebn.*, III, 179.

[54] C.S., *Rem.*, II, 218.

[55] Unless one should so interpret a letter from N. H. Jorgensen, of Fond du Lac, also foreign-born, who gave him some apparently unsolicited and superfluous advice, to the effect that, with even the foreign vote divided, and with the antiforeign feeling still strong, the risk of defeat would be too great and he ought not to run for the office of governor (C.S. MSS., L.C., August 23, 1860).

[56] C.S., *Rem.*, II, 196.

will adapt herself to the White House cleverly enough. Lincoln's boys are typical Western youngsters. One of them insisted on going about barefooted.[57]

In the evening they were escorted by the Wide-awakes to the grounds of the capitol, Lincoln, clad in his old linen duster, marching arm in arm with Schurz, thus making what Schurz said was his first public appearance of that sort since his nomination. Even then, Lincoln did not speak. Schurz wrote that his own German speech on that occasion was "about the best" he had ever made. After it, he made another, in English, at the conclusion of which Lincoln shook his hand, and said: "You are an awful fellow. I understand your power, now."[58]

The Springfield appearance was one of a very strenuous series in Illinois, including speeches in Quincy, Peoria, Pekin, Havana, Beardstown, Meredosia, Springfield, and Alton, in as many days. Mrs. Schurz was evidently much concerned about his endurance; and her worries were not quite all so unfounded as those in answer to which he had written, on July 6, from Philadelphia:

As you see, I have fortunately escaped all the dangers which threaten the stranger in the great city of New York, the city where one can so easily get lost, and where so many wicked

[57] From Alton, Illinois, dated July 25, in C.S., *S.C.&P.P.*, I, 120; *Lebn.*, III, 180.

[58] *Ibid.*

men live; also that I have survived the Fourth of July unshot, unburnt, unstabbed, and unslain, and have happily run into the safe haven of the doctor's home.[59]

As the campaign went on, he repeatedly assured her that he was not overtaxing his strength, and was "like a fish in water"; but he as often complained of the difficulty of finding an hour to be alone, to work on the more important speeches he was writing. The worst feature was the inevitable serenade, "to haul one out of bed" long after the evening meeting—"that dreadful Bum! Bum!" He rather liked the idea of being literally "drummed and trumpeted" from place to place, but the lover of Wagner found campaign band music rather terrible, and the man who felt that he had earned his rest resolved to make no more serenade speeches, no matter how urgently they were insisted upon. The Wide-awakes, with their torches and their black glazed caps and oilcloth capes, formed the unvarying background of a fine series of word-pictures, typical of the campaign; but by their very ubiquity, they wore him out.[60]

From Springfield, he worked down into the southern part of Illinois, where scarcely any Republican votes had been cast in 1856, even though both Hecker and Koerner lived there. From Koerner's home in Belleville, where he had been entertained in grand

[59] Probably Dr. Tiedemann. Cf. chap. iii. In New York, the Jacobi home had been his haven. C.S. MSS., W.H.S.

[60] Series of letters to Mrs. Schurz, in C.S. MSS., W.H.S.

style, he wrote: "The Germans are coming over to our side by hundreds and thousands. If things go everywhere as they did in Egypt, Lincoln's election is inevitable."[61] His impression was afterward confirmed by Koerner.[62]

Meanwhile he was working on what he then called his "masterpiece," the second of two speeches to be delivered in St. Louis. "This evening I speak German, tomorrow English. Oh woe! I work like a horse."[63] Of his reception at the German meeting, that night, the *St. Louis Democrat* wrote that between five and ten thousand people were present and that no such ovation had ever been seen in St. Louis.[64] But his best speech of the entire campaign was the one in English on August 1, published at first under the name of "The Irrepressible Conflict and the Dissolution of the Union," later as "The Doom of Slavery."

In it, he canvassed the questions in debate between the sections in a more thorough fashion than he had done since his Chicago speech on "The Irrepressible Conflict," nearly two years before. While disclaiming for his party any intention of attacking slavery in the states where it existed, he predicted that it would soon

[61] Letter to Mrs. Schurz, July 29, in C.S., *S.C.&P.P.*, I, 121; *Lebn.*, III, 181.

[62] Koerner, *op. cit.*, II, 98, 99.

[63] Letter to Mrs. Schurz, from St. Louis, July 31, in C.S. MSS., W.H.S.

[64] Quoted by *Mil. Sen.*, August 4.

die, as an anachronistic institution, under pressure of economic forces. He consciously addressed himself to the slaveholders, hoping to undermine their confidence in the economic soundness of their "peculiar institution," an effort in which at least one slaveholder later told him he had been successful.[65] But he addressed them with great moderation and wasted no breath in idle denunciations.

In his introduction, he defended himself against a possible charge of incendiarism by saying that opponents of reform only charged those who defined the nature of an existing difficulty with having originated it, and tried to make those who spoke of an "irrepressible conflict" responsible for its existence. He promised to stress only the practical arguments against slavery, rather than the moral, though he said that the latter were to him quite sufficient.

He showed how, in self-preservation, slaveholders must insist on political control of their states as a check on the national government. Having identified their social existence with the existence of slavery, they could not act otherwise. But slavery was incompatible with our form of government.

A social institution which is in antagonism with the principles of democratic government cannot be protected and maintained by means which are in accordance with those principles; and on the other hand, a social institution that cannot be protected by means that are in accordance with the democratic prin-

[65] C.S., *Rem.*, II, 204.

ciples of our government must, essentially, be in antagonism to those principles. It proves that the people in the slave-holding states, although pretending to be free men, are, by the necessities arising from their condition, the slaves of slavery. That is all.

Southern policies in federal affairs were also governed by their peculiar necessities, but Schurz acquitted the slave interest of wilful aggression. He was "willing to concede that it struggled for existence."

The great and varied industrial strength of the North was due, he said, to its free labor system and freedom of thought and inquiry. Free labor demanded freedom of inquiry, safeguards of individual liberty, good foreign relations, free soil, and harmony of all interests. On the other hand,

Slavery demands, for its protection and perpetuation, a system of policy which is utterly incompatible with the principles upon which the organization of free-labor society rests. There is the antagonism. That is the essence of the "irrepressible conflict." It is a conflict of principles underlying interests, always the same, whether appearing as a moral, economic, or political question. Mr. Douglas boasted that he could repress it with police measures; he might as well try to fetter the winds with a rope. The South means to repress it with decisions of the Supreme Court; they might as well, like Xerxes, try to subdue the waves of the ocean by throwing chains into the water. . . . . .

Thus the all-pervading antagonism stands before us, gigantic in its dimensions, growing every day in the awful proportions of its problems; involving the character of our institutions; involving our relations with the world abroad; involving our peace, our rights, our liberties at home; involving our growth and prosperity; involving our moral and political ex-

istence as a nation. How short-sighted, how childish, are those
who find its origin in artificial agitation! . . . . [It could not
be ignored.] However severely it may disturb the nerves of
timid gentlemen, there it stands and speaks the hard, stern language of fact. . . . . They cannot ignore the conflict if they
would, but have not nerve enough to decide it if they could.

In Kansas and in Congress, he said, the Douglas
principle, which had "set aside the construction put
upon the constitution by those who framed it," had
failed. He quoted Douglas on the extension of slavery
into the states of Northern Mexico—"when they are
annexed"—and proceeded to a statement of the southern demands.

The program is as follows: The agitation of the slavery
question, North and South, is to be arrested; the fugitive slave
law, in its present form, is to be strictly carried out, and all
state legislation impeding its execution to be repealed; the Constitutional right of slavery to occupy the territories of the United States and to be protected there is to be acknowledged; all
measures tending to impede the ingress of slavery and its establishment in the territories, are to be abandoned; the opposition to
the conquest and annexation of foreign countries, out of which
more slave states can be formed, is to be given up; the economic
policy of the planting interest, to the exclusion of the encouragement of home industry, is to become the ruling policy of the
country.

This is the Southern solution to the "Irrepressible Conflict."

This program possesses at least the merit of logic,—the
logic of slavery and despotism against the logic of free labor
and liberty. The issue is plainly made up. Free labor is summoned to submit to the measures which slavery deems necessary
for its perpetuation.

The tendency of the age, however, was all toward free labor. The whole northern economic and social system demanded it, in the territories and elsewhere. The Republican solution of the difficulty was "to adopt a policy which will work the peaceful and gradual extinction of slavery . . . . for if we do not, we shall have to submit to a policy which will work the gradual extinction of liberty. . . . ."

He gave a bold reply to southern threats of disunion. These he enumerated, with the reasons given for them, and his answers.

1. Because we do not stop agitation of the slavery question. We do discuss every social problem that presents itself to our consideration; we agitate it, and we do not mean to stop.

2. We do not show sufficient alacrity in the catching of fugitive slaves. True, we are not much inclined to perform for the slave-holder a menial, dirty service, which he would hardly stoop to do for himself. . . . .

3. Because we do not surrender the territories to slavery! True, we mean to use every constitutional means within our reach, to save them for free labor. . . . . The territories are the property of the Union as such; those who in a revolutionary way desert the Union, give up their right to the property of the Union. . . . . The slave power would do well first to consider how much blood it can spare, before it attempts to strip the Union of a single square foot of ground. . . . .

4. You want to establish the industrial and economic independence of the slave-holding states. . . . . [Attempts to create factories, shipyards, etc., had failed and would fail.] The very same institution for the protection and perpetuation of which you want to establish your commercial and industrial independence, is incompatible with commercial and industrial labor and enterprise. . . . .

Slave labor was unfit for industry. The South must still depend upon the North economically; a policy of friendship would be its wisest one.

The danger of a slave insurrection was greatly exaggerated by Schurz, who thought that the necessity of guarding against it would prevent the concentration of southern troops, and that slavery would disappear wherever the Union armies went. Slavery, which might die a slow, gradual death in the Union, would certainly die an instantaneous and violent death if the Southern states should attempt to break out of the Union.

In case of a Republican victory, the men of the South should submit, "not to Northern dictation, but to their own good sense." They would find the North friendly, though slavery would die out "as surely as freedom will [would] not die out." It had long been an anachronism, already; and America lagged behind the world in clinging to it.

> Slave-holders of America, I appeal to you. Are you really in earnest when you speak of perpetuating slavery? Shall it never cease? Never? Stop and consider where you are and in what day you live. . . . . The labor of the brain has exalted to a mere bridling and controlling of natural forces the labor of hand; and you think you can perpetuate a system which reduces man, however degraded, yet capable of development, to the level of a soulless machine? . . . .

He recognized the pride of the southern people but urged that a concession to the overpowering forces of modernization and industrialization would be in no way humiliating, that it was "not dishonorable to give up the errors of yesterday for the truth of today," and that Missouri should adopt emancipation as an example in modernization to her sister-states.[66]

It was, by that time, a rare thing if any northern editor spoke of Schurz in anything but superlatives— of friendly or hostile sort. The one bit of friendly but unfavorable criticism yielded by a survey of representative newspapers of the period is of enhanced interest on that account. L. W. Reavis wrote from Beardstown, Illinois, as follows: "His genius towered among his people like a monument. . . . . When his spleen shall have become fully expended, he will truly be a representative man of the age."[67]

Until he spoke in St. Louis, he had won some favorable comment from at least one slave state. The *Louisville Journal* had written:

Although a Black Republican and a radical, Mr. Schurz is one of the most profound and most philosophical and powerful thinkers of the age; and he always gives utterance to his views in language remarkable for its clearness, its classical accuracy, and its eloquence.[68]

[66] C.S., *S.C.&P.P.*, I, 122 ff. Republican campaign document; widely printed in newspapers; C.S., *Speeches* (Lippincott ed.); quoted briefly by McMaster, VI, 247. Most popular *Chicago Tribune* pamphlet.

[67] Letter to *Chicago Press and Tribune*, printed July 28.

[68] Quoted by *Mil. Sen.*, July 24.

But in spite of the fact that his "spleen" was kept fairly well repressed on the occasion of this "Doom of Slavery" speech, he was thenceforth considered as an archenemy of the slave interest.[69]

But he had not yet finished with Douglas. His program took him back into Indiana, where he had been urged by the state committee to spend six or seven weeks,[70] and did spend most of August, speaking almost every day—presumably answering the scores of letters now filed in the Library of Congress collection, most of them urging him to speak in various places—and spending every free half-day at work on his "Douglas speech." Whenever he spoke, he made more or less of a "Douglas speech"; but he used the phrase in his letters to designate a special one he was preparing to be delivered in New York, September 13. The date was set so that he would follow right on the heels of Douglas, there.

The long interview with Lincoln, in Springfield, had apparently touched to some purpose on that subject; for it was only a few days later that Lincoln sent Schurz the Douglas scrapbook mentioned above, with a note to the effect that it contained the New Orleans speech for which he had asked, and also those made at

[69] Compare speech of William B. Reed, Democrat, Philadelphia, September 4, in bound pamphlets, *Campaign of 1860*, p. 77.

[70] Letter from A. H. Conner, Indianapolis, August 4, in C.S. MSS., L.C.

Chicago, St. Louis, and Memphis, just after the election of 1858.[71] It was in them that Douglas had tried so hard and so unsuccessfully to undo the damage done by his references to "unfriendly legislation." Six weeks intervened between Schurz's greatest speech of the campaign, "The Doom of Slavery," and the third and most virulent of his attacks upon Douglas; and his letters of that whole period testify to the thoroughness with which he studied the record of the man whom he tried so hard to destroy, and with which he prepared what he meant to say—even memorizing much of it.[72]

Most of his speeches were extemporaneous, and naturally used, again and again, much of the same material. They do show, however, a surprising amount of variety—enough to acquit him of the charge of living in a glass house when throwing a stone at Douglas for being under the punishment of Tantalus, "condemned to deliver that old speech of his, over and over

[71] Letter, Lincoln to C.S., July 28, 1860, C.S. MSS., L.C. Sometime near that date, the Republican committee put into circulation a pamphlet reviewing the whole career of Douglas with relation to slavery, consisting almost entirely of quotations.

[72] Letter to Mrs. Schurz, from Pittsburgh, September 10. He had spent a whole day on shipboard between Detroit and Cleveland in memorizing it. Of the same voyage he wrote that the captain of the boat had found out, from another passenger, who he was, and had then insisted upon moving him into his own cabin, refunding his passage money, and showering upon him every possible attention, saying that it was an honor for which he could not charge. So fame was worth something, after all. *"Ruhm ist doch etwas wert, nicht?"*

again."[73] The more important ones were written out with care and partly memorized; copies were sometimes given or dictated in very modern fashion to the newspaper men, in advance;[74] and pamphlet copies were at once made, to be used as campaign documents.

The reader of the "Bill of Indictment," so called, will find in it plenty of basis for the criticism of Reavis that his philippics against Douglas would have been more effective if somewhat less splenetic. He seemed bent not merely on the defeat but on the destruction of his man, and found satisfaction in hearing the speech afterward spoken of as his "dissection" of Douglas. But his hearers liked it. He wrote to Mrs. Schurz that the storms of applause with which he was frequently interrupted took up almost as much time as the speech;[75] and the *New York Tribune* account of the affair stated that so great a crowd had never listened to a man so long, in New York, or with such enthusiasm. There again, as in the joint meeting with Hobart the year before, he gave free rein to his unusual powers of irony and sarcastic wit, which the *Tribune* wrote had "overcome the most serious dyspeptic." He was not usually a funny man. The speech took about two

[73] Speech at New York, September 13, 1860, "The Bill of Indictment," below.

[74] Letter to Mrs. Schurz from New York, September 14, C.S. MSS., W.H.S.

[75] *Ibid.; Lebn.*, III, 183.

hours and a half to deliver, and filled ten of Greeley's closely packed columns.[76]

The friends of Douglas had called him "the true champion of freedom" and "the greatest living statesman"; and those extravagant terms furnished Schurz his points of attack, with the record of Douglas in his hand. One would expect to find Schurz at a loss for new criticisms of Douglas by that time; but he found some new ways of saying things, at least. Douglas' Freeport remark about "unfriendly legislation," Schurz called authorization of the people "to annoy or tease slavery out of a territory," if they could.

He noted also the insistence of Douglas that the Dred Scott Decision be accepted, as made on a question which it was proper for the courts to decide.

And after having struck down the freedom of the territory, this "Champion of Freedom" will sneak behind the judicial despotism of the Supreme Court, and, like the murderer of Banquo, tell you that "Thou canst not say I did it." But I say *he did do it.* . . . . Strike the word demagogism out of your dictionaries, if you do not want to apply it here. . . . .

Going on to a discussion of Douglas as a statesman, the speaker got so excited that he slipped, for once, back into faulty word-order, as if he were still learning English, and started a sentence with "But already Jefferson told you . . . . etc." Quotations

[76] *New York Trib.*, September 14; *Albany Evening Journal Tracts*, No. 14; *Speeches* (Lippincott ed.), pp. 162–221; other newspapers. First printed under the unwieldy title of "Douglasism Exposed and Republicanism Vindicated."

from Jefferson were used to combat the proposals of Douglas for strengthening the discretionary powers of the president, with a view to suppressing the antislavery agitation which he held responsible for John Brown's raid. Douglas had said: "I will show the Senator from New York that there is a constitutional mode of repressing the 'Irrepressible Conflict.'" He would "open the prison doors, and let the conspirators select their cells."

Schurz replied:

If you want a *safe* man to administer your laws, select him from among those who understand their spirit, not one who means to cushion his Presidential chair with imperial powers, and who would take delight in playing like a reckless boy with the club of Hercules. . . . .

Parties must fight with arguments, not with indictments; and the power to persecute rivals in revenge must be denied them. . . . . There is one kind of despotism more terrible than that of kings—that is the despotism of political parties. . . . . Preventive laws are the poison with which freedom is killed. . . . . Place the power to indict for combination and for criminal intent in political matters into the hands of our Federal judges, those petty proconsuls who feel big when they can show their power, and we shall soon have a little Star Chamber in every little judicial district. . . . .

In 1858 Douglas had said: "Uniformity in our institutions is neither possible nor desirable." Prevalence of free labor would be uniformity. . . . . What benefactors were the men who introduced slavery! Schurz pitied the Europeans. "Poor people, that have no variety, no slaves, among them: they can never

be free. . . . ." The slave could console himself
with the thought that he was being whipped "for variety," for "a very great principle. . . . ." "It cannot be denied that there is some of the profundity of
the illustrious Dogberry in Mr. Douglas's philosophical
doctrines. . . . ."

The "Bill of Indictment," itself:

But, as to Judge Douglas, here I stand up before the great
jury of the sovereign people, and bring my bill of indictment.

I arraign him for having changed his position in regard to
the Missouri restriction, time and again, according to the interests of slavery.

I arraign him for having broken the plighted faith of the
people, by the repeal of the Compromise of 1820.

I arraign him for having upheld the most atrocious violations of the ballot box; for having trampled upon the most sacred rights of the people of Kansas, so long as the struggle between freedom and slavery was doubtful.

I arraign him for having committed a fraud upon the people by forging and adulterating the principle of popular sovereignty and making it the machine of slavery propagandism.

I arraign him for having deserted the cause of Free Kansas when the people, having complied with all reasonable conditions, applied for admission into the Union.

I arraign him for having repeatedly made the attempt to
disturb the system of constitutional checks and balances, by placing the war-making power in the hands of the President.

I arraign him for having attempted, by his conspiracies
[resolution of 1860], a thing more outrageous than the Sedi-
tion Law of 1798, to put the liberties of speech and press at the
mercy of a political inquisition, and to make the judicial persecution of opinions a standard system of policy.

I arraign him, lastly, for having tried to pass off upon the people the doctrines of a political philosophy which is an insult to the popular understanding. No, I beg your pardon; I do not arraign him for that, for this is a free country, where everybody has a right to make himself as ridiculous as he pleases, subject only to the Constitution of the United States. [Loud laughter.] And yet, I arraign him for that also, for I protest that he has no right to make the Republic ridiculous with him.

Here is the charge. It is for the people to give the verdict.

Even there he did not conclude, but went on to a discussion of Douglas as a presidential candidate. The remainder of the speech really adds little to it but length; but his party liked it, as his hearers did. Preston King, head of the document committee, told him that this one was more in demand than any other document.[77]

As three lengthy speeches, all devoted wholly or in part to denunciations of Douglas, have been reviewed, and as the rather unfavorable descriptions of him in the *Reminiscences* have been mentioned earlier, it seems proper at this time to balance them somewhat by including another description of Douglas, found in a lecture on Lincoln, delivered about twenty years later:

Douglas was called the "Little Giant,"—short of stature, with his coat tails a little too near the ground, as Thomas Benton said,—broad-shouldered, deep-chested, with something lion-like in the squareness of his front and jaw, and the shake of his long hair; a mind of strong grasp; with great power of statement; a sort of rough logic,—not seldom hiding rather artful sophistry; audacious, overbearing, sometimes violent in manner

[77] Letter to Mrs. Schurz from Fort Wayne, Indiana, September 28, in C.S., *S.C.&P.P.,* I, 163.

and language; not scrupling in direct appeals to prejudice and passion; genial and rollicking in his social intercourse; the idol of the boys. He had undoubtedly more than Lincoln of those attributes of political leadership that strike the eye. He had all those qualities apt to make a politician successful. He was an honest man withal, a man of patriotic impulses. But the disturbance of the slavery compromise was so utterly wanton an act as to make it charitable to explain it by saying that at that period of his life Mr. Douglas was ill, [with presidential fever].[78]

An even greater danger than Douglasism was to be found in the fusion movement in the Democratic party, a proposal that both factions of it unite on one set of electors, to be instructed to wait until the votes of other states were known, and then to cast their votes for Douglas or Breckenridge, whichever could be elected. If neither could be elected, the electors were to vote as they pleased.[79] It was commonly predicted that Douglas would carry Pennsylvania and New York, with German and Irish support.[80] What the Republicans had most of all to fear was that failure on their part to carry almost any one of the "doubtful states" would throw the election into the House of Representatives, where they would control only four-

[78] C.S. MSS., L.C. For other observations by Mr. Schurz on the devastating effects of presidential fever on the psychology and political acument of its victims, see his *Reminiscences*, II, 171, and *Henry Clay*, I, 310, 368; II, 168, 407, 412.

[79] McMaster, *op. cit.*, VIII, 462–63.

[80] Cf. *Frank Leslie's Illustrated Newspaper*, July 14.

teen, or at most fifteen, of the thirty-three state delegations, and would almost certainly lose.[81]

The fusion movement was strongest in Pennsylvania, Indiana, Maryland, New York, and New Jer-
sey.[82] Schurz spoke in all of those states except Maryland and, after his Illinois-Missouri tour, occupied
himself in the states just named, and in Connecticut
and Ohio, until after the October elections. Then, at
last he yielded to insistent urging from Rublee and
others, and spoke daily in Wisconsin from October 24
to election day, ending the canvass in Potter's district.[83]

Rather than attempt a detailed, or even summary,
further review of his participation in the campaign, it
seems best merely to cite a few of the most significant
incidents and letters.

One of the latter was from a Kentucky committeeman, asking him to speak in Louisville but caution-
ing him: "We do not designate the opposition to Republicanism as slave-holders, for upon the whole, there
is as much political liberality among the slave-holders
as among the non-slave-holders of Kentucky."[84] Schurz
did not go.

Another interesting letter of the period was one

[81] W. E. Dodd, "Fight for the Northwest," *A.H.R.*, XVI, 779.

[82] McMaster, *op. cit.*, VIII, 463.

[83] Letters and newspaper announcements and comments. Mostly
those in C.S. MSS., L.C. and W.H.S., and in *Mil. Sen.*

[84] Dated October 12, C.S. MSS., L.C.

of his own to Mrs. Schurz, written after he had stolen
time from the campaign for a sentimental return to
Bethlehem, Pennsylvania, where they had lived for a
time during their first years in America. The affec-
tionate, home-loving nature of the striving young politician was most strikingly revealed in it.[85]

His German speeches were not very fully reported,
but a fair sample of them seems to have been that delivered at Buffalo. In it, he addressed the Germans on
the "American" movement; but while stating his own
unequivocal opposition to it, he said that it had its
natural origin in the tendency of the foreign-born to
vote in blocs, in unthinking and uncritical fashion. As
fast as the foreign-born showed themselves capable of
intelligent independent thought and Americanized
themselves, the proscriptive spirit was sure to lose its
basis and its point and disappear.[86]

One of his greatest personal triumphs, after that
in New York in September, was at a second meeting in
the same city, five weeks later, when he delivered a
German address upon the preparation of which he
had worked, whenever he could, throughout the interim.[87] The chairman of that meeting, and his host at

[85] Letter to Mrs. Schurz from Philadelphia, September 17, in
C.S. MSS., W.H.S.

[86] *Buffalo Commercial Advertiser*, October 13. Quoted by *Mil.
Sen.*, October 18, and in weekly edition, October 29.

[87] Letter to Mrs. Schurz, from Philadelphia, September 24, in
C.S. MSS., W.H.S.

dinner next evening, was another of the greatest of the German-Americans, Francis Lieber.[88]

Another triumph was at a tremendously enthusiastic ovation given him personally by the Republicans of Milwaukee on the occasion of his return there to participate in the Wisconsin elections after the "October states" were safely stowed away.[89] They had been busy for weeks on their preparations, and outdid themselves with torchlight processions, transparents, fireworks, etc. He had never been so popular in the state.[90]

The Wisconsin committee had plenty for him to do. He spoke there mostly in German, as in some places no Republican had yet addressed the Germans in their own language.[91] At most of the later meetings he appeared along with Potter;[92] and with his col-

[88] *New York Tribune*, October 18, 19; letter from "Franz" Lieber, October 19, in C.S. MSS., L.C.; *New York Evening Post; Mil. Sen.*

[89] Until then, he had been detained by incidents such as the following: "I shall not be able to go home on Sunday. A delegation came to me in Pittsburgh to assure me that my appearance in Erie might make a difference of five hundred votes, which might decide the result of the October election" (letter to Mrs. Schurz, September 26, in C.S., *S.C.&P.P.*, I, 163. Letters from A. H. Connor, of the Indiana committee were also especially urgent. "One week's work from you is worth more than all the German help we have in the state" (September 18, C.S. MSS., L.C.).

[90] *Mil. Sen.*, October 15–25. Letter to Mrs. Schurz, October 25, C.S. MSS., W.H.S.

[91] Letter from Rublee, October 11, in C.S. MSS., L.C.

[92] Letter to Mrs. Schurz, November 3, in C.S. MSS., W.H.S.; *Lebn.*, III, 185.

leagues, gathered in the rooms of the chamber of commerce of Milwaukee, he received the news of the victory in New York state, which for him meant "love, peace, family, fortune."[93]

Schurz had called the campaign "my [his] fight."[94] To what extent was the victory, also, his victory? It is perhaps impossible to say with any degree of definiteness; but the detailed studies of Dr. Joseph Schafer, in Wisconsin, in so far as Wisconsin conditions may be typical, furnish significant indications.

In 1856 Fremont had a majority of 12,669 in Wisconsin over Buchanan; Lincoln carried the state with a majority of 21,000 over Douglas. Of the Republican increase, the four German counties, Milwaukee, Ozaukee, Sheboygan, and Manitowoc, furnished more than half—4,357. In Milwaukee and Jefferson counties alone, the Republican gain was 3,000.[95] Jefferson County contained the first, and Milwaukee the second, place of residence of Schurz in Wisconsin. Jefferson County had to be carried without Water-

[93] Letter to Mrs. Schurz, November 7, in C.S. MSS., W.H.S.

[94] Letter to Mrs. Schurz, September 24, *loc. cit.*

[95] Schafer, MS. paper, "Carl Schurz, Immigrant Statesman." Note also the returns in five German wards in Cincinnati:

        1854—Democratic majority—4,000
        1856—Democratic majority— 369
        1858—Republican majority— 420
        1860—Republican majority—1,730

Quoted from *Cincinnati Volksblatt* by *Mil. Sen.*, December 4, 1860.

town, however. No other Republican had yet duplicated Schurz's feat of carrying that Democratic stronghold. The vote of the fifth ward was 100 to 33; and
that of Watertown as a whole, 631 to 450 in favor of
Douglas.[96]

It is generally conceded that a portion of the German voters of the whole state moved over from the
Democratic to the Republican side, much as in the
four counties mentioned above, except in the strongly Catholic districts. It is Jensen's estimate that at
least 40,000 Wisconsin Germans voted for Lincoln.[97]
While in the country as a whole, less dependence was
placed than formerly upon editorials and pamphlets,[98]
it is Dr. Schafer's opinion that the rural Germans were
still prone to follow the shifts in political sentiment of
their newspaper editors.[99] If they did, many of them
turned Republican; for after even the *Madison Demokrat* did so, on October 19, it repeatedly published
long lists of others, in Wisconsin and elsewhere, that
were doing the same thing.

It is also generally conceded that in other states
more doubtful than Wisconsin similar gains were made
among the Germans. Dr. Schafer believes that a full
quota of the converts from Democracy were Ger-

[96] *Watertown Dem.*, November 8, 1860.

[97] Jensen, *Wis. Deutschamerikaner*, I, 181.

[98] Rhodes, *op. cit.*, II, 484; McMaster, *op. cit.*, VIII, 459–61.

[99] Schafer, *Four Wisconsin Counties*, p. 149.

man.[100] Writers of the German-American group estimate the total number of German voters at 450,000,[101]
of whom 120,000 to 150,000 would have been voting
in their first presidential election in that year and likely
to be influenced in favor of Republicanism only
through the other Germans or by special circumstances.[102]

Such special circumstances were the Republican
policies of free land and internal improvements at
public expense,[103] and the railroads. In Illinois, Indiana, and Iowa, where a change of one vote in twen-
ty-seven would have given those states to Douglas, the
maps showing changes from the Democratic to the
Republican columns show them to have been made
mostly in those counties where new railroads had recently brought in new immigrants.[104]

What did Carl Schurz have to do with all that?
He built no railroads. Neither did he, alone, dictate
Republican policy. But it has been shown that he was
strongly influential in securing the adoption of those
policies which are conceded to have been most attractive to his newly arrived countrymen, and that he did
much to counteract the deterrent influence which the
suspicion of nativism would otherwise have exerted

[100] MS. "Carl Schurz."

[101] F. F. Schrader, *The Germans in the Making of America*,
p. 194.

[102] Jensen, *Wis. Deutschamerikaner*, I, 181.

[103] Channing, *op. cit.*, VI, 250.

[104] W. E. Dodd, "Fight for the Northwest," *A.H.R.*, XVI, 788.

against the party, while at the same time steadily advocating independence of thought which, under the circumstances, could only mean revolt against the party discipline and the herd instinct which were keeping those of the earlier migrations Democratic.

He was considered, and considered himself, the leader of the German element; while he did not control it, he influenced it more than any other man could do.

His influence with the Germans, however, was but a very small part of his usefulness to the Republican party. With the American-born, "the gifted foreigner" began by being something of a novelty and ended by being more popular than among those of his own nativity, many of whom were envious of his rapid rise and were hostile to him. From reams of testimonials, earned not as a German but as an American, only a few of the most worthwhile can be quoted here.

William Cullen Bryant wrote in the *New York Evening Post:*

> Young, ardent, aspiring, the romances connected with his life and escape from his father-land, his scholarly attainments, and above all, his devotion to the principles which cast him an exile on our shores, have all combined to render him dear to the hearts of his countrymen, and to place him in the foremost rank of their leaders.[105]

No one worked harder than Carl Schurz. . . . . No one touched the people more deeply.[106]

[105] Quoted by Ida M. Tarbell, *Life of Abraham Lincoln* (4 vols. New York, 1907), II, 163.

[106] *Ibid.*

Andrew D. White, who regularly read the campaign literature to his aged father, concurred in his judgment that the speeches of Schurz were the best of all, although the elder White had idolized Seward.[107]

Just after his St. Louis speech of August 1 "an eminent gentleman of Massachusetts" was quoted as having written to "a gentleman in Madison":

> No one, not even Seward, makes speeches which are, in my mind, equal to those of Carl Schurz. I am amazed at his power. I read and re-read everything he says. The speech at St. Louis was a masterpiece of political philosophy. . . . . Don't make him Governor of Wisconsin. His place is in the United States Senate. Let him bide his time, and he will there find his appropriate sphere. Sumner said today that he ought to be in the Senate; a year ago, old Josiah Quincy told me his first speech in Boston was a remarkable one. I sincerely think that, today, no man in this country is doing the effective work that Schurz is.[108]

Clearly, not only Wisconsin but much of the northern part of the United States was ready to adopt Carl Schurz, and proud to call him an American. Clearly, too, in the minds of many of his contemporaries, as well as in the judgment of later students of the period, he had done much toward the election of Lincoln. Exactly how much, it would still be very difficult to say with certainty; but certainly his contribu-

[107] Andrew D. White, *Autobiography* (New York, 1905), I, 86, 87.

[108] *St. Jour.*, August 28, 1860. Possibly E. L. Pierce to Rublee(?).

tion was second to few, if any, of those of his colleagues, and it may well have been decisive.

He made no attempt, himself, to say exactly to what extent he claimed credit for the Republican victory. Nearly three years later, he wrote:

> I am told that I made Lincoln President. That is, of course, not true; but that people say so indicates that I contributed something toward raising the breeze that carried Lincoln into the presidential chair, and thereby shook slavery in its foundations.[109]

In the midst of the campaign he had written, with equal truth and perfect justification in fact: "It seems as if victory could not fail us—and by Jove! I have done my share towards it."[110] He had.

[109] Letter to Petrasch, September 24, 1863, in *Lebn.*, III, 225.

[110] Letter to Mrs. Schurz, September 24, 1860, in C.S., *S.C.&P.P.*, I, 160.

CHAPTER X

CARL SCHURZ, U.S.A.

THE victory which was to have meant "peace, family, and fortune" to Schurz, actually brought him none of those blessings immediately. His anxiety for fear the fruits of victory should be lost by a compromise policy, and his impatience at being barred from Congress by constitutional ineligibility, having been for but eight years a resident and three years a citizen of the United States, gave him no rest. Dire financial distress, owing to long-continued neglect of his private business, forced him out on another extended lecture tour, which kept him away from his family, much against his will, even at Christmas time. And the salary of a foreign minister, while it looked large in anticipation, fell far short of affluence, when he got it; while the anticipated period of quiet happiness in Madrid never materialized.

Directly after the election, he went out to Watertown, well in body but overwrought in mind and spirit.[1] But he was back at work at once, writing a speech for the Milwaukee celebration meeting soon to be held, and playing one final part in Wisconsin politics. The latter incident shows how far he had gone in half a

[1] *"Geistig gespannt."* Letter, November 14, to Mrs. Schurz, who was still in the East, in C.S. MSS., W.H.S.; *Lebn.*, III, 187.

year from his old State-rights position. He had been
assured by his friends that his voice would be decisive
in the choice of a new Senator to take the place of
Senator Durkee. Before going to a conference with
Potter, Senator Doolittle, and Judge Howe to discuss
the matter, he wrote to Mrs. Schurz that he expected
to see to it that Randall did not get the place; but he
wrote no word of objection to his old opponent on the
State-rights question, Judge Timothy Howe, who did
get it.[2] This, too, in spite of the fact that but little
more than a year had elapsed since Judge Howe had
headed those standing in the way of his progress to the
governor's chair of the state.

During the same period he was so harassed by the
urgent demands of office-seekers, asking him to inter-
cede for them with Lincoln, that he adopted the expedient of having a stock reply printed, to be sent to
those whom he could not help[3]—somewhat like the
one Nicolay, as Lincoln's secretary, was writing to so
many. But he never succeeded in freeing himself from
their importunities.

His greatest concern was about the conduct of the
national government. It was one of his virtues, and
one which he always tried to cultivate in others—
though in himself it sometimes carried him somewhat
beyond the bounds which a more modest man would

[2] Letter to Mrs. Schurz, November 10, 1860, in C.S. MSS.,
W.H.S.; *Mil. Sen.*, January 27, 1861.

[3] Letter to Mrs. Schurz, November 14, *supra*, n. 1.

have set upon himself—that he felt a sense of personal
responsibility for the conduct of the whole party, for
that of a Congress of which he could not be a member,
and of an administration not yet even formed. If one
did not admire his ideal of an active and earnest type
of citizenship, one would be tempted to smile at the
conceit of the young Atlas who tried so hard to carry
the whole Republican world on his shoulders in the
months between Lincoln's election and his inauguration, while the chosen leader of the party formulated,
but was slow to make a public announcement of, his
policy.

The speech of Schurz at the Milwaukee celebration meeting reads like a president's inaugural address—in many places, in fact, strikingly like Lincoln's
first one. There was the same firm insistence that the
result of the election must be accepted and the Union
preserved, the same hope that, as the North would not
attack the South, the South would conquer its own resentment and refrain from attacking the North, the
same combination of determined intent and conciliatory tone, the same absence of exultation.

With Schurz even the slavery question had become
momentarily subordinate to that of the preservation of
the Union and the original principles upon which it
was founded. The issue of paramount importance was
the acceptance of the result of the election. If the defeated minority could refuse to accept the verdict of
the election, or could bargain for compromises as the

price of their acquiescence, then the whole basis of democratic government would be destroyed, and the United States would be "Mexicanized." Endless disorders would result in the future.[4]

So, after a sermon to the Republicans, to the effect that their victory was no end in itself but simply made possible the performance of the positive part of the mission of the party, involving responsibilities toward the whole country and duties which should be performed with a sympathetic understanding of the circumstances of the South, he addressed himself to the southerners themselves.

While the North would resist an attack upon the integrity of the Union, it would make none upon the institutions of the South. The secession movement was merely heading that section toward ruin, "to guard against aggressions which nobody intends [intended] to make. . . . ." As in St. Louis, however, he underestimated the strength of the South and overestimated the danger of a servile uprising.

We recognize the constitutional rights of the states, and will respect them as sacred and inviolable. Where slavery exists by virtue of state legislation, there it exists upon the responsibility of the people of those states. There we claim no control over it. . . . .[5]

[4] See also C.S., *Rem.*, II, 212–16, and compare with Lincoln's attitude on the same matter, at the same time. Letter, C.S. to Mrs. Schurz, January 29, 1861, in C.S. MSS., W.H.S.; *Lebn.*, III, 191.

[5] Compare with resolutions sent to Senators Trumbull and Seward by Lincoln, by the hand of Thurlow Weed, in December, 1860, to

Southerners were warned that those who had elected Lincoln were determined to see him inaugurated. It was better that they should understand that the moderation being shown was that of conscious strength. The secessionists were leading their section into a mistake.

If to recede from a mistake requires any sacrifice of pride, it is the kind of pride which a true man will be proud to sacrifice. . . . . We do not ask of you any act of self-humiliation, for a ready acquiescence in the will of the majority will never deserve that name in a republic like ours. But we do expect you to recognize the necessities of your situation, as every man of sense will do, and to follow the dictates of loyalty and patriotism, which no man of honor can disregard. . . . .[6]

Then a return to his old theme:

It is decreed that no interest, no power, can rule the destinies of this country, which is incompatible with a free expression of public sentiment. . . . . It [the Republican party] has maintained the principles upon which this government was founded, and I trust it will be able to maintain the government to which these principles have given birth."[7]

He felt it safe to promise not to interfere with slavery in the states where it existed, because he was so sure that, if denied the right to spread farther, it would

be introduced by Seward, to make interference with slavery in the slave states unconstitutional but to give fugitive slaves a jury trial, while asking the northern states to review their "personal liberty laws" (Sandburg, *Abraham Lincoln*, II, 395).

[6] He was speaking there, of course, as one of the victorious party.

[7] *Mil. Sen.*, November 20, 1860; C.S. MSS., L.C.

die out. But no further concession must be made. He wrote to Potter, soon after the Milwaukee celebration:

> If slavery in its present form and strength exists in this republic ten years hence, the Republican party will be to blame for it. We have got them at last; do not let them escape us once more. If no compromise had been made in 1833, we should never again have heard the disunion cry. Let not that mistake be repeated. The future of the country, the repose of the nation, depends on our firmness.[8]

He could not have entertained any real fear as to the firmness of the man who had earned the sobriquet of "Bowie-knife Potter" in the famous Pryor-Lovejoy incident. But he was hoping, if not actually to use Potter as a mouthpiece, at least to influence other members of Congress, through him, and so to make himself heard on the floors of the national legislature. In December he actually wrote a speech for delivery by a member of the House of Representatives,[9] and wrote to Mrs. Shurz: "I wish I were a member of the Senate, if only for a few days; I would sing them a new song."[10]

Barred from actual participation by his ineligibility, and even from lobbying by the financial necessities which kept him at work on a lecture tour

[8] Letter dated November 30, 1860, in C.S., *S.C.&P.P.*, I, 165.

[9] Letters to Potter, December 17, 24, *ibid.*, p. 168, 175; to Mrs. Schurz, December 24, C.S. MSS., W.H.S.; C.S., *S.C.&P.P.*, I, 177; *Lebn.*, III, 189; Jensen, *Wis. Deutschamerikaner*, I, 328, 330.

[10] Letter to Mrs. Schurz, December 17, fom Boston, C.S., *S.C.&P.P.*, I, 168; *Lebn.*, III, 188.

through nearly the entire North, he was forced to exert
what influence he could by correspondence. So he
continually urged on, in Congress, those who opposed
compromise, and in a series of letters to Mrs. Shurz
bemoaned the numerous defections, as man after man
went over to the compromise group.

When the Corwin resolutions for the Committee
of Thirty-three were proposed, he wrote:

> As soon as these resolutions, or anything like them, are
> adopted, the Republican party has ceased to exist. I have been
> traveling all over Pennsylvania, New York, and New England,
> lately; and outside of the large commercial cities, I have not
> found one single Republican who did not scorn the idea of re-
> ceding from a single principle laid down in the Chicago plat-
> form.[11]

In November, he had thought that no coercive
measures would be necessary but that it would be sufficient for the North to display an attitude of firmness,
or at worst one of armed preparedness; the secessionists, if given "rope enough to hang themselves," would
"accomplish that necessary and praiseworthy task with
their own hands."[12] In December he was less sure of
that but insisted upon "the prompt and vigorous execution of the laws as against the seceders."[13] It was his
belief, then and even after the war, that such an atti-

[11] Letter to Potter, December 17, 1860, in C.S., *S.C.&P.P.*, I,
168; Jensen, *op. cit.*, p. 328.

[12] Letter to Mrs. Schurz, November 10, 1860, in C.S. MSS.,
W.H.S.

[13] Letter of December 17 to Potter, *supra*, n. 9.

tude of firmness, if generally shown and consistently
adhered to, would have prevented secession, and that
Buchanan's failure to insist upon execution of the laws
amounted to criminal sanction of secession.[14]

So he even took it upon himself to work out a plan
of military organization, for submission to Lincoln and
the northern governors.[15]

Meanwhile, one by one, men on whom he had
counted in Congress joined the compromisers; and
Schurz was alternately furious and sad.

One day he was cheered by a newspaper account
that Lincoln had said in private conversation that he
had no idea of taking part in any such flight of the
conquerors before the conquered as would be constituted by any abandonment of the Chicago platform.[16]
Two days later Cassius M. Clay had convinced him
that he could trust no one but himself. Clay, too, had
become an advocate of compromise, after inducing
Schurz to write a letter to Lincoln recommending him
for a cabinet position and giving Schurz, as the ground
of such action, "the absolute necessity in Lincoln's

[14] Letters to Potter, December 24, 1860, in C.S., *S.C.&P.P.*, I,
172; Jensen, *op. cit.*, p. 330; to Mrs. Schurz, in C.S. MSS., W.H.S.;
C.S., *S.C.&P.P.*, 174; *Lebn.*, III, 190; C.S., *Rem.*, II, 210, 211.

[15] Letters to Mrs. Schurz, from Boston, December 24, 27, 1860,
in C.S., *S.C.&P.P.*, I, 177, 199. Some expressions used in these letters
indicate that he may have contemplated the possibility of his being offered a cabinet position. Such a matter, however, seems never to have
been discussed.

[16] Letter to Mrs. Schurz, from Toledo, January 29, 1861, in C.S.
MSS., W.H.S.

cabinet of a firm and energetic man who could uphold him against throwing the Republican cause out of equilibrium by compromise."[17]

Within another week it was Seward who had dropped out of his firmament:

This star also paled! That is hard. We believed in him so firmly, and were so affectionately attached to him! . . . . Between us, it would not surprise me, if Lincoln should recall his invitation to Seward to head the cabinet. It would be a sharp, perhaps a dangerous stroke, but a just one; for Seward, no matter what he may think, privately, has no right, on his own responsibility, to compromise the future policy of the President, against his will and opinion.[18] Where is our "Seward enthusiasm" of the Chicago Convention? Where are the lovely oratorical bouquets with which we covered his defeat? [19]

Only Sumner, Wade, Chase, and Lincoln were left. He urged Chase not to refuse a cabinet position, and counted upon him as a "staff and support" there; while every report from Springfield strengthened his faith in Lincoln.[20] Soon he was in Springfield himself, and talked with Lincoln before his lecture.

[17] Letter to Mrs. Schurz, from Sandusky, January 31, 1861, in C.S. MSS., W.H.S.

[18] Seward had gone far beyond Lincoln's conciliatory proposals, but Schurz apparently did not know that Lincoln had ever made them. In any case, there was a great difference between conciliation and compromise.

[19] Letter to Mrs. Schurz, from Hillsdale, Michigan, February 4, in C.S. MSS., W.H.S.; *Lebn.*, III, 193.

[20] *Ibid.*

He is a true man [*ein ganzer Mann*], firm as a stone wall, and clear as crystal. He told me that Seward has made all his speeches without consulting him.[21] He himself will not hear of concessions and compromises, and says so openly, to everyone who asks him.[22]

Next day Lincoln read him the draft of his inaugural address, and the two "discussed it point by point."[23]

His growing admiration for Lincoln, and perhaps an unconscious reaction to criticisms of himself, led him to write the following:

This is not merely an age of adventurers and upstarts whom strength of intellect and favoring circumstances have raised up, but rather the age of men of conscience who, purely by sheer force of honesty dominate affairs and overcome all obstacles.[24]

[21] The following remarks of Seward, if authentic, will explain his independence of Lincoln at that period. "You think I can save the country by sacrificing myself.—Suppose I were to save the country as you wish. I should have put an end to my power for good or evil, forever. I should have to go back to Auburn and amuse myself with writing history the rest of my life. I am not so blind to history as to suppose that I can sacrifice myself and remain leader at the same time. Now, do you want me to retire from public life?" . . . . "No, Governor, we cannot do without you." . . . . "Then you must let me save the Union in my own way." Quoted by *Boston Advertiser, New York Times, Mil. Sen.* (February 12, 1861). At the last moment, Seward withdrew his acceptance of a cabinet position, then reconsidered his withdrawal,—which causes one to marvel more and more at Lincoln's patience.

[22] Letter to Mrs. Schurz from Springfield, Illinois., February 9, 1861, in C.S. MSS., W.H.S.

[23] Letter to Mrs. Schurz from Springfield, Illinois, February 10, 1861, in C.S., *S.C.&P.P.*, I, 179; *Lebn.*, III, 195.

[24] Letter to Mrs. Schurz from Toledo, January 29, 1861. Written in French. German translation in C.S. MSS., W.H.S.

Schurz himself favored acceptance of the Virginia proposals for a compromise conference. But his reasons for doing so were based upon no expectation that the conference would be successful, but upon his hopes that time would be gained thereby and the secession movement delayed until nearer to the time of Lincoln's inauguration, and that the strong demands which the Southern delegates were sure to make would "set a limit on the cowardice" of the Republicans. He hoped that some determined antislavery men would attend, and offered to go as a member of the Wisconsin delegation. Some little further friction developed between him and Governor Randall over that; but the conference had broken up before the Wisconsin legislature decided whether to send delegates to it or not, so Randall was relieved of the necessity of a choice between appointing him and refusing to do so.[25] The failure of the radical northern states to send delegates led him, and the Governor of Michigan, to fear that before Lincoln could get to Washington, the Republicans would have "eaten dust."[26] Since only believers in compromise attended the compromise conference—as was, after all, not unnatural—he was relieved when the conference broke up. No one welcomed more gladly than he the inauguration of Lincoln.

[25] Letters to Mrs. Schurz, February 4, 7, 9, 15, in C.S. MSS., W.H.S.; to J. A. Hadley, February 7, *Mil. Sen.*, February 16, 18.

[26] Letter to Mrs. Schurz, from Ottawa, Illinois, February 15, C.S. MSS., W.H.S.

In the meanwhile, matters of a more personal nature had been as acutely disturbing. He was still kept uncomfortable by the necessity of paying, painfully, for an unfortunate financial past; his future was not yet assured; and both for his past and for his prospects, he was still subject to much criticism, which pained him.

It has been said above that the land he had purchased at Watertown was bought on mortgage, in a time of rapidly rising prices, just before the period of deflation which began in 1857 and which prevented him from reselling it as he had expected to do. His collected correspondence contains a number of letters—three in 1860—from John Jackson, who sold him the land; and others from Halbert Paine and various lawyers, which show him to have been struggling, even during the campaign of 1860, to meet the notes still falling due on it.[27]

Both his law business, such as it was, and his more lucrative lyceum engagements were entirely neglected from May until November, during which time he considered himself in the employ of the National Executive Committee. But even there, there seems to have been some misunderstanding about the amount of his compensation, in which Norman B. Judd, committeeman from Illinois, supported him against Governor Morgan of New York, chairman of the committee.[28]

[27] C.S. MSS., L.C.

[28] Letter, Judd to C.S., August 15, 1860, in C.S. MSS., L.C.

During the campaign the letters urging him to speak in various places sometimes contained promises to pay his expenses, and sometimes offers of fixed amounts, up to $50, for the same purpose. One offer, from Michigan, which he did not accept, was of $25 per day;[29] he asked Rublee for $15 per day while in Wisconsin, October 24 to November 6.[30] The letters do not show how many of the offers were accepted, or whether he used passes on more than one railroad. One case has already been cited where he paid boat fare as a matter of course and made its refunding a matter of comment.[31]

The most convincing statements on the subject are his own. To Rublee he wrote: "I wish I could offer my services gratis, and foot the bills in addition; but unfortunately, *'les jours des fêtes sont passés'*; I am not in a position to do so."[32] After the campaign, in answer to a direct question from J. P. Sanderson, he replied that he had, during the campaign, been constrained by his financial embarrassments to take fees for his services. He said that he had received a total of $1,800, mostly from the national committee and the state committees of Indiana and Pennsylvania, while traveling 21,000 miles at a cost of $800 for railway fare alone.

[29] C.S. MSS., L.C.

[30] Letter to Rublee, October 14, 1860, in C.S., *S.C.&P.P.*, II, 164.

[31] Letter to Mrs. Schurz, September 10, 1860, in C.S. MSS., W.H.S., *supra,* chap. ix, n. 72.

[32] Letter of October 14, *supra,* n. 30.

He had been barely able to support his family on the balance of his fees after his expenses were paid, and, immediately after the close of the campaign, had been forced to take the road again, to meet his debts with lecture fees.[33]

Of the truth of the last statement there is abundant testimony in his letters to Mrs. Schurz and to Potter; and one is inclined to accept the accuracy of his others. But during every campaign he had been accused by his enemies of serving only for fees; and during and after that of 1860, wild stories of their amount were kept afloat by his calumniators. One of them called him "a hair-lipped renegade, who left his country for his country's good, and has been furnished money and means by the Black Republicans to stump the country for Lincoln. He is a red Republican, all but his heart; that is black."[34]

Schurz had passed the point where such criticism could do him real harm; but the Sanderson letter, and his later statements in his *Reminiscences*,[35] show that it never ceased to cause him real pain.

Constant lecturing, too, was a hard life, particularly when he found no pleasure in it because he was

---

[33] Letter to J. P. Sanderson, from Boston, December 22, 1860, in C.S., *S.C.&P.P.*, I, 170.

[34] *Cleveland Plain Dealer*, quoted by *Mil. Sen.*, October 3, 1860. Other attacks by *Mil. News* quoted by *Mil. Sen.*, March 27, 1861.

[35] C.S., *Rem.*, II, 135–38.

so engrossed in political matters. While on earlier tours, he had complained of the discomforts of travel:

The life on the train is abominable; for breakfast, indescribable beefsteak, tough as tanned leather, warmed-up potatoes, and "saleratus" biscuits that smell like green soap. Ditto at noon; ditto at night; then the lecture and the same answers to the same compliments, and finally to bed, quite worn out; and the next morning, I am on the train again.[36]

On the tour of December, and of January following the election of Lincoln, he was more impatient than ever at the necessity that held him to it, and chafed at "saying a thousand times the things that have already been said about American Civilization or France,"[37] when so much more interested in the political situation and in his own prospects.

Once he had varied his subject sharply and on short notice. Four days before the date of a lecture in Boston, an abolitionist meeting there was broken up by a mob actuated by the prevalent idea that antislavery agitation was responsible for the secession movement. Not only disinterested Unionists, but business men with large pecuniary interests in the South, were so perturbed by the secession movement that public opinion was strongly opposed to anything which might irritate the South.[38]

[36] Letter to Mrs. Schurz, March 9, 1860, in C.S., *S.C.&P.P.*, I, 110; *Lebn.*, III, 176.

[37] Letter to Mrs. Schurz, January 31, 1861, in C.S. MSS., W.H.S.

[38] Letter to Mrs. Schurz, December 11, 1860, in C.S. MSS., W.H.S.

As once before, when he invaded Boston to fight the two-year amendment, Schurz accepted the incident as a challenge and favored his hearers with a spirited defense of free speech, filled with flashing periods.

> Free discussion has always been an uneasy thing to those who were wrong and knew it. . . . . Intrigue has lost its life-element, when in the open light of day argument struggles with argument. . . . . Why not by free speech counteract the mischief free speech threatened to accomplish? . . . . [If people really wanted to demonstrate their loyalty to their slaveholding customers], *the thing* would have been to tar and feather James Redpath, to hang Wendell Phillips, and to burn Fred Douglas alive. That would have been a sign of loyalty worth a gracious compliment. . . . . There was never a despot on earth who refused to tolerate opinions which exactly agreed with his own. . . . . The freedom of thought and the freedom of utterance . . . . [were] the firmest bulwark of peace and order, ... the greatest moderator of strife, ... and the great safety-valve of the social machinery.[39]

The address was reported as having caused a considerable sensation among his hearers but as having been warmly applauded throughout.[40]

Meanwhile, the question of an appointment for him from Lincoln went unsettled but not unmentioned. In that, as in other political matters, Potter was his confidant and, in a sense, his Washington manager. While making it quite clear that he desired an appointment, he yet wrote to Potter that if anything were offered to him, it must be spontaneously done.

[39] C.S., *Speeches* (Lippincott, 1865), pp. 222 ff.

[40] *Boston Courier*, quoted by *Mil. Sen.*, December 17, 1860.

To ask for an office is, in my opinion, to pay too high a price for it. I shall not do that myself, nor do I wish to have others do it for me. I will tell you why I am somewhat scrupulous on that point. If I ask for a place, I lose part of my independence; if I merely accept what is spontaneously offered, I am bound by no obligations; and I must confess my independence in political life is worth more to me than all the favors which a government can shower upon a man.[41]

But that did not mean that he would not be glad to accept a good offer, under the proper omens. He would have preferred the Sardinian mission[42] and, for a time, was encouraged to think that it would be his.[43] He was not alone in thinking so, for he was told by the Sardinian minister in Washington that that official had written to his government four months before that he would be sent there.

He felt confident of Lincoln's friendship. In addition to the assurance of it which he had received during the campaign, he had been promised by Lincoln, in February, offices for whatever friends he should recommend, and whatever he asked for himself.[44] In March, he was told that the new president, speaking to Senator Grimes, had called him the greatest man in America

[41] From Boston, December 24, in C.S., *S.C.&P.P.*, I, 176; Jensen, *op. cit.*, p. 330.

[42] Letter to Potter, November 30, 1860, in C.S., *S.C.&P.P.*, I, 165.

[43] Letter to Mrs. Schurz, December 11, 1860. Written in French. German translation in C.S. MSS., W.H.S.

[44] Letter to Mrs. Schurz from Springfield, Illinois, February 10, 1861; C.S., *S.C.&P.P.*, I, 179; *Lebn.*, III, 195.

and had said that his wish alone would command compliance, without other support.[45]

He had himself talked with the president often, as freely and informally as before, about the appointments of others, but never about his own.[46] It was Lincoln, in fact, who raised the question, in a letter to Seward: "And then what about Carl Schurz; or in other words, what about our German friends?" In addition to fitness, Lincoln's reasons for approving C. F. Adams had been Seward's recommendation; and "the intense pressure of their respective states" had aided Burlingame and March.[47] The latter was named for Sardinia, and Cassius M. Clay and his nephew had already been suggested as minister and secretary of legation at Madrid.

"What about Carl Schurz?" indeed! Only Rome, Prussia, and Russia were left, in Europe. Certainly the first two would have been closed to him, and the third would have been none too hospitable. For a time he was talked of for Brazil, and tried to reconcile himself to the idea. Finally Clay was offered the Russian post instead of the Spanish, and Schurz was given the benefit of the vacancy so created.

Greeley had ardently supported him for the Sar-

[45] Letter to Mrs. Schurz, March 8, 1861, in C.S. MSS., W.H.S.; *Lebn.*, III, 196.

[46] C.S., *Rem.*, II, 219.

[47] Letter, Lincoln to Seward, March 18, 1861, in *Works of Abraham Lincoln* (Federal ed.), V, 273.

dinian mission and had objected even to the suggestion
that Wisconsin reward him, saying that he had ceased
to be a state character and become a national figure,
"known to and loved by the Republicans of three-
fourths of the Union," and that it was his due, as,
though some were more conspicuous, no one was more
effective in support of Seward at Chicago, and "no
man got so many votes for Lincoln."[48] But he might
have been more strongly supported for a desirable appointment if he had been more of a "state" man and
had had fewer scruples about the use of "intense pressure."

Sumner also favored his appointment;[49] and Douglas, whom he had attacked so often, made no objection
in the Senate to its confirmation.[50] He was surprised,
later, to learn from Potter and other Washington
friends that the real opposition to it had come from
Seward. In his *Reminiscences* he said that Seward's
objection was due only to fear that his revolutionary
antecedents might make him unwelcome at a conservative court, and that, in Seward's place, he would
have felt the same way.[51] But a study of their relations
while he kept the Spanish mission causes one to wonder
whether the Secretary was not affected rather by fear

[48] *New York Tribune,* March 11, 1861.

[49] E. L. Pierce, *Memoir and Letters of Charles Sumner* (4 vols.;
Boston, 1894), IV, 26.

[50] C.S., *Rem.,* II, 221.

[51] *Ibid.,* 221–22.

of what did arise—a difference of opinion over the relation of the slavery question to foreign policy.

At the time, ignorant of Seward's opposition, and relieved to have ended his distasteful experience among the place-chasers in "this hunt in which the hunters shoot at one another,"[52] he decided to be pleased with what he was offered, as a substitute for what he had wanted.[53] Lincoln told him of it with pleasure. His friends professed to be pleased, also; while the *Milwaukee News* wailed:

Impudence has triumphed over all obstacles. . . . . An audacity that could not be repulsed. . . . . This foreign adventurer and mercenary soldier, this impudent mendicant. . . . . He who entered the Presidential mansion a homeless vagrant, went forth clothed with the high dignity of a first-class ambassador of state.[54]

At least, his worst enemies had to recognize that he would return to Europe clothed with a higher dignity than when he left there, nine years before. The exile from Germany would be known as "Carl Schurz of the United States of America."

Before Schurz actually went abroad to take up his Spanish mission, there intervened a brief military interlude, the record of which contains a number of vig-

[52] Letter to Mrs. Schurz, from Washington, in C.S. MSS., W.H.S.; *Lebn.*, III, 197.

[53] Letter to Mrs. Schurz, from Washington, in C.S. MSS., W.H.S.; *Lebn.*, III, 198.

[54] Quoted by *Mil. Sen.*, April 11, 1861.

nettes of the characters of the day and presents a striking picture of the confusion of ideas which prevailed
everywhere, especially after the firing on Fort Sumter.
They would be highly diverting if the reader did not
know the farce to have been such a tragic one. Plans,
organization, conception of the work to be done, were
lacking; for a time there was only enthusiasm on
which to build the defense of the Union.

Schurz hurried home to Wisconsin, after the confirmation of his appointment, to settle up his affairs.
Thereupon, E. S. Williams, of the Young Men's Club
of Chicago, urged him to come there to speak—"the
time, subject, and terms" to be fixed by him. Differing
therein from Editor Ballou of Watertown, who had
objected to all of his first lecture that was not a mere
historical record, Williams wrote: "You might throw
in a few remarks specially adapted to the times, and in
favor of the Stars and Stripes."[55]

When, at last, it became clear that war was actually inevitable, Schurz dashed back to Washington to
offer Lincoln his resignation and ask permission to
raise troops instead of going abroad. He reached the
city only by way of Annapolis, avoiding Baltimore, and
traveling on a pass and by courtesy of General B. F.
Butler,[56] who "thoroughly enjoyed his position of

[55] Letters from E. S. Williams, Chicago, April 3 and 18, 1861, in
C.S. MSS., L.C.

[56] Copy of pass, with envelope indorsed by General Butler, in
C.S. MSS., L.C.

power, which, of course, was new to him, and . . . . keenly appreciated its theatrical possibilities." Young Governor Sprague of Rhode Island, with a "waving yellow plume" in his hat, also appears in the same picture, taking the field with the volunteers from his state.[57]

In Washington an epidemic of irrational volunteering was raging. Cassius M. Clay, like W. J. Bryan in a later crisis, volunteered to serve as a private soldier. Denied that permission, he was placed in command of an ephemeral military organization which must have been a great comfort to General Scott and the president in their time of trouble—the Strangers' Guard, a gallant company of a hundred men, including "Bowie-knife" Potter, Colonel Rufus King of Milwaukee (who, like Clay, was asking for leave from a diplomatic appointment, and eventually went back to Milwaukee to lead his regiment), Carl Roeser, the impulsive German from Manitowoc, and a dozen other Wisconsin men.[58]

Schurz was received with favor by the administration. On April 27 a letter was written by Cameron, Secretary of War, to the governors of the several states, recommending that they avail themselves of the services of Carl Schurz in effecting transfers of volunteers to those branches of the service for which their experience best fitted them.[59]

[57] C.S., *Rem.*, II, 226.
[58] *Mil. Sen.*, April 26, 1861.   [59] C.S. MSS., L.C.

He might have begun with the Strangers' Guard; but other Germans were setting him a better example. Blenker and Max Weber of Baden, and Von Gilsa of Prussia were busy in New York, Schimmelpfennig in Pittsburgh, Mahler in Philadelphia, and Franz Sigel in St. Louis, raising German regiments for actual service.[60]

His own idea was to go to New York, where he hoped to raise a regiment of cavalrymen, already trained in Germany, who could be very quickly prepared for field service. General Scott frowned upon the scheme. It was his view that the war, if any, would be a short one; the regular dragoons would be sufficient; and Virginia was so cut up with fences that cavalry could not be used there to advantage, anyway.[61]

In spite of the skepticism of Scott, Schurz obtained three months' leave from his duties as minister,[62] and was authorized to raise a regiment of five squadrons, the men to furnish their own horses and horse equipment, and to be paid fifty cents per day for their use and risk. Only old cavalrymen were urged to apply for enlistment.[63] John Hay, who had seen him often at the White House, wrote admiringly that he would make "a wonderful land pirate, bold, quick, brilliant,

[60] Cf. chap. ii, nn. 20 and 21.

[61] C.S., *Rem.*, II, 230.

[62] Letter to Mrs. Schurz, April 30, 1861, in C.S. MSS., W.H.S.; *Lebn.*, III, 200.

[63] *Cincinnati Gazette*, quoted by *Mil. Sen.*, May 21, 1861.

and reckless,—hard to control and difficult to direct"; and later, that he had "gone home to arm his clansmen for the wars."[64]

The "Lincoln Cavalry" was duly formed, though not exactly as proposed. After the departure of Schurz for Spain, it served under Colonel McReynolds as the "First New York Volunteer Cavalry." Meanwhile, evidence of further difficulties of organization and another illustration of the things that seemed really to matter were given by the following letter from Lincoln to the Secretary of War.

You see on the other side of this sheet that four German regiments already raised in New York wish to form a brigade and have Carl Schurz for their Brigadier-General. Why should it not be done at once? By the plan of organization, I see that I am to appoint the generals. Schurz says he would, if allowed, go immediately to Fortress Monroe; and if it would be an objection that, by rank, he would command the garrison there, he would, of choice, waive that.

I am for it, unless there should be some solid reason against it. Answer soon.[65]

Apparently there was; for three days later, the President wrote to Schurz:

[I have been] . . . . hoping to get the matter of which we spoke into satisfactory shape; but at last, I have not suc-

[64] From which figurative remark the indexer of Thayer's *Life and Letters of John Hay* has it that Schurz returned to Germany to raise a regiment of recruits! (*op. cit.*, II, 443).

[65] Letter, Lincoln to Secretary of War, May 13, 1861, in Nicolay and Hay, *Complete Works of Abraham Lincoln*, II, 46.

ceeded. On Monday, I was about to telegraph you to proceed, but was arrested in it on the question of rank, as it would put you in command at Fortress Monroe.[66]

The danger of his ranking someone else out of a command at Fortress Monroe was evidently quite a solid obstacle, in spite of his having offered to waive that privilege. For Lincoln continued: "I still hope you may be made Brigadier-General of them; but I cannot make it move smoothly just yet."[67]

During the same period, his friend and partner, H. E. Paine, called on Schurz for significant services. Paine had volunteered in April, when Schurz was in Milwaukee, and Schurz had had an impulse to join him. Soon Paine was urging Schurz, then in Washington, to use his influence with Secretary Cameron to secure equipment for the Wisconsin troops. The government was supposed (by Paine) to have plenty of guns, caissons, and side-arms; while in Wisconsin, he said, there were "only five pieces in the whole state, and not a single caisson."[68]

Paine's personal equipment, however, was his own affair; and that should not be lacking. In May, having meanwhile become a colonel, he wrote from Camp Randall to Schurz, then in New York, full instructions as to uniforms to be purchased for him. Weighty ques-

[66] Letter, Lincoln to C.S., May 16, 1861, in C.S. MSS., L.C.

[67] *Ibid.*; cf. letter, C.S. to Lincoln, May 19, C.S., *S.C.&P.P.*, I, 180.

[68] Letter, H. E. Paine to C.S., April 24, 1861, in C.S. MSS., L.C.

tions as to braid and plumes were taken up with great seriousness.[69] Schurz later sent him, as a gift, a handsome sword.[70]

He had proposed to take his friend with him to Spain as secretary of legation. For that Paine thanked him, but said he was not interested. Assuming that Schurz had resigned his diplomatic post instead of being given only a brief leave of absence from it, he wrote that he did not doubt that he would prefer the command of a New York brigade to such a duty. "Certainly I would."[71]

So, thought Schurz, would he; but Seward insisted that the state of affairs in Europe demanded the presence in Madrid of a minister of full rank.[72] So, reluctantly, he went.

The attitude in which Schurz approached his work in Spain had been expressed by him in a letter to Lincoln in April, concerning the appointment of a secretary of legation. He had written:

It is needless to say, I shall be strictly governed by my instructions, but in carrying them out, I shall follow ideas of my own which may not always run in the beaten track of our former diplomatic representatives. . . . .

I cannot lose sight of the fact that my appointment was

[69] Letter, H. E. Paine to C.S., May 27, 1861, in C.S. MSS., L.C.

[70] Letter, H. E. Paine to C.S., October 10, 1861, in C.S. MSS., L.C.

[71] Letter, H. E. Paine to C.S., April 24, 1861, *supra*, n. 68.

[72] Letter, C.S. to his parents, June 2, 1861, in C.S. MSS., W.H.S.; *Lebn.*, III, 201.

your own work, and that you, in a certain measure, will be held answerable for the success or failure of my mission. If anything were necessary to sharpen the keenness of my sense of responsibility, the knowledge of this fact would supply the deficiency. This mission is to me a trust of friendship, and it is my highest ambition to discharge all its obligations. I shall never forget that in gaining credit for myself, I shall have to justify your choice.[73]

With a parting admonition from the president that it should be his first duty to watch public sentiment abroad as closely as possible, and report directly to him whatever he thought it necessary for him to know, the new minister started off to Spain. He went first, for orientation, to London for an interview with Charles Francis Adams;[74] then to Paris, where he parted reluctantly from his family, as on account of the health of Mrs. Schurz it was feared that Spain would be dangerous to her, in summer. She and the children then turned aside to Hamburg; while he, after ordering in Paris, under protest, the necessary court costumes, went on to Madrid.[75]

He arrived there on July 12, 1861.[76] In a letter to his parents[77] and in his *Reminiscences*[78] he wrote some

[73] From Milwaukee, April 13, 1861. Draft copy in C.S. MSS., L.C.

[74] C.S., *Rem.*, II, 245–46.

[75] Letter to Adolph Meyer from Paris, July 3, 1861, in C.S., *S.C.&P.P.*, I, 182; *Lebn.*, III, 202.

[76] Letter, Seward to Fifth Comptroller, January 28, 1862, in C.S. MSS., L.C.

[77] From Madrid, August 19, 1861, in C.S. MSS., W.H.S.

[78] C.S., *Rem.*, II, 245–46.

highly amusing accounts of the consternation caused
by his being received at court in civilian dress instead
of the usual court costume. Such unusual action had
been necessitated by the circumstances that the royal
family was just on the point of departure from Madrid
for the summer[79] and that the costumes ordered in
Paris had not arrived. Schurz could never take the
punctilious formality of court life seriously; so, in
writing about the incident, he made the most of it, and
reported to his parents a month later that his embroid-
ered coat had at last arrived and European equilibrium
was again restored.[80]

The man who piloted him through his hectic presentation was one in whom he soon placed the highest
confidence, apparently with good reason, though he had
not been his first choice.[81] Horatio Perry had been in
Spain for more than ten years and had served twice
before as secretary of legation.[82] By his conduct in that
capacity under Pierre Soulé, Schurz's predecessor, he
had become involved in serious trouble with his superior, and had been discharged under the accusation of

[79] Letter, Horatio Perry, secretary of legation, to C.S., July 9,
1861, in C.S. MSS., L.C.

[80] Letter, C.S., to his parents, from Madrid, August 19, 1861.

[81] His preference for Paine has been stated above. The German,
Reinhold Solger, had also begged Seward to send him "as consul-general with Carl Schurz, where at all events, I may pursue my ethnologi-
cal studies to advantage" (letter of March 10, 1861, in C.S. MSS.,
L.C.).

[82] C.S., *Rem.*, II, 254–65.

revealing the minister's instructions to the Spanish government and dealing directly with it in defiance of him. Reports of that incident, and a letter written by Perry in his own defense and published in the *New York Evening Post*,[83] had caused Schurz to write a vigorous protest against his reappointment. Recognizing that Mr. Perry's knowledge of the politics and the people of Spain would be of value to the legation (Mr. Perry had married a Spanish lady and established his permanent residence there), Schurz felt that his conduct had shown him to be a man unworthy of trust, and did not wish to be associated with him.[84] He seems later to have come to the belief that the purposes of the secretary had been correct in the quarrel, and those of the minister wrong, and that Perry's offense had been a technical one only and prompted by zealous patriotism. Without directly accusing Soulé of treasonable pro-southern activities, he conveyed the impression that he was not pleased with the state in which Spanish relations had been left by his predecessor. His relations with Perry continued to be cordial for years after his return to the United States.[85]

The small diplomatic crisis which had caused Seward to think the presence of the minister in Madrid urgently necessary, although Perry had handled the

[83] *Watertown Dem.*, May 17, 1861.

[84] Letter, C.S. to Lincoln from Milwaukee, April 13, 1861. Draft copy in C.S. MSS., L.C., *supra*, n. 73.

[85] Compare letter from Perry to C.S., April 2, 1877, *infra*, n. 94.

negotiations with skill and diligence, was that arising
out of Spanish intervention in Santo Domingo. Taking
advantage of disorder in the island, Spain tried to
establish control of it. Seward protested sharply to
Tassara, the Spanish minister in Washington, who returned a discreet reply; but the course of his government continued unaltered. Seward then instructed
Perry at Madrid to make a sharp protest which the
United States should "in every case . . . . expect to
maintain." Schurz asked whether the government
would have approved if Perry had broken off diplomatic relations. He was told both then and later to confine his action to protests. Seward finally left the matter in the hands of Congress, which did nothing. So
Spain tried vainly for four years to control the island.[86]

It was another of the duties of the minister to
guard against the abandonment of a position of neutrality by Spain; but as he saw a great danger to Cuba
in an independent slaveholding Confederacy, and supposed that the Spanish government saw it also, he was
not particularly fearful on that point—unless France
and England should recognize the Confederacy. The
real danger, he thought, was to be found in the policies
of England and France.[87] But he kept himself in-

[86] Bancroft, *Seward*, II, 158 (based on *Diplomatic Correspondence of the United States*); Seward to Perry, May 21, 1861, MS.;
Schurz to Seward, June 5, 1861, MS.; Seward to Schurz, June 10,
1861, MS.; Seward to Schurz, June 22, 1861, MS.; Seward to Schurz,
July 2, 1861, MS.; Seward to Schurz, August 14, 1861, MS.

[87] C.S., *Rem.*, II, 272–75.

formed as well as possible on policy and opinion in
Spain, and wrote to Lincoln, through the secretary, his
advice as to the best treatment of Spanish questions in
presidential messages and by Congress.[88] Extended reports of a similar character were sent, with information about the joint punitive expedition of the three nations against Mexico.[89]

While not greatly perturbed about the neutrality
of Spain alone, he was very much concerned about the
attitude of Europe generally, as he saw it affected by
the subordination of the slavery issue to the constitutional one of the preservation of the Union. As an
ardent antislavery man, and as one still viewing America somewhat through European spectacles, more particularly while again resident abroad, he was irked by
his instructions as to the attitude he was to take officially
toward slavery. The secretary had made it a part of the
instructions of all foreign ministers that they were to
give foreign powers to understand that the war was
not one for the abolition of slavery and that the status
of the slaves in both states and territories would remain
unchanged by it.[90]

Schurz, on the other hand, in common with most
of his colleagues in the foreign service, quickly became
convinced that nothing could hurt the Union cause

[88] Letter to Seward and Lincoln, November 11, 1861; copy in
C.S. MSS., L.C.

[89] C.S., *S.C.&P.P.*, I, 200–206; C.S., *Rem.*, II, 289–99.

[90] C.S., *Rem.*, II, 280–82.

more than the giving of just that impression. Adams had told him, in London, of "hostile influences, the strength of which depended in a great measure upon the strength of the widespread belief that the existence of slavery was not involved in our home struggle.[91]

N. B. Judd, his former colleague on the Republican national executive committee, wrote to him from the legation in Berlin:

The mass of the Diplomatic Corps here believe that our Union is finally and permanently destroyed, and I am fearful that the governments of Europe will soon act upon that supposition. . . . . The worst part of it is that [even] the Liberals sneer at us.[92]

Bigelow, first consul-general and then minister to France, wrote to Seward that there was serious danger of foreign recognition of the Confederacy, which could best be averted by immediate emancipation.

There is no government in Europe that could stand a month in alliance with the South, if the people could be made to understand that the struggle with us was between free and slave labor. Of this I am satisfied.[93]

The seriousness with which the American diplomats then in Europe regarded the danger is further illustrated by the following, written long afterward, by Perry: "Even President Lincoln died with a very

[91] *Ibid.*, pp. 245–46.

[92] September 3, 1861, in C.S. MSS., L.C.

[93] October 3, 1861. Quoted from the Seward MSS. by Bancroft, *op. cit.*, p. 324, n. 1.

imperfect knowledge of the risks we had run in Europe, or how or why they had been averted."[94]

Their view was doubtless affected by their peculiar position. Closer to Europe than their countrymen, they may have seen the foreign danger too close and too large; farther away from the domestic political considerations bound up with emancipation, they may have minimized the difficulties in its way. But their concern was none the less real, on that account; and when emancipation was proclaimed, the effect upon public opinion abroad justified their predictions.

One of the first and most forcible warnings of what American representatives abroad thought to be a real danger was sent to the Secretary of State by Schurz in a letter from San Ildefonso dated September 14. Disclaiming any intention of questioning the wisdom of the government, but "bearing witness to the effect its attitude produced upon public opinion in Europe," he pointed out that while European opinion was unsympathetic toward a war for the subjection of the South, it was sure to react favorably to one in the interest of free labor and to control the policies of governments accordingly. Union defeats were attributed by many to lack of moral faith in the Union cause, which appeared as one of repression. Danger of a rupture with foreign powers could be averted, he said, only by striking military successes or by "such measures as will place the war against the rebellious slave states

[94] Letter to C.S. from Madrid, April 2, 1877, in C.S. MSS., L.C.

upon a higher moral basis, and thereby give us the control of public opinion in Europe." Immediate emancipation was urged as the surest means not only of securing success at home but of averting a menace from abroad. He further argued that if successes were not to be quickly won, emancipation became doubly necessary as a defense measure.[95]

Evidently the Secretary did not wish to discuss the question.[96] The boldness of his tone in addressing foreign powers seems to have been the product of fear that they would, for the sake of cotton, intervene to re-establish slavery, if it were abolished.[97] His reply to Schurz's letter urging speedy emancipation began with generalities about the necessity of determining domestic policy in the light of domestic, not foreign, conditions and opinion, and ended with empty self-assurances that the Union could maintain itself, if necessary, against foreign enemies as well as domestic ones.[98]

Schurz felt sure that his dispatch had never been transmitted to the president by the Secretary; so he wrote to Lincoln, asking leave to come home,[99] and,

[95] No. 18, C.S., *S.C.&P.P.*, I, 189; quoted also by Bancroft, *op. cit.*, p. 324.

[96] *Ibid.*

[97] Compare Stanton's memorandum of a cabinet meeting, July 22, 1862, and Seward's dispatch to Motley, July 24, 1862.

[98] Letter, Seward to C.S., October 10, 1861, in C.S., *S.C.&P.P.*, I, 191.

[99] Letter to Lincoln from Madrid, November 11, 1861, *ibid.*, p. 193.

without waiting for an answer, wrote also to Sumner that he would soon be on his way and that Sumner should delay action on any Spanish matters by the Senate Committee on Foreign Affairs until he got back to Washington.[100] In Sumner, he knew that he was writing to another strong antislavery man, one congenial with himself. Since May, Sumner had publicly urged emancipation.[101] To him Schurz wrote that, but for the danger, he would be willing to wait; for he was sure slavery would die anyway, as a result of the war; but that he considered the danger such as to make it imperative that the Union avail itself of the powerful weapon of abolition without delay.[102]

Less than a week after the date of his letter to Lincoln above mentioned, he wrote again even more urgently to Seward. He had decided to resign; but Perry had persuaded him to ask for leave, only, so as to create no unfavorable impression in Madrid. Having once been tacitly refused, he seemed to hope for little sympathy from Seward, and wrote: "I have but one favor to ask of you, and that is to be permitted to return to the United States, either one way or the other, and to have your reply as soon as possible. Do not refuse me that."[103]

[100] Letter to Sumner from Madrid, November 14, 1861, *ibid.*, p. 198.

[101] George N. Hayes, *Charles Sumner* (Philadelphia, 1909), pp. 248–50.

[102] Letter, C.S. to Sumner, November 14, 1861, *supra*, n. 100.

[103] Letter, C. S. to Seward, November 17, 1861; copy in C.S. MSS., L.C.

He wrote like a man who was homesick and distressed. He was. In practically every one of the letters above quoted, there appeared statements, like that made to Lincoln before his departure, to the effect that he felt it his duty to help to maintain in the field the administration which he had helped to elect at the polls. He rebelled at the quiet, elegant leisure to which he was condemned while others were in active service. His private letters express the same sentiments even more forcibly.

He was humiliated, too, by the news of defeats suffered by the people whose representative he felt himself to be in the eyes of Europe. The Spanish pun about the battle of *Patassas* ("feet"), for Manassas ("hands"), stuck to him until it found its way into his *Reminiscences.*[104] To his parents, he wrote:

> You must perform better in America, so that we in Europe need not be ashamed. I would ten times rather fight in America along with the rest than here in Europe to extenuate our defeats. That is a hateful task.[105]

He would probably not have been at home or really happy in Spain, in any case. The ignorance and poverty of the poorer classes appalled him; and bull-fighting, which he took as indicative of their plane of culture, disgusted him. Even in the highest circles, he said, he found superstition over which, in America, the

[104] C.S., *Rem.*, II, 271–73.

[105] Letter, C.S. to his parents, from Madrid, August 19, 1861, in C.S. MSS., W.H.S.; *Lebn.*, III, 205.

children would make merry. He judged Spain to be
about a hundred years behind the rest of Europe; and
for all her backwardness, the doctrinaire democrat held
his twin demons—kingcraft and priestcraft—to be
responsible.

Of the nobility whom he met at court, and for
whom he had almost equally little use, he wrote:

> Great titles are as common as blackberries, here; but there
> is ordinarily little behind them. . . . . I cannot deny that I
> wish I were at home again. I would prefer to work ten times
> harder, there, rather than go idle here. I cannot endure people
> who abase themselves as they do here; and I am embarrassed
> when all manner of honors and reverences are hurled at my
> head. Nowhere can I feel right save in a country where the
> people stand erect in their boots.[106]

It is very probable that, added to all of the foregoing causes of discontent, ambition played its part in
urging Schurz to come home where more exciting
work was to be done, and where opportunity seemed to
beckon him on to fame. He made diligent use of his
leisure in renewing the military studies begun under
the instruction of Prussian officers in Switzerland,
years before, and made of himself as good a self-
taught book-soldier and strategist as possible. The feel
of civilian clothes upon his shoulders was probably
made more irksome than ever by the receipt of a letter
from H. E. Paine, written from a camp in Maryland,
telling with the greatest enthusiasm how he had "had

[106] *Ibid.*

to do everything, and at the same time learn how to do it," but had succeeded "as well as the average of Colonels." Paine expected to be (and was) soon promoted again, and predicted that Schurz would soon be a major-general if he would come home and enter the army.[107]

But he might have learned to endure having marks of respect flung at his head and jibes at his nation's army had he felt his work in Madrid to be really vital, any more, and had there not been that insistent idea of the urgent necessity of immediate emancipation and the conviction that he should go home at once, in order to urge that policy directly upon Lincoln in person.

In August, he wrote to his German brother-in-law that he was "more in Washington than in Madrid, in thought," and would "give much to be in the President's cabinet, if only for a day."[108] To Althaus, he declared that, if he were at home, he would carry on an agitation among the people on his own responsibility, and build up a public opinion that would bring the government to the point of emancipation. He saw in slavery the source of the secession movement, and in the end of slavery the only means of stopping it. He had become convinced that the cabinet lacked courage,

[107] Letter, H. E. Paine to C.S., October 12, 1861, in C.S. MSS., L.C.

[108] Letter to Adolph Meyer, August 13, 1861, in C.S. MSS., W.H.S.; *Lebn.*, III, 204.

and that either no one in it saw the truth, or no one had the courage to tell it to Lincoln.[109]

So, being sure that he did see the truth and did have the courage to tell it to the President, he came home as soon as permission was granted. Since August he had been in correspondence with Judd, in Berlin, in an attempt to secure permission to visit Hamburg on business in connection with the property of Mrs. Schurz and in order to bring her back to Madrid with him.[110] When the tardy permission came, it was used for a visit to Hamburg, whence Mrs. Schurz accompanied him back to the United States, in January, 1862.[111]

Back in America, he hurried to Lincoln, and, in a long interview, laid his views before him. In the midst of it, Seward started to enter the room, but was asked

[109] Letters to Friedrich Althaus, from Madrid, October 11 and December 9, 1861; *Lebn.*, III, 208–11. Cf. n. 120 *infra*, and chap. ii, n. 71, p. 45.

[110] Letters, C.S. to Judd, August 27, and Judd to C.S., September 3, 21, 23, 1861, in C.S. MSS., L.C. In conjunction with Schurz's views of Spain, and his complaints of the high cost of diplomatic life, the impressions of the other amateur diplomatist, in Berlin, are interesting. Judd wrote (September 3): "The streets and buildings are full of all sorts of statuary, good, bad, and indifferent. The city is growing—the women are homely—the police are thick, and the military thicker—badges of servitude meet me in every station—beer is essential to a man's (German) existence—and a man in official position has to pay for it."

[111] Letter, C.S. to Adolph Meyer, written on the voyage, January 14, 1862, in C.S. MSS., W.H.S.

by the President to excuse them while they talked. Lincoln listened as if he had never heard of the matter before, and Schurz felt his suspicion to be confirmed, that his most urgent dispatch of September 14, 1861, had never reached the President's hands.[112]

Lincoln did make him see, however, what obstacles there still were to the immediate performance of what he proposed, and enlisted him to do, with presidential approval, what he had told Althaus he would do if given an opportunity. Lincoln, too, wanted a public opinion in favor of emancipation built up; if justified by it, he would need no pressure from it, to do what he had wanted to do, all along, only less than he wanted to hold together the body of opinion necessary for the maintenance of the Union. So while the questions of his resignation and of a brigadier-general's commission for him were pending, Lincoln commissioned him privately to make one more of his stirring appeals to the popular mind and conscience against slavery.

On the evening of March 6, 1862, in Cooper Institute, New York, the scene of some of his greatest earlier oratorical triumphs, Schurz went once more before the public with a speech which was a worthy successor to the best of his previous ones. The draft of it had been seen by Lincoln, and approved by him, with the promise that something might be heard from him on the same day.[113]

[112] C.S., *Rem.*, II, 309, 310; cf. n. 95.
[113] *Ibid.*, p. 322; Tarbell, *Lincoln*, II, 370.

The two great problems with which the government was faced, said Schurz, were the suppression of the rebellion and the restoration of the Union. Of the two, the second was the more important, for, unless the Union were restored on a really permanent basis, the suppression of the rebellion could be only temporary. Without the destruction of slavery, such a restoration would be impossible.

This rebellion did not commence on the day that the secession flag was hoisted at Charleston; it commenced on the day when the slave power first threatened to break up this Union. . . . .

Would the rebellion have broken out, if slavery had not existed? Did the rebellion raise its head at any place where slavery did not exist? Did it not find sympathy and support wherever slavery did exist? . . . .

The South would never be really loyal, again, with slavery. . . . . The war should produce such a reform of Southern society as will make loyalty to the Union its natural temper and disposition. . . . .

I am an anti-slavery man. All the moral impulses of my heart have made me so, and all the working of my brain has confirmed me in my faith. . . . ."

But he would have been content to see the gradual extinction of slavery brought about by restricting its spread and limiting the political power of the slaveholding interest. . . . .

This rebellion has uprooted the very foundations of the system, and slavery is not far from its death. It will die, and if you would, you could not prevent it. And thus, as an anti-slavery man, I might wait and look on with equanimity. . . . .

[But] it shall not entangle the Union in its downfall, and there-fore, the Union must deliver itself of its pernicious embrace.
. . . . [With slavery abolished, the Southerner eventually] will understand and appreciate the advantage of this new order of things, and loyalty will become as natural to him as disloyalty was before. . . . .

Schurz proposed:

Let slavery, in the District of Columbia and wherever the Government has immediate authority, be abolished. Let the slaves of rebels be confiscated by the General Government and then emancipated, and let fair compensation be offered to loyal slave states and masters, who will agree upon some system of emancipation. . . . ."

Or he would accept any similar measure to make the restoration of slave power impossible.

The Constitution had already been violated many times, he said, under stress of necessity. Should prop-erty rights in slaves be better protected by the Consti-tution than other rights? Besides, this action would really be within the war powers granted by the Con-stitution.

As to the punishment of rebels, he said just as Lincoln would have done:

As for me, it will be to me supremely indifferent whether any one of the rebels meets a punishment adequate to his crime, provided that the great source of disloyalty be punished in itself. The best revenge for the past is that which furnishes us the best assurance for the future.

All his sarcasm and anger, none of which were wasted on those in rebellion, were reserved for the timid and the pusillanimous in the North. The government was told, he said, that it must not "irritate the rebels" by touching slavery; but if so desirable an end could be attained by doing so, would it not be best to support their anger with equanimity, and do it? . . . .

And yet it is difficult for a man of heart to preserve . . . . coolness and moderation when looking at the position this proud nation is at present occupying before the world; when I hear in this great crisis the miserable cant of party; when I see the small politicians busy to gain a point on their opponents; when I see great men fluttering in trepidation lest they spoil their "record" or lose their little capital of consistency.

He closed by drawing, with colorful word-imagery, two contrasting pictures—one of the Union in disruption and despair, the other of a united, happy, and prosperous country—and bade his countrymen be true to themselves, "for once," in making their choice between them.[114]

At the conclusion of the address, a telegram from the president was brought in and read, announcing his special message to Congress asking for a joint resolution proposing gradual, compensated emancipation, with government co-operation. Both the speech and the announcement were received with the greatest enthusiasm.[115]

Lincoln later expressed himself, to Schurz, as pleased with the results of the meeting and as "not

[114] C.S., *Speeches* (Lippincott ed., 1865), pp. 240 ff.
[115] C.S., *Rem.*, II, 322.

without hope" of the acceptance of his own proposal. At least, something had been done by both to prepare the public mind for the more drastic emancipation measures which were to come, and which, without such preparation, would have been doubly hazardous.

Perry wrote at once from Spain that opinion there had been favorably affected by the news from America and that there Schurz was commonly credited with a share of responsibility, even for the prompting of the President's message. Quite generally, he said, he heard: "Now, we know what Carl Schurz has been doing"; or "Now, you see what Mr. Schurz went home for."[116]

"What Mr. Schurz went home for" was in truth partly accomplished. He had got back once more into the active fight against slavery; he had got once more into close touch and accord with his great chief. He had, also, again redressed the balance of his views on national policy by learning, under the expert tutelage of Lincoln, how to bring domestic conditions as well as foreign opinion into the range of his vision, in well-balanced proportions.

He had already made some progress along the road to the more comprehensive understanding of Lincoln's problems which enabled him, later, to write the following revised estimates of his own position, on

[116] Letter, Horatio Perry to C.S., from Madrid, March 24, 1862, in C.S. MSS., L.C.

those points wherein he had differed in opinion from Lincoln: "Many of these anti-slavery men will now, after a calm retrospect, be willing to admit that it would have been a hazardous policy to endanger, by precipitating a demonstrative fight against slavery, the success of the struggle for the Union." They had reversed their judgment, and admitted that "the heroic measures they favored would have broken down under any disaster, and his way was best."[117]

His own fears were apparently classed, later, in his mind, with the doubts of the European statesmen, one of whom had written to Sumner, pointing out that never in the history of the world had such a war been successful. Sumner had exclaimed: "Thank God, they don't know any history in Washington." With perfect urbanity, though he had himself once seen some of the dangers in exaggerated dimensions, Schurz commented: "Thus the war was made successful, and the Union saved, in profound ignorance of what historically could not be done."[118]

Seward desired him to return to Spain;[119] but Lincoln complied with Schurz's own wish and secured

[117] C.S., *Abraham Lincoln, a Biographical Essay* (Boston and New York, 1907), pp. 105, 116–17.

[118] C.S. lecture on Lincoln, in C.S. MSS., L.C.

[119] C.S., *Rem.*, II, 329. He was very cordial in his praise of Schurz's performance of his duties, generally; but he did not mention the slavery question.

him a military commission instead. At last, he could take the field, "along with the others." While waiting for the confirmation of his new appointment, he wrote to his mother:

> I know well, dear Mother, that you could not rejoice in the thought of my being in the army, instead of in a foreign country; but when one has fought, as I have, for a good cause, to which he is bound with all the force of conviction, it is hard to desert it just at the moment when it is about to come to a final decision.

He was already looking forward to reconstruction, which was the weightiest business, in his estimation, because of its vital importance to the future of the country. The voice of the army would have great weight in that time to come; and if he were to play a prominent part in the making of decisions then, he must as a prerequisite have served in the army.[120] It was not merely for military promotion that he was a "political general."

Before he left Spain, his letters to Meyer and Althaus had shown disappointment that the peace and qu'et which he had hoped to find there had been illusive. He was giving up a fairly comfortable salary, safety, and bodily comfort, because he wanted to come home, where his vital interests had come to be. To Althaus, he exclaimed, in a letter, "It is an uncom-

---

[120] Letter, C.S. to his parents from Philadelphia, May 5, 1862, in C.S. MSS., W.H.S.; *Lebn.*, III, 214.

fortable business to bind one's fate up with that of
a people."[121] But he had done it; and to that people he
returned.

The story of Schurz's first decade in the United
States is a record of a phenomenal rise in status, accompanied by corresponding growth in character. By
September, 1863, after some chastening experiences in
the Army of the Potomac, he had even learned to see
himself in perspective, and, in a revival of his boyhood
correspondence with Petrasch, wrote the following remarkable summary of his own career:

I ended my refugee life in London in the year 1852, because I found its instability unendurable and longed for a productive activity. I lived here in America for several years in
quiet retirement in the happiest family circle. I wish you knew
my wife. She is much better than I, and we have two precious
children. I studied, observed, and learned much.

Finally, in the year 1856, as the movement against slavery
spread tremendously, I found myself drawn into public life. I
knew that I could accomplish something worth while. America
is the country for striving talent, and the foreigner who studies
conditions here fundamentally and knows how to appreciate
them can open for himself an even greater career than the native born. My success surprised even me. I saw my boldest
expectations exceeded. I found suddenly that I had become a
celebrity in America. I threw myself unreservedly into the antislavery movement and therein showed the Americans something
new. The broad German conception of life which opens to
them wider horizons; the peculiar speech of the foreigner which,

[121] From Madrid, December 9, 1861; *Lebn.*, III, 211. Cf. n.
109 *supra,* and chap. ii, n. 71, p. 45.

although modeled upon the best patterns of English literature, still indulged in a multitude of unfamiliar variations; the power of true conviction which is not found too often in its purity;—all of these things had a rare attraction for Americans; and so I won, perhaps more quickly than anyone here in the country, a continental reputation,—a reputation which in many particulars exceeded my deserts. My activities were very extended and had a large and direct influence upon the political development of the country. I have been told that I made Lincoln President. That is of course not true, but that people say so indicates that I contributed something toward raising the breeze which carried Lincoln into the presidential chair and thereby shook slavery in its foundations. I devoted my whole strength to it and became exceedingly wearied with the Herculean labor.

As happens in moments of exhaustion, I sought rest. Therefore I went as minister to Spain, but I soon found that rest at a time like this was for me the most irritating exertion. The rebellion which is to decide the future of this country quickly reached enormous proportions. The noise of the struggle penetrated even to my hermitage in Madrid. It became uncanny to me in my quiet. The enforced apathy of insipid diplomatic life was terribly oppressive to my temperament and my conscience. Then the news of the first great disaster to our army, the battle of Bull Run, came like a thunder clap. I immediately begged the President to recall me. I belonged to the party which had brought on the crisis; I could not avoid the chances of the struggle. Finally, in December '61, I received a leave of absence, returned hither at once, laid down my ministership, made another effort to induce the government to adopt the policy of emancipation, thus smoothing the way among the people, and then entered the army. In the course of the summer campaign of 1862, I was advanced to the position of Major General, the highest rank one can attain in the army of the United States. I shall doubtless continue in service to the end of the war. Then I shall return to my old activities with the satisfaction not only of having labored definitely for the future of this country, but also of having loyally shared its fate. In the political phases of the new developments which this revolution must produce, I shall undoubtedly have an important part and my voice will be heard.

This is the bright external side of my life. I have labored much, struggled much, endured much, and also suffered much—so much that I needed strong convictions to keep me upright. How often in moments of irritation have I wished I could be of those who, in humble occupation, can eat their bread in quiet peace with their loved ones! The petty jealousy of the German who would rather subordinate himself to natives than to a fellow countryman who as he sees has come to overtop him; the ambitions of the native who begrudges the foreigner his influence and his distinction; the poisonous slanderousness of the political opponent to whom not even personal honor is sacred;—all of this has caused me many bitter hours. I might have worked myself up to that sovereign contempt of men which is said to make a man great, but that is against my nature. I would rather remain insignificant. I love people in spite of themselves and possess that invincible confidence which, deceived a thousand times, is a thousand times revived. This is perhaps artless but I cannot do otherwise and that keeps me young and cheerful and hopeful.

The main thing is this: That in a position in life such as mine, a man should not permit himself to be ruled by a false ambition. The ambition to *do* something can be boundless, but it must free itself from the ambition to *be* something. I am glad to have won official positions which, according to the usual interpretation, are brilliant. I have learned to recognize their worthlessness; for they have never contributed to my inner satisfaction. I believe that I could now, without regret, cast from me a crown if I had it. Such things are only means to an end, and as such are perhaps sometimes of consequence. I have happily come to the point where externalities no longer have any temptation for me. I believe I am able to say that in practice I have become a better republican even than in theory.[122]

Both in practice and in theory he had become a good American. He had not given up his affection for the old fatherland; he never did; he never needed to do so, to be a valuable citizen of the new. But there was no longer any but a quite remote chance that he would revoke his decision to stay in America.

The immigrant who had learned to feel at home in America had returned as minister of state to Europe and had been homesick there. His feeling of personal responsibility for the preservation of the Union, and his sense of the identity of his personal interest with the success of the government which he had chosen to serve and with the welfare of the people who had adopted him as one of themselves, had brought him home. America had claimed him. While still a German, he had become an American.

[122] Letter to Petrasch, from Camp at Catlett Station, Virginia, September 24, 1863; *Lebn.*, III, 225. Cf. chap. i, n. 31, p. 14.

BIBLIOGRAPHY

A. SCHURZ

Schurz Manuscripts, Wisconsin Historical Society. German letters.

Schurz Manuscripts, Library of Congress. Letters in German and English, manuscripts of political speeches, lectures, etc.

Lebenserinnerungen von Carl Schurz. 3 vols. Berlin: Georg Reimer, 1912.

Speeches, Correspondence, and Political Papers of Carl Schurz. Selected and edited by Frederic Bancroft on behalf of the Carl Schurz Memorial Committee. 6 vols. New York: G. P. Putnam's Sons, 1913.

Speeches. Edited by Carl Schurz. Twelve early political speeches. Philadelphia: Lippincott, 1865.

Schurz, Carl. *Reminiscences.* 3 vols. New York: McClure Company, 1906–8.

Abraham Lincoln. A biographical essay. Boston and New York: Houghton Mifflin Co., 1907.

Henry Clay. 2 vols. Edinburgh: David Douglas, 1887.

B. NEWSPAPERS

Boston Daily Advertiser, April 10, 1859—April 28, 1859.

Chicago Press and Tribune, July–December, 1858; January–December, 1860.

Frank Leslie's Illustrated Newspaper, November, 1859—December, 1860.

Harper's Weekly, January–December, 1860.

Manitowoc (Wisconsin, daily) *Tribune*, August–November, 1859.

Madison (Wisconsin, weekly) *Demokrat*, German, February, 1858—October, 1860.

Madison *Wisconsin Daily State Journal*, January, 1856—December, 1860.

Memphis (Tennessee, weekly) *Avalanche*, January, 1859—December, 1860.

Milwaukee (daily) *Atlas*, German, May, 1860.

Milwaukee (weekly) *Atlas*, German, August–October, 1857.

Milwaukee (daily) *Banner und Volksfreund*, German, April and May, 1860.

Milwaukee Daily Sentinel, July, 1855—June, 1861.

New York (daily) *Tribune*, April 15–30, 1859; May–November, 1860; January–April, 1861.

Watertown (weekly) *Democrat*, January, 1855—April, 1861.

C. PAMPHLETS

Albany Evening Journal, Tracts, of 1860.

Beloit College miscellaneous pamphlets, Wisconsin historical section.

Bound pamphlets, "Campaign of 1860," No. 77, Wisconsin Historical Society.

Greene, E. B., *Lieber and Schurz*. "War Information Series," 1918.

Halstead, Murat. *Conventions of 1860*. Columbus: Follet, Foster, & Co., 1860.

D. GERMAN-AMERICAN LITERATURE

Betz, Gottlieb. *Die deutschamerikanische patriotische Lyrik der Achtundvierziger und ihre historische Grundlage*. Publications of the University of Pennsylvania.

Bruncken, Ernest. "The Germans in America," *American Historical Association Report, 1898*.

―――. "Political Activities of Wisconsin Germans, 1854–1860," *Proceedings of the State Historical Society of Wisconsin, 1901*.

―――. *The Germans in Wisconsin Politics*, "Parkman Club Papers," No. 9 (1896).

Deutsch-Amerikanisches National-Bund. *Das Buch der Deutschen in Amerika*. Philadelphia: Walthers Buchdruckerei, 1909.

Faust, Albert Bernhardt. *The German Element in the United States*. Boston and New York: Houghton Mifflin Co., 1909.

Fröbel, Julius. *Aus Amerika*. 2 vols. Leipzig, 1856, 1857.

Hense-Jensen, Wilhelm, and Bruncken, Ernest. *Wisconsins deutsch-amerikanischer bis zum Schluss des neunzehnten Jahrhunderts*. Milwaukee: Verlage der Deutschen Gesellschaft, 1900.

Lacher, John H. S. *The German Element in Wisconsin*. Muehlenberg University Pamphlet, No. 36. Milwaukee, Steuben Society, 1925.

Schrader, Frederick Franklin. *The Germans in the Making of America*. Boston: Stratford Co., 1924.

Von Bosse, Georg. *Das deutsche Element in den Vereinigten Staaten*. Stuttgart: Chr. Velsersche Verlagsbuchhandlung, 1908.

―――. *History of German Immigration in the United States; and Successful German-Americans and their Descendants*. New York: F. T. and J. C. Smiley, 1908.

E. SPECIAL ACCOUNTS

Becker, Carl. *The Declaration of Independence*. New York: Harcourt, Brace & Co., 1922.

Dodd, W. E. "The Fight for the Northwest in 1860," *American Historical Review*, XVI, 774–88.

Julian, George W. "The First Republican National Convention," *ibid.*, IV, 315–22.

North American Review, 1856.

Schafer, Joseph. "Four Wisconsin Counties," *Wisconsin Domesday Book*. Madison: State Historical Society of Wisconsin, 1927.

Thompson, Alexander McDonald. *A Political History of Wisconsin*. Milwaukee: C. N. Caspar Co., 1902.

Whyte, William F. "Chronicles of Early Watertown," *Wisconsin Magazine of History*, Vol. IV, No. 3 (March, 1921).

Winn, Bessie Sara. "The Wisconsin Railroad Scandal. 1856," Manuscript thesis, University of Wisconsin, 1928.

F. LINCOLN

Beveridge, Albert J. *Abraham Lincoln*, 2 vols., Houghton Mifflin Co., 1928.

Newton, Joseph Fort. *Lincoln and Herndon*. Cedar Rapids, Iowa: The Torch Press, 1910.

Nicolay and Hay. *Abraham Lincoln—A History*. 10 vols. New York: Century Co., 1920.

Sandburg, Carl. *Abraham Lincoln, The Prairie Years*. New York: Harcourt, Brace & Co., 1926.

Stephenson, Nathaniel W. *Abraham Lincoln*. Indianapolis: Bobbs-Merrill Co., 1924.

Tarbell, Ida M. *Life of Abraham Lincoln*. 4 vols. New York: Lincoln Historical Society, 1907.

Works of Abraham Lincoln (Federal ed.). Edited by Arthur Brooks Lapsley. New York: G. P. Putnam's Sons, 1906.

Letters and State Papers of Abraham Lincoln. Edited by Nicolay and Hay. New York: Century Co., 1894.

G. OTHER BIOGRAPHIES AND AUTOBIOGRAPHIES

Bancroft, Frederic. *Life of William H. Seward.* 2 vols. New York and London: Harper & Bros., 1900.

Gardner, William. *Stephen A. Douglas.* Boston: Roxburgh Press, 1905.

Haynes, George H. *Charles Sumner.* Philadelphia: George W. Jacobs Co., 1909.

Koerner, Gustave. *Memoirs.* 2 vols. Cedar Rapids, Iowa: The Torch Press, 1909.

Pierce, Edward L. *Memoirs and Letters of Charles Sumner.* 4 vols. Boston: Roberts Bros., 1894.

Stevens, Frank E. "Stephen A. Douglas," *Journal of Illinois Historical Society,* 1923–24, Joint Number 2–3.

Thayer, W. R. *Life and Letters of John Hay.* 2 vols. Boston and New York: Houghton, Mifflin Co., 1915.

White, Andrew D. *Autobiography.* New York: Century Co., 1905.

Willis, Henry Parker. *Stephen A. Douglas.* Philadelphia: George W. Jacobs Co., 1910.

H. GENERAL ACCOUNTS

Channing, Edward. *A History of the United States,* Vol. VI. 6 vols. New York: Macmillan Co., 1905–25.

McMaster, John Bach. *A History of the People of the United States, From the Revolution to the Civil War.* Vol. VIII. 8 vols. New York: D. Appleton and Co., 1883–1913.

Morison, S. E. *The Oxford History of the United States, 1783–1917.* 2 vols. Oxford University Press, 1927.

Rhodes, James Ford. *History of the United States, from the Compromise of 1850,* Vol. II. 8 vols. New York: Macmillan Co., 1910–13.

I. GERMANY

Becker, Joh. Phil., und Esselen, Chr. *Geschichte der süddeutschen Mai-Revolution des Jahres 1849.* Genf: Gottfried Becker, 1849.

Hays, Carlton J. H. *Political and Social History of Modern Europe,* Vol. II. 2 vols. New York: Macmillan Co., 1924.

Henderson, F. H. *Short History of Germany.* New York: Macmillan Co., 1906.

Marriott, J. A. R., and Robertson, C. Grant. *The Evolution of Prussia.* Oxford: Clarendon Press, 1915.

Priest, George Madison. *Germany since 1740.* New York: Ginn & Co., 1915.

Nachträgliche authentische Aufschlüsse über die badische Revolution von 1849, "Sammlung Socialpolitischer Schriften, Bd. XX. Zurich, 1876.

J. ITEMS TAKEN FROM THE FOLLOWING PAPERS, AS FOUND IN CLIPPINGS IN THE LIBRARIES OR AS QUOTED IN OTHER PAPERS

Boston: *Courier, Liberator.*
Buffalo: *Express, Commercial Advertiser.*
Chicago: *Times.*
Cincinnati: *Commercial, Gazette, Volksblatt, Criminal Zeitung.*
Cleveland: *Herald, Plain Dealer, Deutscher Pionier.*
Easton, Pennsylvania: *Times.*
Fond du Lac: *Commonwealth.*
Janesville: *Gazette, Standard.*
Louisville: *Journal.*
Madison: *Argus.*
Manitowoc: *Democrat, Pilot.*
Milwaukee: *American, Evening Wisconsin, Germania Herold, News, Seebote.*

New York: *Evening Post, Times.*
Oshkosh: *Democrat.*
Philadelphia: *Press.*
Racine: *Advocate, Volksblatt.*
San Francisco: *Journal.*
Sheboygan: *Times.*
St. Paul: *Minnesotian.*
St. Louis: *Democrat, Turnzeitung, Vossische Zeitung.*
Watertown: *Deutsch Volks-Zeitung, Register, Wisconsin Dem-okrat.*

INDEX

367